INNOVATIONS
in COMPUTERIZED ASSESSMENT

◆ ℬ ◆ ℬ ◆

INNOVATIONS
in COMPUTERIZED ASSESSMENT

◆℘◆℘◆

Edited by
Fritz Drasgow
University of Illinois, Urbana-Champaign
Julie B. Olson-Buchanan
California State University, Fresno

 LAWRENCE ERLBAUM ASSOCIATES, PUBLISHERS
1999 Mahwah, New Jersey   London

Lawrence Erlbaum Associates, Inc., Publishers
10 Industrial Avenue
Mahwah, New Jersey 07430-2262

Cover design by Kathryn Houghtaling Lacey

Library of Congress Cataloging-in-Publication Data

Innovations in computerized assessment / edited by Fritz Drasgow, Julie B. Olson-Buchanan.
      p. cm.
   Includes bibliographical references and index.
   ISBN 0-8058-2876-1 (cloth : alk paper). — ISBN 0-8058-2877-X (pbk. : alk. paper)
   1. Psychometrics—Data processing. 2. Psychological tests—Data processing. 3. Behavioral assessment—Data processing. 4. Educational tests and measurements—Data processing. 5. Personnel management—Data processing. I. Drasgow, Fritz. II. Olson-Buchanan, Julie B.
BF39.5.I55 1999
153.9'3'0285—dc21   98-29600
                                                        CIP

Books published by Lawrence Erlbaum Associates are printed on acid-free paper, and their bindings are chosen for strength and durability.

Printed in the United States of America
10 9 8 7 6 5 4 3 2 1

♦ To our families ♦

Contents

Preface

It is hard to believe how much computer technology has changed since we started to develop our interactive video assessment in 1989. At the time we were barely able to purchase what was the state-of-the-art in interactive video: a laser disc player, a full-motion video adaptor, and a personal computer with a 16 MHz microprocessor. To reduce development time, we produced a prototype of the video clips for our assessment while we simultaneously developed software and grappled with the psychometric and theoretical issues underlying the assessment.

In 1991, we presented a symposium on our project at the Society for Industrial and Organizational Psychology conference in St. Louis. We hauled bulky equipment and prototype materials to the conference so we could demonstrate the technology. Our symposium was at 8:00 a.m., so we were there early to connect our equipment to the video projection system. We held our breath, crossed our fingers, and prayed to the computer assessment gods that it would work. Our equipment worked, but the projection system was able to display only 16 colors at a rate much less than 30 frames per second. It was too late to change, so we gave our presentations and explained our research. When it was time to demonstrate the prototype, we first apologized for the poor quality of the projection and started the interactive video assessment. There was an audible gasp from the audience; most had not previously seen full-motion video presented on a personal computer. Today, just 8 years later, video presented by computer is commonplace.

Although computer technology has changed dramatically, our knowledge about how to use it for assessment has not. Several conference presentations have focused on developmental and psychometric issues; very little, if any, written information about developing computerized assessments is available. One of the principal reasons for this book is to provide an answer to the question asked repeatedly, "How do I develop a computerized test?"

The chapters of this book present the challenges and dilemmas faced by leading researchers as they created their new computerized assessments; much less emphasis has been placed on examining characteristics of the finished products. Particular attention has been given to dilemmas: What were the choices that were faced in developing, scoring, and administering the assessments? What were the advantages and drawbacks of the choices? How did the researchers resolve their dilemmas? Were their solutions good ones? Thus, the sage advice from some of the "pioneers" in computerized assessment is offered as a type of blueprint for others who are considering computerization of their assessment program.

OVERVIEW OF CHAPTERS

The potential for computerized assessment is reflected in the variety of innovative applications described in this book. As we note in chapter 1, the chapters may appear to be widely different. The authors represent a variety of disciplines including psychometrics, industrial–organizational psychology, and educational measurement. Similarly, the computerized assessments described in the chapters have varying target populations including military recruits, primary and secondary school students, applicants for graduate school, computer programmers, managers, and other professionals. However, all chapters share one common thread: All describe how computers were used in an innovative way to assess individuals.

Using Computers to Present Standard Items

Chapters 2 through 5 describe projects that use computers to present standard text or math items in a novel way. Specifically, the assessments are adaptive tests that tailor the difficulty of the items to be appropriate for the test-taker's skill level. These tests use item response theory (IRT) as the psychometric basis for the assessment (see Hambleton & Swaminathan, 1985, or Hulin, Drasgow, & Parsons, 1983, for introductions to IRT). Briefly, IRT is based on the idea that a test attempts to measure a latent trait, usually denoted by the Greek letter theta (θ), such as verbal aptitude or mathematics achievement. Each item on the test is linked to θ via its item characteristic curve, which gives the conditional probability $P_i(\theta)$ of answering item i correctly as a function of the latent trait θ. An item is discriminating in a range of θ values if its item characteristic curve rises rapidly (so that higher ability examinees have noticeably higher probabilities of answering correctly than lower ability examinees). Using IRT, an adaptive test attempts to administer only discriminating items; given a tentative estimate of ability, it inspects the pool of available items and selects one that should be very discriminating. This item is administered and the examinee answers, the ability estimate is updated based on the examinee's response, and another highly discriminating item is selected. This process continues until the examinee's ability estimate reaches some prespecified level of precision or a fixed number of items has been administered.

In chapter 2, Zicker, Overton, Taylor, and Harms describe how a newly commissioned math reasoning ability test was used as the basis for an adaptive test for selecting computer programmers at State Farm Insurance Companies. The chapter includes a discussion of how incumbent computer programmers were used to calibrate the item pool and to conduct a concurrent validity study. Given its intended use, the authors paid special attention to issues relating to how the content of the test could be kept secure, how an adaptive test might affect applicants' reactions to the organization, and keeping the time needed to complete the test to an acceptable amount while providing examinees with enough time to answer.

In chapter 3, Segall and Moreno describe the issues raised and decisions made over a 20-year development period for the computerized adaptive test to select and place military recruits. The chapter includes a detailed discussion of numerous studies designed and conducted to address the military's concerns about characteristics of the computerized version of the enlistment test battery. These include some of the earliest empirical studies to address the question of whether the psychometric theory underlying adaptive testing would actually work with real people. Given the length and scope of the project, the authors pay special attention to changing hardware and software requirements (and availability), human factors, and economic (utility) analyses.

In chapter 4, Bergstrom and Lunz draw on their experience in developing computerized adaptive tests for certification and licensing purposes. The chapter identifies several steps in the development process and includes a discussion of issues that need to be considered at each step as well as the authors' recommendations. The authors also include a discussion of how the use of computerized adaptive tests changes the examination committee members' work requirements, as well as the procedures for challenging exam scores, and test maintenance procedures.

In chapter 5, Kingsbury and Houser chronicle the development and implementation of computerized testing in the Portland Public Schools. The authors describe the computerization of a math achievement test in detail, including the development of the item pool, the measurement model selected, the scale used for score reporting, and the item selection algorithm and its constraints. In addition, practical considerations, such as the test's interface, the hardware platform, and the software used for the assessment, are stressed.

In the sixth chapter, Mills details the process of converting a large-scale, high-stakes academic admissions test, the Graduate Record Examination, to a computer-adaptive format. This chapter also describes numerous issues that had to be resolved during the development of the assessment. For example, the chapter discusses using several questions with a single item stem (i.e., a reading passage followed by several questions), item exposure, omitting, reviewing previously answered items, and scoring incomplete exams. Great care was taken as these issues were considered by the test developers due to the importance of this test for examinees.

Using Computers to Present Audio and/or Video

The next three chapters describe projects that use computers to present innovative visual, audio, or audio/video assessments. In the seventh chapter, Ackerman, Evans, Park, Tamassia, and Turner describe how a test of dermatology knowledge was developed that uses digitized images of skin with different disorders. Students are given a brief patient history along with the digitized image and are asked to select the appropriate disorder from a list. The chapter includes a discussion of the hardware/software issues that were encountered as well as several ways in which the assessment might be enhanced.

In chapter 8, Vispoel explains how he used the audio presentation capabilities of computers to develop the first computerized adaptive test for assessing music aptitude. The author describes how the stimuli were developed and how the items were calibrated. Given the length of time over which the assessment was validated, Vispoel gives special attention to how the changes in available hardware and software affected the evolution of the assessment.

In chapter 9, we describe the development of a multimedia assessment of conflict resolution skills for managers based on a theoretical model. We include a discussion of the steps needed to develop such an assessment, including writing scripts for the vignettes, taping the vignettes, and preparing them for laser disc or CD, and scoring performance. Special attention is devoted to the struggle to maintain the integrity of the original scripts and to keeping up with the changes in hardware and software.

Using Computers to Assess a Criterion Measure

In chapter 10, Hanson, Borman, Mogilka, Manning, and Hedge describe how they used the audio and video capabilities of computers to develop an innovative work sample measure of the job performance of air traffic control specialists. The chapter describes the steps the researchers took to develop the content of the simulation, to translate it into a computerized assessment, to revise it, and to pilot-test the measure. The authors pay special attention to how construct validity was assessed.

Using Computers for Administrative Purposes

In chapter 11, Burroughs et al. describe how Wilson Learning Corporation has used computers to streamline the assessment process. The chapter includes a discussion of how to decide which aspects of the assessment process would best be served by computerization and which aspects are best performed by humans. For example, they use multiple human judgments on noncomputerized assessment tasks to rate performance and identify material to be used for feedback purposes. Computers are used to tabulate these ratings, integrate across raters, and create feedback reports. Attention is paid to how computerization saves time and money.

Final Chapter

Finally, in Chapter 12 we discuss and integrate the 10 core chapters of this volume. Specifically, we identify some commonalities across the chapters such as the emphasis on addressing the psychometric issues raised by innovative assessments and a relative lack of emphasis on software development. In addition, we discuss whether the time and effort needed to develop novel computerized assessments is worthwhile, and propose some ways in which computers can be used to improve assessment measures further.

SUMMARY

Taken as a set, we believe the chapters of this book provide a representative and detailed description of the process of developing a computerized assessment. They illustrate numerous advantages of computerized measurement, and they honestly describe a variety of difficulties and challenges that are likely to be encountered. It is our belief that the adage "Nothing ventured, nothing gained" applies here: Real improvements in our ability to precisely assess a wide range of human skills are possible with computerization.

A FINAL NOTE

We wish we could also introduce a chapter by Patricia J. Dyer and her colleagues on IBM's experience in developing an innovative computerized battery of tests. We are greatly saddened by Pat's untimely death—on both a personal and professional level. Pat was the consummate research–practitioner who held her work to the highest standards. The field of computerized assessment will suffer without her continued insight and "embracing of the technology."

—*Fritz Drasgow*
—*Julie B. Olson-Buchanan*

REFERENCES

Hambleton, R. K., & Swaminathan, H. (1985). *Item response theory: Principles and applications.* Boston: Kluwer-Nijhoff Publishing.

Hulin, C. L., Drasgow, F., & Parsons, C. K. (1983). *Item response theory: Applications to psychological measurement.* Homewood, IL: Dow Jones–Irwin.

1

Beyond Bells and Whistles: An Introduction to Computerized Assessment

Julie B. Olson-Buchanan
California State University, Fresno

Fritz Drasgow
University of Illinois, Urbana-Champaign

The changes in computers since their inception have been staggering. Just a few decades ago, they were rare, curious, astronomically expensive machines that were so massive that they literally filled large rooms. Mainframe computers of the mid-1970s cost millions of dollars and served hundreds of users but were equipped with just a few hundred kilobytes of memory; today, memory costs just a few dollars per megabyte and personal computers designed for individual users have dozens of megabytes. Similarly, in the early 1980s, a 500 megabyte disk drive cost approximately $25,000; in contrast, multigigabyte disks now cost just a few hundred dollars.

Today, computers have become ubiquitous, affordable machines that are commonly desktop-sized; laptop computers, weighing less than 10 pounds, are even smaller. Accordingly, attitudes toward computers have also changed. Fear, apprehension, and awe toward these machines have turned into acceptance, dependence, and even, to some extent, nonchalance. Indeed, in this era where many people have their own home page, the bells and whistles of computers seem commonplace.

1

POTENTIAL OF COMPUTERIZED ASSESSMENTS

Although the existence and capabilities of modern computers may barely elicit a nod from most people, their potential for psychological assessment can still raise an eyebrow from measurement practitioners and academicians. No longer limited to static paper-and-pencil methods, computers can be used for assessment in myriad ways. Computer programming affords test developers the flexibility of dynamic selection of items to be presented and allows variations in the presentation of stimulus materials. For example, computers can present single test items for a limited period of time (to limit exposure) or tailor the exam to the examinee's ability (i.e., adaptive testing).

The dynamic technological capabilities of computers also allow *different types* of test items to be created and presented. As a result, test developers are not limited to text statements and graphics. For example, computers enable test developers to portray motion. Consequently, spatial ability test items can use objects moving in space, instead of traditional items such as pictures of stationary unfolded boxes. Tracking tests can use target stimuli that move in unpredictable patterns. Similarly, the computer can be used to create complex items that change over time to measure problem-solving skills.

With the addition of a laserdisc player or a compact disk (CD) drive and audio speakers, computers can present full motion video and stereo sound. As a result, the methods of standardized psychological measurement can be utilized to evaluate skills previously assessed using live actors role-playing with test-takers or written descriptions of situations. For example, suppose a test developer is interested in measuring how well someone perceives and interprets nonverbal information. The test could consist of several realistic, compelling vignettes—and the test-taker would be asked to identify and interpret the actors' nonverbal behaviors. This multimedia test may be a much more relevant and construct-valid measure of this interpersonal skill than a written test that describes the behaviors and more standardized than its role-playing counterpart.

This video–audio capability can be taken one step further through the use of interactive video. An assessment tool can be designed and developed to interact with the assessee's responses. That is, a test developer can present an initial scene to all test-takers. At the end of the scene, the test-takers could be shown a set of possible responses to the initial scene. An individual test-taker's response could determine which scene is shown to that test-taker next. Thus, the test-taker would see continuing scenes based on how he or she responded to earlier scenes. This dynamic branching may add realism and improve the assessment's fidelity to real world situations.

Computers can also expand the types of actions test-takers make in response to stimulus materials and automate the collection of measures of these actions. Thus, test developers are not limited to using traditional multiple-choice questions, an assessment format that has long been a source of concern for the measurement community. For example, the computer can be used to measure the test-taker's movements (via a joystick or mouse) or the elapsed time between the presentation of the item and the test-taker's response. Moreover, underlying processes used to answer items may be examined by collecting information about how an assessee goes about answering a question; the computer can record what information the assessee requests before responding, the amount of time spent consulting that information, and the order in which the information is provided.

Motion, time, and process can provide very important information for the assessment of a wide variety of educational and job skills. A pilot selection program would certainly want to avoid an individual who could answer paper-and-pencil spatial skill items very accurately, but was too slow to use a joystick to guide a simulated airplane in real time. Similarly, the veracity of a correct response might be questioned if information critical to the solution of the problem was not presented to the examinee or if the examinee answered an item in just a few milliseconds (i.e., without reading the question).

Finally, the availability of affordable, reliable computers can change the way we administer assessments. That is, in many cases computers can administer and score tests with greater convenience, reliability, standardization, and affordability than human test administrators. In fact, assessees may be able to initiate, complete, and even score an assessment with little or no intervention from a test administrator. Computer test administration has many potential benefits to organizations and educational institutions, including reductions in labor costs, decreased scoring errors, increased standardization in test administration, increased test security, and increased speed in processing assessees' answers.

THE CHALLENGE OF COMPUTERIZED ASSESSMENTS

The bells and whistles of innovative computerized assessments are not without costs. Perhaps the most omnipresent challenge occurs because these types of assessments are still relatively new; there is not a standard methodology for developing, say, an interactive video assessment or an adaptive test. Although some aspects of the development and implementation of these types of tests may parallel traditional measures, the flexibility inherent in computer technology introduces novel issues as well.

A test developer encounters a variety of dilemmas in developing and implementing computerized assessments. For example, in creating an interactive video measure, the test developer needs to decide how to develop realistic stimuli that are appropriate for the assessment (including writing dialogue, selecting actors, videotaping, etc.), how to score the assessment, how to appropriately measure reliability, and how to prepare the assessment for videotaping. In developing an adaptive test, the test developer needs to determine how the assessees are likely to respond to such a test, what legal issues might be raised, and so forth.

Unfortunately, traditional texts such as Nunnally's (1978) *Psychometric Theory* and Guilford's (1954) *Psychometric Methods* have only limited relevance to the development of innovative computerized assessments. Consequently, test developers have had to create their new assessments with little theoretical and empirical research to guide them.

Although the potential uses of computers for assessment seem promising, the number of researchers who have attempted to explore this technology is surprisingly small. Certainly several researchers have used computers as page-turners to administer paper-and-pencil tests (see Mead & Drasgow, 1993, for a review); however, there are only a handful of researchers who have used computers to devise new types of assessments (i.e., assessments that are *not* computerized versions of previously developed paper-and-pencil assessments).

There are several possible reasons for this. First, only recently have computers become affordable yet sufficiently powerful for this type of research; the initial cost of personal computers and multimedia technology was prohibitive. Second, the development time for these types of assessments is notoriously long; indeed, some assessments' development spanned decades. Finally, the lack of methodological guides and information about how others have addressed issues arising during test development has greatly increased the difficulty of exploring new and innovative assessments.

MEETING THE CHALLENGE

The bells and whistles of computers are seductive, yet there is not much available literature that helps practitioners and researchers to develop innovative assessments. So, how can others make use of the dynamic capabilities of computers without reinventing the wheel? The purpose of the following 10 chapters is to provide leading researchers' developmental and methodological guidance for the creation and use of innovative computerized assessments.

Clearly, innovative use of computers for assessment presents a host of psychometric, administrative, and technological issues that are typically not encountered in traditional assessment. Moreover, information about developing these types of assessments is extremely scarce. Academic journals provide a means for summarizing the characteristics of assessment tools after they have been developed, but provide almost no detail about how the assessments were created. Thus, the following chapters address this lack of information by focusing on how leading researchers have (a) computerized already existing assessment tools; (b) developed innovative new measurement tools; and (c) used computers to assist the assessment process.

REFERENCES

Guilford, J. P. (1954). *Psychometric methods*. New York: McGraw-Hill.

Mead, A. D., & Drasgow, F. (1993). Equivalence of computerized and paper-and-pencil cognitive ability tests: A meta-analysis. *Psychological Bulletin, 114*, 449–458.

Nunnally, J. C. (1978). *Psychometric theory* (2nd ed.). New York: McGraw-Hill.

2

The Development of a Computerized Selection System for Computer Programmers in a Financial Services Company

Michael J. Zickar
Bowling Green State University

Randall C. Overton
L. Rogers Taylor
Harvey J. Harms
State Farm Insurance Companies, Bloomington, IL

The computer has dramatically altered the landscape of selection testing, its impact ranging from the practical to the theoretical. Among the former, the advantages of administering tests on computer include increased standardization of test administration procedures, immediate scoring, elimination of manual errors in scoring, and reduced time required of human resources personnel to proctor tests. Mead and Drasgow's (1993) meta-analytic finding that power tests can be transported from paper-and-pencil to computer without compromising the tests' construct integrity makes the advantages of computerization even more beneficial. Although the construct meaning of speeded tests may be altered by the mode of administration, technological advances such as pen-based computers may ultimately eliminate these differences as well (Overton, Taylor, Zickar, & Harms, 1996).

Yet, the computer offers much more than a functionally equivalent platform to paper-and-pencil for delivering tests. The theoretical impact of the computer on testing has been demonstrated in at least two major areas. The first is an expansion of the types of skills that are amenable to standardized assessment, such as perceptual–psychomotor tests (McHenry, Hough, Toquam, Hanson, & Ashworth, 1990) and multimedia work sample tests (Schmitt, Gilliland, Landis, & Devine, 1993). The second is in enabling advances in measurement theory to be operationalized. Item Response Theory (IRT) provides a much more powerful measurement framework for testing than does classical test theory (Lord, 1980), but until it became possible to utilize computers in the testing situation, many of the purported advantages were impractical to implement. IRT and its property of parameter invariance, which spawned the concept of adaptive testing, have become a reality with today's high speed computers.

This chapter describes the development and validation of a system for selecting entry-level computer programmers at a large financial services corporation. An important component of the selection system is a computer adaptive test (CAT). The practical and psychometric reasons for choosing an adaptive testing format are described, the reasoning behind the choices is emphasized, and the extent to which the project's objectives were achieved is discussed. In the selection system, the adaptive test was combined with a biodata form and with a semistructured, behavior-oriented interview to maximize the criterion variance predicted.

RATIONALE FOR "GOING ADAPTIVE"

State Farm Insurance Companies made a decision in the late 1980s to revise and update its selection procedures for entry-level computer programmers and analysts. For many years, the company had used a 20-minute paper-and-pencil test of math ability along with a relatively unstructured interview as programmer selection tools. The growth of the company's data processing operation in the late 1980s and early 1990s made an improved system for selecting programmers and analysts a research priority. We decided to hire an outside consulting company that specialized in test development to build a new cognitive ability test that would be proprietary to State Farm. The consultant performed a detailed job analysis of the jobs for which the new test would be used, identified the skills and abilities needed for successful job performance and constructed a fair and valid paper-and-pencil test that measured math reasoning ability. Looking toward the future, the items created for the new test were developed with computer screen limitations in mind so that, should State Farm proceed to computerize test administration, the items of the new test would be transferable, without modification.

The new cognitive test, a 20-item, 25-minute *power* test of math reasoning ability, was introduced into the company's employee selection program in 1990. In addition to having increased face validity, with all items appearing to tap skills required for computer programming, the test also employed word problems rather than the math calculation items exclusively used by the previous test. Word problems were introduced in order to recognize the importance of language skills as well as math skills to successful performance in the State Farm computer programmer jobs. After the initial form of the test was implemented, the consultant was asked to develop alternate forms of the new test utilizing items remaining in the initial item pool. Those alternate forms were never implemented, however, because they were not entirely satisfactory in the judgment of the company's research staff.

Despite being pleased in general with the new test, it possessed several features that concerned the company researchers because they suggested that the new test was unreasonably susceptible to compromise. First, the test was relatively short, only 20 items in length, so that it might be easy for test-takers to remember specific item stems. Second, as mentioned, there was no satisfactory alternate form available. Third, only four item stems were used in the test. Each of the stems consisted of a problem scenario, followed by five questions. Obviously, prior knowledge of the scenarios would have been very beneficial to someone wanting to cheat on the test. Fourth and finally, the job of computer programmer for State Farm was a very attractive entry-level position for new college graduates in the local community. This was in part due to the company's practice of hiring inexperienced individuals and providing them with extensive and highly marketable training in programming and due to the company's reputation as a very desirable place to work. Thus, there appeared to be considerable incentive for individuals to compromise the test's integrity to increase their chances of employment. Unfortunately, the researcher's concerns were heightened soon after the new test was introduced. Only 3 months after the test was implemented, information was received that the test may have been compromised. Although convincing evidence that the test's security was in fact compromised never developed, investigating the security scare early in the life of the new test led to the decision to proceed quickly to the next phase of research.

External consultants conducted the job analysis of the computer programmer position, which identified six final performance areas as important to the job of programmer–analyst. These were labeled: problem solving and innovation; planning, organizing, coordinating, and assigning work; communications skills; interacting with others; work orientation and dedication; and technical knowledge of data processing. The test developed by the consultant was targeted at predicting the cognitive components of the job: problem solving and innovation; planning, organizing, coordinating, and assigning work; and, technical knowledge. of data processing. The cognitive test was not expected, however, to be helpful in predicting performance in the "softer" job components such as communication skills, work orientation and dedication; and, interacting with others. Those aspects of the job were targeted for prediction using a content-valid, behavior-oriented job interview and a specially constructed biodata form, or life history inventory, both of which were developed after the cognitive test was initially validated and implemented.

Research on the selection interview has shown it to be most useful in predicting interpersonal aspects of the job such as communication skills and interacting with others (Harris, 1989). Life history or biodata items seemed to be a good candidate for measuring the technical knowledge of data processing job dimension, while perhaps also adding to the prediction of some of the softer aspects of the jobs. Reviews of the personnel selection literature have consistently shown biodata to be among the best predictors of most performance criteria (Barge & Hough, 1988; Ghiselli, 1966; Reilly & Chao, 1982; Schmitt, Gooding, Noe, & Kirsch, 1984). Thus, it was decided that in addition to improving the security of the cognitive test, the next step in the project would include expanding the number of predictors and then validating these additional measures.

State Farm's recognition of the need to replace its new paper-and-pencil math reasoning test closely followed the computerization of the two most frequently administered test batteries at State Farm (Overton, Taylor, Zickar, & Harms, 1996). It seemed reasonable that a selection test for computer programmers also should be computerized. Next, the purported benefits of adding an adaptive structure to the computerized test had to be weighed against the extra support and commitment of resources that are required to develop an adaptive test. Fortunately, support for this effort existed, both internally and externally. The executive-level management of the Data Processing Department had expressed interest in developing a "state of the art" selection system. Accordingly, the project was aided considerably by the (then) Vice President of Data Processing (DP) who held a PhD in industrial–organizational psychology and was very visible in his support of the work. Also, technical advice and assistance in the area of adaptive testing was conveniently available at the University of Illinois, located only 45 miles from State Farm's Corporate Headquarters. All of these factors motivated us to develop and implement a computerized adaptive test (CAT) as part of the "state of the art" selection system requested.

Three of the major purported benefits of CAT are increased test security, reduced testing time, and increased measurement precision. Test security is enhanced because it is not likely that any two applicants will receive the same set of test items. The CAT selects items for administration that progressively target an individual's ability level. Increasingly difficult items follow correct responses and easier items follow incorrect responses.

Through this process, the items administered successively move the assessment toward the individual's ability level, and rarely will two test-takers receive the same sequence of items.

The second purported benefit of CAT is reduced testing time. Fewer items are needed to assess ability with the same precision achieved by a longer, conventionally administered test. By restricting items to those that are most informative in estimating an examinee's ability level, items that are either too difficult or too easy are excluded. In effect, the easy items of a fixed-item, conventional test are seen as consuming test time while contributing little or no information when administered to high ability test-takers. The same argument holds regarding the presentation of difficult items to low ability examinees. According to Mislevy and Bock (1989), adaptive testing "enables testing time to be reduced to a half or a third of that required for a conventional test of the same precision" (p. 1-1).

A reduction in testing time was seen as a very desirable outcome from the perspective of the DP department; this reduction would help improve the recruitment process. Candidates that have passed an initial screening interview by on-campus recruiters are invited to the corporate headquarters for interviewing, tours, and selection testing. Reducing testing time would allow more time for other events, such as a longer community tour and/or more lengthy meetings with prospective coworkers. Also, with reduced testing time, candidates may have a more positive experience on their corporate visit, which might result in an increased likelihood to accept a tendered job offer.

The third purported benefit of a CAT is the capacity to tailor measurement precision of the test at a targeted ability level. In this case, the DP department wanted to exclude moderately low to low ability applicants from further hiring consideration. Applicants of average ability or higher were expected to be able to perform at acceptable levels because of the extensive training given to new employees. By using IRT to evaluate test items, the test pool could include items that discriminated best near an ability range slightly below the average. Therefore, an adaptive test with a pool of items near the critical decision point should provide more accurate identification of these poor math ability applicants than a traditional paper-and-pencil test.

In passing, it may be noted that tailoring measurement precision through IRT also suggested an alternative to adaptive testing. Only the most informative items for the ability level near the cutoff could have been administered. Although this alternative approach would have required less development time and cost, adaptive testing was preferred because it was desired that the test be flexible to allow DP to adjust the cutoff in response to changing labor market conditions. Furthermore, the CAT allowed a second, upper cutoff to be set in order to identify exceptional candidates.

Additional Benefits and Costs

It was expected that some additional benefits of the proposed new selection system would be derived simply because it was computerized. Benefits of computerizing the biodata–cognitive test battery included instant scoring, standardization of timing, reduced personnel time for administration, and increased face validity. Instructions are given on the computer, minimizing concerns about lack of standardization and allowing clerical staff that previously administered the tests to work on other tasks. These benefits solely due to computerization were very valuable to State Farm.

Costs were also considered in the decision to make the test computerized and adaptive. First, the costs of developing an adaptive test would be higher than that of developing a conventionally administered test because a large pool of items was needed for a CAT. Adaptive tests work best when the items sufficiently cover the range of ability to be assessed, and for test security reasons, many good items are needed at each ability level so that individuals of the same ability do not receive the same set of items. If there is a large range of abilities in the applicant group, the item pool may need to be many times larger than that used for conventional testing. Of course, a large pool of items implies an even larger number of trial items. Items must often be eliminated because they are either too easy or too difficult, do not load on the same dimension as the majority of other items (i.e., are poor measures of the intended construct), or are low in information value (i.e., do not sufficiently discriminate between lower and higher ability examinees).

A second cost is attributable to the large sample of test-takers needed to calibrate the test items. IRT item analysis traditionally has required sample sizes much larger than are needed in classical test theory analyses. Thus, to collect the necessary calibration data, a large number of trial items must be administered to a large sample of test-takers. In our case, test-takers were incumbent computer programmers, and the hourly compensation (including salary and benefits) for a computer programmer was high. The company had already spent money to develop the paper-and-pencil test and could computerize that test relatively cheaply. Substantial additional costs were incurred in order to calibrate the additional items needed for the test to be made adaptive.

Last, there were other costs that also had to be considered. A full-time programmer was required for the labor intensive job of developing the computer code that performed the calculations for updating ability estimates during the test and using these estimates to select items. Clearly, much more is involved than entering items into a computer software program that presents items and records responses. Also, testing sites were required to purchase computers to administer the test if they did not already possess a suitable computer. This concern was minimal, though, because the primary test administration site already possessed the necessary computers.

A balancing of the pros and cons weighed in favor of the CAT, especially considering that research had recently been published suggesting that estimation procedures for calibrating items required much smaller sample sizes than had historically been true. Under certain conditions, a sample size of approximately 200 was found to be sufficient (Drasgow, 1989). Although the costs remained considerable, the company's research development of a CAT, with its many potential benefits, seemed feasible.

DESIGN OF THE NEW SELECTION SYSTEM

As mentioned previously, the job analysis conducted by the test development consultant identified six performance areas that were important to success in the computer programmer positions at State Farm. These dimensions and the strategy chosen for their assessment appear in Table 2.1. Specifically, the project team proposed that an adaptive test of math reasoning ability be combined with a computerized biographical data questionnaire that would evaluate an applicant's technical knowledge, work habits, and interpersonal skills. Finally, a structured interview was proposed to replace the existing interview process. The structured interview would provide an additional assessment of many of the performance dimensions and would provide the only assessment of a candidate's communication skills. The final piece to the proposed new selection system involved a second behaviorally oriented interview to be used by campus recruiters to screen applicants before they were invited to visit the com-

TABLE 2.1
Strategy for Linking Performance Areas to Selection Instruments

| | Selection Instruments | | |
| | Computerized Test | | |
Aptitude Performance Areas	*Biodata*	*Cognitive*	*Structured Interview*
Technical knowledge of data processing	X		X
Problem solving and innovation	X	X	
Planning and organizing work	X	X	X
Work orientation and dedication	X		X
Communication skills			X
Interacting with others	X		X

pany. Both interview portions of the selection system were developed by an outside consultant. The biodata form was constructed by the State Farm research team. Because this chapter deals primarily with the CAT development and its validation, the methods used to develop the interviews and biodata form will be only alluded to here.

TEST DEVELOPMENT

CAT Item Pool

The external consultant who developed the previous math reasoning test had culled the 20 items in this test from a pool of 112 items, all of which had been written specifically for the State Farm programmer job. This item pool was considered as an initial source of questions for the adaptive test, but pilot tests involving the administration of these items via computer to a sample of experienced Research Department personnel caused this idea to be rejected quickly. Several of the participants in the pilot sample expressed concern that the items were too difficult, complicated, and ambiguous. In fact, several of the items took over 5 minutes to complete, even for test-takers who had completed a master's degree in computer science. One pilot test-taker wrote a six-page memo to the Vice President of Research, expressing frustration with the length and difficulty of these items. Consequently, new items were written and the difficult items were simplified, and an effort was made to eliminate ambiguity from all the items. In addition, multiple questions dependent on a single item stem were eliminated.

To construct new items, test specifications had to be developed to serve as a blueprint for item writers. The following guidelines were adopted:

1. The items should measure math reasoning ability.
2. The items should not require advanced knowledge of statistics or mathematics, such as trigonometry or calculus.
3. The items should have a verbal component. Items such as "Solve for X when $X^2 + 6X + 9 = 0$" were to be avoided.
4. The job analysis had highlighted four specific aspects of the math reasoning cognitive factor: problem solving; decision making; information processing; and planning, scheduling, and coordinating. Approximately equal numbers of items should be written for each of these four content areas. Although math reasoning ability was the dominant construct underlying these areas, this requirement was included to increase the test's face validity. Sample items were provided to supplement the definitions of the content areas and to help clarify their differences.

5. Items were to target below average levels of ability because this would be the range that the test was intended to measure best. Equal numbers of moderately easy (80% of applicants with a bachelor's degree in computer science should answer these items correctly) and average difficulty (50% correct) were to be written.

Many of the items were written by graduate students in industrial–organizational psychology at the University of Illinois. All had experience in writing items. The remaining items were drafted by members of State Farm's Research Department staff. This combination of internal staff and experienced graduate students was able to generate a large item pool of high quality at a lower cost than hiring professional item writers or having incumbent programmers (inexperienced in item writing) write items.

The resulting 200 items were pretested for clarity, conciseness, and difficulty level. After appropriate revisions were made and poor items eliminated, the number of items in the initial pool was reduced to 164. Two relatively easy sample items that show the structure of these items are presented here:

Sample Items

#1. At 8:00 in the morning your electronic mail has the following messages:

LUIS: Can we start our meeting at 10:00? It should take two hours to get the ALR presentation sharpened up. As planned, we should finish our presentation in just an hour-and-a-half, leaving a half hour for questions.

ANN: Could we meet for an hour-and-a-half today? My schedule is free from 9:30 to noon, and after 3:00.

KAREN: The ALR presentation has been moved up an hour to 1:00.

JAMES: Can you interview a job applicant this morning? She can talk with you between 9:00 and 10:30. It should take about an hour.

What is the earliest time you can meet with Ann?

A) 9:30
B) 2:00
C) 3:00*
D) It is not possible.

#2. Modem A carries one-half the information that Modem B carries. Modem B carries one-fourth the information that Modem C carries. If the total information load the three modems working together can carry is 440 pieces per second, how many pieces per second are carried by Modem B?

A) 80*
B) 88
C) 132
D) 160

* Correct answer.

Design of the CAT Testing Software

The test administration software was designed to run on IBM desktop personal computers using either a DOS or Windows 3.1 operating system. The display features of the test were designed to facilitate navigation through the test while at the same time not distracting the test-taker with fancy graphics or complicated features. Although all applicants were expected to have extensive computer experience (after all, many would be computer programming undergraduate majors), it was desirable to maintain a simple feel for the software so that differences in experiences with computers and types of computers would not impact the results.

Several measures were taken to ensure test security and to make it difficult for hackers to crack into the item pool. On booting up the computers, administrators had to enter a password to load the testing software. Item files and program files were encrypted and keyed to particular computers so that files could not be copied onto other computers and be studied.

Detailed instructions were given to familiarize test-takers with the navigational properties of the test. For the test, keys that had no functions (i.e., not used for navigation or coding answers) were deactivated. To guide test-takers through the features of this test, all keys that were functional for the test were highlighted in the directions. After a key was highlighted and its navigational feature displayed, the test-taker was required to press that key before continuing. This process forced test-takers to locate each key and minimized unfamiliarity with the particular keyboard used for the test.

Test-takers were required to complete five practice items that assessed math reasoning and were similar in format to items in the item pool. After keying in their response, test-takers were informed of the correct answers. If the answer they had chosen was incorrect, they were required to press the key corresponding to the correct answer. This step was included to guarantee that all test-takers were familiar with the keyboard layout and could register the response that they intended to make.

A digital clock was displayed in the upper-right corner of the screen, showing the number of minutes remaining in the testing session. This clock was included because some of the testing rooms would not have clocks on the walls. Participants in pretesting had requested such a clock. It is unclear if there were any disadvantages (e.g., heightened test anxiety) to making the remaining time salient. Test-takers were given scratch paper and pencils to perform calculations. The number of unadministered items was also displayed to make the computer test similar to paper-and-pencil testing. Participants with paper-and-pencil tests can estimate the number of items remaining due to the pages in the test booklet that are left to complete.

One of the difficulties involved with displaying the items in an attractive format was the need to minimize item length. Each screen allowed 25 lines of text. Of these 25 lines of text, 11 were dedicated to the options and instructions. Each item stem had to fit in the remaining 14 lines. We decided not to allow test scrolling so that exposure time per item and navigational complexities could be kept to a minimum. Also, by not allowing scrolling, item complexity was reduced. A couple of items had to be edited to fit on the screen but otherwise there was little problem in meeting the length requirements. The standard text-mode font was used because it was simple to program and all computers would have this font available. Participants in pretesting found a white font on a black background to be easiest to read.

Test-takers were not allowed to return to previously answered items. Because of the adaptive nature of the test, changing a previous item response might alter the choice of which item was presented next. Test-takers were allowed to return to the instructions during the test, although doing so counted against the time limit.

Design of the CAT

In adaptive testing, an algorithm is used to select items based on specific statistical criteria. Typically, items are chosen based on the IRT concept of information. Information is defined by the amount of uncertainty in an ability estimate (i.e., the standard error of measurement) that is reduced by a correct or incorrect response to a particular item. Easy items provide little information in distinguishing between above average and very high ability test-takers because both groups have a high probability of answering these items correctly. Easy items, however, can be very informative in discriminating average ability test-takers from very low ability test-takers. Item selection algorithms can be written to select the most informative item at each stage of the test. A CAT with this item selection routine would provide the most accurate ability estimates. However, one disadvantage is that the best items would tend to be administered frequently, whereas items that were slightly less informative would rarely be administered. Because test security was a prime consideration in the decision to construct an adaptive test, an item selection algorithm was needed that would both maintain measurement precision and minimize exposure of the most discriminating items.

A procedure was implemented that incorporated a stochastic process into the item selection routine. The INFO4 algorithm (Segall, 1994) computed the probability of an item being selected based on a transformation of the information value at the examinee's current estimated ability level. This transformation involves raising the information value to the power of four. The probability that an individual item is selected is the ratio of this item's INFO4 value to the sum of the values computed for all items that have not already been presented. This transformation has been found to strike a balance between the need to select items that are informative and the need to avoid overadministering the most informative items. Using a stochastic process necessitated the saving of the random seed used to generate the random numbers that were used to select items; by saving this random seed, it was possible to reconstruct the item selection process if a particular administration was challenged.

Computerized Biodata Administration

The navigational features for the computerized biodata form differed from those for the adaptive test. For example, there was no time limit to complete the biodata items. Also, test-takers could return to skipped items or review previously answered items. When test-takers desired to return to a previously skipped item, they were instructed to press a key that would access a review screen. On this review page, item numbers were listed for items that had been skipped along with numbers corresponding to the items that had not yet been administered. Entry of an item number would access the item. We decided to allow test-takers to skip biodata items because experience had shown that some test-takers feel uncomfortable answering some biodata questions. When exiting the test, participants again encountered the review screen if any items had been skipped in order to encourage their completion.

Hardware Considerations

The hardware system to be used for the item calibration data and for administering the adaptive test and computerized biodata form was required to meet several criteria. First, it was strongly desired that the same computer system be used for both the research and the later implementation of the test so that generalizability of results would be assured. Testing would be performed primarily at the centralized corporate headquarters, but some testing might be conducted at remote regional administrative offices. In 1992, the lowest common denominator computer that would satisfy multisite administration and be able to adequately handle the computational demands of adaptive testing was an IBM personal computer with 8 megabytes of RAM and a 486 MHz microprocessor. Because it was probable that the testing program would outlive this microprocessor, steps were taken to make the program run equivalently on future faster computers. Specifically, the testing clock was turned off after a keyed response and restarted with the presentation of the next item. Faster processors would be able to cycle through the item selection algorithms more quickly than the 486 processor. We did not want to penalize applicants that completed the test on relatively slow processors by giving them less time to answer items.

Additional considerations were monitor size, keyboard size, and administration platform. The monitor size was fixed at 13 inches and standard IBM keyboards were used. Although we had considered laptop computers because of their administrative flexibility, there were ergonomic concerns about keyboard standardization and limited display size as well as questions about product availability. Thus, it was decided that desktop personal computers would be the administration platform.

The remainder of this chapter describes the three-phased evaluation of the new selection system. The objectives of Phase 1 were to compute the IRT item statistics needed for adaptive testing and to evaluate the biodata items. In this phase, math reasoning items were administered via computer whereas the biodata items were administered in a paper booklet. Job performance criterion data were collected for a first check on test validity. Phase 2 was a concurrent validity study with the math reasoning test being administered adaptively and the biodata form being administered conventionally, both via the computer. The job incumbents who participated in this second phase had not served in Phase 1, and performance criterion data were collected for them. Phase 3, in progress, is a predictive, in-use validity study. The tests are being administered to actual job applicants, and criterion data (supervisors' ratings) are being collected for those hired under the new selection system. A second goal of Phase 3 research is to validate the behavior-based structured interview.

PHASE 1: ITEM POOL CALIBRATION

Data Collection Design

The backbone of adaptive testing is IRT. Items are identified that provide the most information about a person's estimated ability. For adaptive testing to be successful, detailed statistics are needed to judge which items are most appropriate for a given test taker. Classical item statistics generally are not appropriate because they are sample-dependent. This limitation of classical test theory underscores a strength of IRT, that being its property of parameter invariance. An implication of parameter invariance is that examinee ability estimates may be obtained without having to administer a common set of items to all the examinees.

To estimate IRT item parameters, response data for each item must be obtained from a large sample of test-takers. The data collection traditionally has conformed to one of two designs: Either all items are administered to all participants, or overlapping subsets of items are administered to different subsamples of examinees. The first design lowers sample size, but requires a major time commitment from each participant. In the second design, the subsets taken by different respondents have items in common with other subsets so that the measurement scale can be linked. Although this approach requires less time for each individual, a very large sample of respondents is needed.

The first design was chosen due to the limited number of computer programmer employees that were available. As noted earlier, only about one half of the eligible programmers could be selected for Phase 1 because a second sample was needed for Phase 2. Because all employees in the calibration sample would be asked to complete all 164 items, a research schedule was needed that would minimize the effects of fatigue and decreased motivation.

The data collection procedures also had to be designed to be as similar as possible to the operational adaptive test. Serious questions of generalizability arise when item data are collected under conditions that differ from the conditions in which the items ultimately will be administered (e.g., item statistics derived from paper-and-pencil testing may not accurately estimate the items' characteristics when administered on computer). Thus, the structure of the adaptive test had to be decided before the Phase 1 research could be designed.

The first decision was that the adaptive test would be of fixed length. IRT provides an estimate of measurement error for each individual test. Once a prescribed level of measurement precision is reached, the adaptive test may be terminated, meaning that different examinees may receive differing numbers of items. Examinees who fall in the ability range where high information items have been written will receive fewer items compared to examinees who lie outside this range. However, the perceived fairness of this testing strategy can be an issue, especially for candidates who are administered only a few items and fail. Accordingly, the adaptive test initially was set to administer 16 items and employed a 40-minute time limit. Pilot testing had suggested that most examinees would complete 16 items in 40 minutes, which was near the testing time management desired. If the number of items is too large for the time allotted, the resulting speeded conditions tend to introduce outside factors, such as test taking strategies and personality characteristics that contaminate measurement of the intended construct. Finally, as noted previously, examinees would not be allowed to skip questions or to return to previously answered questions.

In accordance with these decisions, the design for collecting the calibration data involved administering the 164 pool items as a series of 16-item, 40-minute subtests with the restrictions that items could not be skipped and previously answered items could not be reviewed. To minimize missing data, the subtests for each Phase 1 employee were progressively redefined. For example, if only 13 items were answered in Subtest 1 before 40 minutes expired, Subtest 2 consisted of items 14 to 29. Thus, an employee who always completed 16 items within the time limit received 10 subtests of 16 items, and Subtest 11 contained only 4 items. An employee who averaged 14 items received 11 subtests, and Subtest 12 presented the remaining 10 items.

Also, the ordering of the 164 items was varied across the Phase 1 test-takers. The items first were divided into four 41-item blocks, and the sequence of these blocks then was counterbalanced across employees (i.e., there were 24 sequences of the four blocks: ABCD, ABDC, ACBD, etc.). Last, the 41 items within each block were randomly reordered for each employee. These counterbalancing and randomization procedures were intended to control for order effects within and across subtests.

The different 164-item sequences were loaded onto diskettes and each employee was assigned a specific diskette. The diskettes recorded the item responses and the time required to answer each item. The participants were allowed 5 weeks to complete all items in the pool and were asked to complete a minimum of one subtest of 16 items at each session. Most respondents completed two or three subtests in a session. To minimize fatigue, respondents were urged not to complete more than three subtests in any given day. Testing was performed in a large room containing 25 computers used exclusively for the item administration. Programmers scheduled their own testing sessions on days and for blocks of time convenient to them. Proctors monitored the room and kept track of the participants' test sequence diskettes.

Sample of Incumbent Programmers

Drasgow (1989) showed that a calibration sample of 200 can be sufficient for estimating the two parameters per item when a two parameter logistic (2PL) IRT model is appropriate. We believed, however, that a 3PL model was needed to properly fit the math reasoning items. Thus, a pseudo-guessing parameter was seen as needed in addition to the discrimination and difficulty level parameters that define the 2PL model. Although the impact of the third parameter on sample size was unknown, the decision was made to collect data from slightly over 200 incumbent programmers and to also perform a follow-up simulation study. The simulation study would be used to evaluate whether the item parameters had been sufficiently well estimated to support the type of selection decisions for which the adaptive test was being designed. If the item parameter estimates were found to be inaccurate, a simpler IRT model would be used (e.g., the pseudo-guessing parameter would be fixed at .25 because the items conformed to a four-alternative, multiple-choice format, while the discrimination and difficulty level parameters would be estimated).

Two hundred and forty programmer–analysts were randomly sampled from an incumbent population with less than 5 years of experience. Minority programmers were over-sampled. Two hundred and two programmers (84%) completed all 164 items, while another 18 programmers completed at least

100 items. The participants also were asked to complete a paper-and-pencil biographical data questionnaire at their own convenience and to return it prior to being tested. The biodata form was not administered via computer because there was not enough time to develop the program before the commencement of Phase 1 testing. Of the 240 programmers sampled, 213 completed the biodata form (response rate = 89%). These high completion rates affirm the strong support upper management showed for this project.

Also remarkable was the uniform performance of the employees across time. The calibration data revealed no evidence of declining motivation. Percent correct and average item response time remained relatively constant across subtests.

Finally, for the purposes of validation, supervisory ratings of job performance data were collected during the time programmers were completing the series of tests. A series of half-day sessions were conducted by the research staff in which supervisors were trained on how to evaluate performance. Examples of typical rating errors, such as halo and central tendency, were given and a member of the research staff was available to answer questions while supervisors completed their ratings. The rating form was developed by an external consultant, based on a job analysis, and assessed three components of job performance: (a) overall performance; (b) six performance area measures anchored by performance examples provided by DP programmer supervisors; and (c) nine job skill areas, consisting of a verbal description of each skill identified by job incumbents as being critical in performing the job.

The programmers and analysts used in this sample worked on different types of projects that would make it difficult to develop objective criterion measures, such as number of lines coded per year. Performance ratings allowed supervisors to consider specific job duties of individual employees and then attempt to place them on a performance continuum common to all programmers. By providing behavioral anchors and skill descriptions, rater subjectivity was thought to be reduced.

Adaptive Test Item Analyses

Several of the 164 items were eliminated because of poor wording discovered during the calibration data collection. Next, item-total correlations were computed and items with low correlations ($r < .15$) were discarded.

Finally, the response data for all remaining items were analyzed through the PC-BILOG, Version 3.0 program (Mislevy & Bock, 1989). Bayesian estimates of the 3PL item parameters were calculated by retaining all of the program's default options, except that the number of quadrature points was raised to 30 to increase the accuracy of analytical integration. Several items had to be deleted because of low discrimination parameters and poor model fit. After the initial screening and analyses, 126 (77%) items remained in the test pool.

Simulated Adaptive Test: Timing and Validity

An adaptive test was simulated using the item response data that had been collected from the Phase 1 employees. Because we had recorded response times for each item, we were able to evaluate the 40-minute time limit in the simulation study. The second purpose was to estimate the validity of the adaptive test that might be expected in Phase 2. A very low validity estimate would raise questions about whether we should continue to pursue an adaptive testing format.

The item selection and ability estimation algorithms of the adaptive test were applied to the item response data each employee had provided. This was accomplished as follows. An item of average difficulty was randomly selected. If the employee had answered this item correctly (incorrectly), the employee's ability estimate was revised upward (downward) and a more difficult (easier) item was "presented" next. This simulation process continued through 16 items with an updated ability estimate recorded after each item response; a cumulative response time was also tracked.

According to these simulations, only 56% of the participants would have completed a 16-item *adaptive* test in 40 minutes. This unexpected finding reflected an item-response time interactive effect. Respondents appeared to need more time to answer items appropriate to their level of ability and less time to answer items that were either easier or more difficult. Because the simulations suggested that 98% of the Phase 1 participants would have completed the adaptive test in 60 minutes, the time limit for Phase 2 adaptive testing was increased from 40 to 60 minutes, while retaining 16-item test length.

The correlation between the ability estimates from the simulated 16-item adaptive test and supervisory ratings of job performance (i.e., the estimate of test validity) was statistically significant and encouraging. For comparison purposes, ability estimates for the Phase 1 employees also were calculated based on the entire 126-item pool. The 16-item adaptive test's validity was only .02 less than the 126-item validity. The biodata scales also correlated with the supervisory ratings.

PHASE 2: CONCURRENT VALIDATION

Phase 1 was conducted to estimate the IRT item parameters that are integral to the item selection and ability estimation procedures of adaptive testing. Phase 2 was performed to validate the adaptive test. Although the results from the simulated adaptive test were favorable, differences were conceivable in how individuals would respond to the same items when presented under actual adaptive testing conditions as compared to the conventional testing format of Phase 1. Such differences could be due to different item orderings across the different tests, though this was minimized by having essentially randomized orders in Phase 1 administration. Also, there could be something about the adaptive testing experience that impacted respondent motivation. For instance, test-takers who are given only challenging items may have reduced self-efficacy because they would be accustomed to answering at least some easy items. Also, if the test-takers are aware that the test they are taking is adaptive and are aware of the branching nature of adaptive tests, they may feel heightened test anxiety because of the implicit feedback given after each item: If an item appears easier, the previous item was probably answered incorrectly. These concerns are purely speculative but they appeared to be of sufficient importance that the validity of the test needed to be demonstrated under actual adaptive testing conditions.

One additional reason to conduct Phase 2 was that the usefulness of an adaptive test partially depends on having sufficiently accurate item parameter estimates to describe the items in the test pool. If the item parameter estimates obtained in Phase 1 could not be generalized to other samples, perhaps due to small sample size, then we would expect that Phase 2 results would not appear favorable for the adaptive test. However, there has been no research showing how much inaccuracy can be tolerated in item parameter estimates before a decrease in adaptive testing performance results. Also, it seemed prudent to evaluate the validity of the adaptive test in a sample independent of the sample used for item calibration.

Phase 2 Sample

The sampling procedure for selecting participants in Phase 2 was identical to Phase 1 sampling, except that participants in Phase 1 were excluded from this study. Two hundred and eight programmer–analysts were tested using a 16-item adaptive version of the math reasoning test and a computerized version of the biodata questionnaire. The computer program used to administer the math reasoning test was identical (e.g., same font and same navigational features) to the Phase 1 presentation software except items were administered adaptively.

Phase 2 Results: Timing Issues

Less than two thirds (64%) of the Phase 2 sample completed 16 questions within the 60-minute time limit. This result was surprising because the time limit was carefully chosen based on the response latency data collected from Phase 1. The average response time per item had not been used because the simulated adaptive test had shown that items near an individual's ability level take longer to answer. To anticipate the extra time required for adaptive testing, the time limit had been increased from 40 minutes to 60 minutes. Yet, this additional time still was not sufficient to complete the 16-item adaptive test.

Several reasons may be offered for this underestimate. The Phase 1 respondents may not have attended as carefully to the items because of the many subtests they were asked to complete over several weeks. In contrast, the Phase 2 participants were informed that they would be taking a single 16-item test. The Phase 1 finding that the percentage of items answered correctly remained constant across subsets, however, argues against the hypothesis of declining motivation. Alternatively, the Phase 1 participants may have developed a more efficient pace for answering items. Another possibility is a cumulative effect of adaptive testing. By continually receiving "challenging" items, fatigue may have built up more quickly and slowed item responses.

Whatever the reason for the underestimate, the more general finding that items likely to be chosen for an adaptive test take longer than the typical item in a test was confirmed across the two samples. To further explore this item-response time finding, the relationship between the "difficulty" of an item and the mean response time was studied for the Phase 1 data. In IRT, it can be shown that the items most informative about a person's ability have about a 50% chance of being answered correctly. For many of the math reasoning items, we observed a concave function relating the probability of answering correctly and the mean response time. Figure 2.1 shows an example of one of these functions. For examinees who are expected to answer the item correctly with a probability of .50, the mean response time is highest. The mean response time tends to be lower for examinees for whom the item is too easy

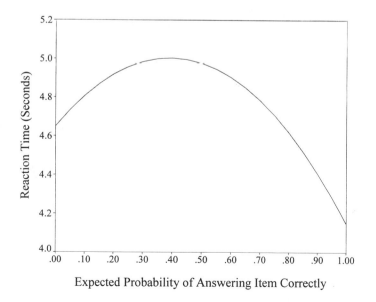

FIG. 2.1. Reaction time as a function of expected probability of correct answer.

$[P(u = 1) > .50]$ and for examinees for whom the item is too difficult $[P(u = 1) < .50]$. Therefore, individuals appear to spend less time on items that are too easy for them, and when faced with items that are too difficult, they tend to also respond quickly, possibly because they realize that they do not know the correct answer and that the best strategy is to "pass" on that item.

To further illustrate this finding, the mean response time was calculated for the five most informative items for each individual (given their final ability estimate). These five items would be items likely to be administered to those persons in an adaptive test. Analyses revealed that for all but the lowest ability persons, response times were longer for the most informative items.

This finding has been replicated for two verbal ability tests, Word Grouping and Verbal Comprehension, and for two personality scales, Adjustment and Achievement, that are part of a test battery State Farm agents use to select their office staff (Zickar, Overton, & Taylor, 1997). Because these tests and scales were administered to a different sample and apply to a different job, this item-response time finding appears to be generalizable.

Revising Test Length.   Because an adaptive test is most effective when administered under unspeeded conditions (i.e., a power test), observing that fewer than two-thirds of the Phase 2 programmers had completed the 16-item adaptive test meant that the test needed to be shortened. It was not possible to increase the time limit because 60 minutes was the maximum management would allow for the cognitive ability test, and furthermore, for practical and psychometric reasons the adaptive test was not intended to measure endurance. Because most (93%) of the Phase 2 test-takers had answered at least 12 items in 60 minutes, the decision was made to examine the statistical properties of a 12-item adaptive test.

The primary question at issue was whether a reduction from 16 to 12 items would adversely affect the test's validity. To first address this question, the Phase 2 data were restricted to those participants who had answered all 16 items. The correlation between their ability estimates based on 12 items and supervisory ratings of their job performance produced a validity that was statistically significant and virtually as high as the validity obtained for their 16-item ability estimates. A more formal comparison of these validities employed a multiple regression analysis. Two scores were computed for each participant: the 12-item ability estimate and the difference between the 16-item and 12-item estimates. Adding this difference to the 12-item estimates yielded an incremental R^2 that was essentially zero ($F < 1$). Thus, dropping four items appeared to have no effect on the test's validity.

The problem with these results, however, was the small sample size available for study. The virtual equivalence of the 12-item and 16-item validities applied only to those who were able to complete the adaptive test, and there was no way of knowing if similar results would have been found for the slower respondents (over one third of the sample). Once again, attention turned to the Phase 1 data to provide a more complete assessment of the effect of test length on validity.

Although the Phase 1 simulated adaptive test had underestimated actual required testing time, the simulation still might accurately capture adaptive conditions when item responses and ability estimates are considered instead of response times. To investigate the fidelity of the simulation, the simulated 12-item adaptive test ability estimates of Phase 1 were compared to the actual 12-item ability estimates of Phase 2. Because the two samples of incumbent programmers were similar, random samples from the same population of programmers, the ability distributions should be similar. As expected, the simulated and the actual ability estimates were remarkably close in their means and standard deviations.

Next, the simulated and actual 12-item estimates were examined for predicting job performance ratings. The two correlations and the two sets of regression analyses (slopes and intercepts) were virtually identical. Therefore, the same analyses of the Phase 1 data 12-item and 16-item ability estimates were conducted as had been carried out for the restricted Phase 2 sample. Again, the correlations and incremental R^2 results revealed 12 items to be as valid as 16 items.

ITEM CALIBRATION SAMPLE SIZE
AND ADAPTIVE TEST VALIDITY

The adaptive test clearly was established to be valid for selecting computer programmers, but the validity for this test did not exceed the validity that had been documented for the previous 20-item, paper-and-pencil test. Admittedly, the expressed aim of IRT and adaptive testing is increased measurement precision, not increased validity. Thus, this finding was not altogether unexpected but was still mildly disappointing.

Perhaps this failure resulted from inaccurate item parameter estimates in Phase 1. Even though the BILOG chi square goodness of fit statistics were favorable, these statistics are limited in their power to detect poor model fits unless sample size is large. An alternative approach to evaluate the sufficiency of the Phase 1 calibration sample size was needed.

Item parameters estimated from a very small calibration sample are likely to have large sampling errors. These large sampling errors in turn can bias test information when items are selected on the basis of their estimated parameters (Hambleton & Jones, 1994). For example, items with overestimated discrimination parameters will tend to be selected too often, and as a result, the precision of ability estimates will be overstated. However, this source of bias should vanish when there is no item selection, and instead, all items contribute to the ability estimates. Furthermore, the collective effects of the item parameter sampling errors should be relatively small when all items are used. The 12-item adaptive test estimate of ability correlated .92 with the IRT 126-item ability estimate for Phase 1 participants, which suggests that the calibration sample size was adequate.

The effect of calibration sample size on the adaptive testing was further investigated through a second simulation study. For this study, the item parameter estimates obtained in Phase 1 were assumed to be true population values. Normally distributed ability scores were randomly generated, to simulate test-takers, and for each ability score (test-taken) correct–incorrect responses to the 126 items were stochastically determined on the basis of the "true" item characteristic curves. The 126 items then were "calibrated" twice, using two different sized samples of simulated test-takers: 200 simulees versus 1,000 simulees. Last, 12-item adaptive test estimates of ability were obtained for an independent group of 1,000 simulees. Ability was estimated three times: first using the "true" item parameters, second using item parameters calibrated from the sample of 200, and third using item parameters calibrated from the sample of 1,000. As may be seen in Table 2.2, the three sets of ability estimates were of almost equal accuracy. Clearly, these results also provide no evidence that the validity of the 12-item adaptive test was compromised by a small calibration sample size.

TABLE 2.2

Results From Simulation Study of Calibration Sample Size

Correlations Between True and Estimated Abilities	
Ability Estimates From Adaptive Test With:	r
True item parameters	.91
Item parameters calibrated from a sample of 200	.90
Item parameters calibrated from a sample of 1,000	.91
Absolute Difference Between True and Estimated Thetas	
Ability Estimates From Adaptive Test With:	Mean Absolute Difference
True item parameters	.32
Item parameters calibrated from a sample of 200	.35
Item parameters calibrated from a sample of 1,000	.32

OPERATIONAL CHARACTERISTICS
OF THE SELECTION SYSTEM

The Phase 1 and Phase 2 results demonstrated that the adaptive math reasoning test and the biodata form were valid and that the correlation between these two instruments was very small. Because each instrument contributed uniquely in predicting supervisor ratings of incumbent job performance, we had to decide how to best combine these two predictors into a final score that could be used for hiring decisions. One approach would have been to optimally combine both predictors using weights derived from a multiple regression equation; however, DP management wanted to ensure that all hired employees had a minimum acceptable level of both math reasoning and the softer skills measured by the biodata questionnaire. Therefore, instead of using a multiple regression approach that assumes a compensatory model (i.e., deficits in one predictor can be alleviated by an above-average score on the other predictor), a multiple hurdle model was employed.

In this model, applicants are required to score above a minimum cut off on both predictors to be considered further for hiring. Cut off points were placed at similar percentile levels for the adaptive test and for the biodata form. The percentiles were based on the incumbent data; the objective of similar percentiles was to weight the predictors equally.

An upper cutoff also was set for each instrument. Applicants who score above the upper cutoffs for the adaptive test and biodata form are identified as exceptional candidates. In short, three grades are used. Applicants who exceed both upper cutoffs receive an "A" as exceptional candidates. Applicants who score below both lower cutoffs receive an "F," or unacceptable grade. Last, applicants who pass both lower cutoffs but fall short of one or both upper cutoffs receive a "B." "A" and "B" candidates are considered further through the structured interview process with "A" candidates favored for hiring given similar interview results.

PHASE 3: PREDICTIVE VALIDATION

Even though data from Phases 1 and 2 provided strong evidence for the validity of the selection battery, it was desirable to conduct a predictive, in-use validity study. In addition to assessing the test battery's validity directly for applicants, Phase 3 was designed to monitor the "A," "B," and "F" percentages to determine if the cutoffs should be adjusted and to evaluate the incremental validity of the structured interview. At least as important, if not more so, the dynamics of contemplated organization changes in the programming department and signs of a changing labor market stressed the importance of Phase 3 as a long-term, ongoing process. A particularly critical issue is whether the changes would lessen the effectiveness of the biodata form and the administration of the battery to applicants rather than incumbents.

The new selection system was implemented in April 1996; and, to date, supervisor ratings of job performance have been collected for a small number of programmers hired under the new system. Despite the relatively small number, the validities of the adaptive test and biodata form were found to be statistically significant and favorable despite the range restriction that resulted from using these tests to make hiring decisions. Furthermore, the structured interview has been found to significantly contribute incremental validity beyond the test battery. Certainly, more data are needed before strong conclusions can be reached, but the preliminary results are highly encouraging.

CONCLUSIONS

The process of developing a computerized test is more complicated than simply entering paper-and-pencil items into a computer readable format and then utilizing commercially available presentation software. The development of an adaptive test adds further complexities. The construction of a sufficiently large item pool, estimation of IRT item parameters, and development of a computer program to select items and update ability estimates all must be completed before validity data can be collected. In addition, powerful computers are required to perform the necessary computations during the adaptive test without creating noticeable delays. From the initial proposal to develop a computerized-adaptive selection system to the first applicant being tested took approximately 3 years.

Due to the meta-analysis finding of Mead and Drasgow (1993), some work was avoided by not having to establish the equivalence of the computerized battery to another paper-and-pencil battery. However, the problem of equivalence will continually arise as computer hardware becomes more advanced. Psychologists need to better understand what features of the computer impact test validity and reliability and also which features can be changed without validity–reliability repercussions. State Farm recently updated one of its tests from a DOS text-based program to a more contemporary Windows version. Does this change in font quality and attractiveness necessitate another validity data collection? We are assuming it does not.

No attempt was made to downplay the development of the new selection system. There were 216 programmers who spent 10 to 12 hours completing the calibration phase and 202 programmers who spent about 1.5 hours completing Phase 2. Development time also required the full-time services of one computer programmer and half-time of clerical staff work to help with data entry, coordination, etc. Two full-time staff industrial–organizational psychologists devoted a large percentage of a year in design issues, meetings with relevant DP personnel, planning, and item writing. A parttime intern from a nearby graduate program also devoted time to data analysis. Temporary employees were hired to staff the testing room used for data collection parts of Phase 1 and Phase 2, and 25 desktop computers were devoted exclusively to testing for a 6-week period. Therefore, the development cost of this program was immense.

It is difficult to assign a dollar value to the benefits of the selection system. The predictive validity for the adaptive test was slightly higher than the previous battery, and so decisions should be slightly better. Although the selection system appeared more sophisticated, and perhaps more attractive to applicants than the previous paper-and-pencil battery, it is unclear if these positive attitudes toward the testing session translate into an increase in the likelihood of accepting an offer if tendered. If there was an increase in this acceptance likelihood, that would be very important because the market for computer programmers has been very tight since the mid-1990s.

On the other hand, applicants' reactions to the new selection system may be less favorable compared to the previous test. Adaptive testing may seem more demanding than a conventional test because the items target a candidate's ability level. The lengthy testing time may also be a negative. Currently, applicant perceptions of the new selection system are being researched.

The adaptive test did result in greater item security than the previous test and that was the primary reason for building an adaptive test. Although the item pool was not as large as other adaptive tests have used, there was still more than a 10 to 1 ratio of items in the pool to items administered. Therefore, test-takers typically do not receive the same items as other test-takers. Also of importance, the order of items differs across administrations so that even if two people received many of the same items, they probably had different orderings. Yet, several of the most discriminating items with average difficulty have a high probability of being administered and future work may be aimed at seeding in new items that could replace these overadministered items.

One last benefit of the testing battery has been the capability in streamlining the selection process. Scores are instantly available to the decision team to be considered in conjunction with the structured interview score. This allows the decision team to make instant offers to candidates, which may increase the probability of these offers being accepted. Previously, answer sheets had to be hand-scored before the testing results were known.

Admittedly, not all anticipated benefits of adaptive testing were realized. Increased, rather than decreased, testing time and the failure to improve validity were the most notable disappointments. A more detailed discussion of these issues can be found in Overton, Harms, Taylor, and Zickar (1997).

In closing, State Farm generally had a positive experience with computerized testing for computer programmers. This onsite interview and the testing portions of this program were recently recognized by "best practices" awards in a benchmarking study conducted by R. S. Wunder Corporation for Bell Atlantic (R.S. Wunder Corporation, 1995). In this recent report the author wrote:

> We liked the inclusion of biodata because it gives a non-cognitive ("soft" skills) balance to the battery when included with the math test, and because our review of the testing literature showed it to be at the very top of test types in terms of its overall validity. It is a computer-administered test battery, which has several nice implications for the administrative security of the test. It is harder to "walk off" with the contents of computerized tests than it is with their paper-and-pencil counterparts. This is especially important when a company has the significant investment in a proprietary test battery. Because administration and scoring are automated, most of the errors that are commonly made by test administrators can be avoided. The math section of the battery uses "computer adaptive testing". This is a newer technology that concentrates on administering test items to candidates keyed to their individual ability levels. Candidates with higher ability get (and receive credit for) harder items. Test security is one clear advantage of computer adaptive testing, since only a subset of the test items are exposed to any given candidate. Another supposed advantage is reduced testing time, since candidates don't take items which are "wasted," i.e., too hard or too easy for their ability level. At this time, however, that presumed advantage has received mixed support by research. Finally, we present this test battery as exemplary because its two component tests are based on what correlates with on-the-job performance by systems professionals: there is no extraneous "flab" in this battery of tests. (p. 36)

The success of this project along with other successful applications of computer-based testing, have convinced Human Resources management at State Farm to computerize all testing programs utilized in the company. At the present time, State Farm is using pen-based computers, desktop computers, and portable computers to administer and score its screening batteries for entry-level support staff, transcription typists, entry-level technical/professional staff, sales agents, sales agents' staffs, claims estimators, and many positions requiring customer service orientation. Although none of these other test batteries is adaptively administered, they all capitalize on the multitude of other benefits that have come from the administration of employment tests by computer.

REFERENCES

Barge, B. N., & Hough, L. M. (1988). Utility of biographical data for the prediction of job performance. In L. M. Hough (Ed.), *Literature review: Utility of temperament, biodata and interest assessment for predicting job performance* (ARI Research Note 88-020). Alexandria, VA: U.S. Army Research Institute.

Drasgow, F. (1989). An evaluation of marginal maximum likelihood estimation for the two-parameter logistic model. *Applied Psychological Measurement, 13*, 77–90.

Ghiselli, E. E. (1966). *The validity of occupational aptitude tests*. New York: Wiley.

Hambleton, R. K., & Jones, R. W. (1994). Item parameter estimation errors and their influence on test information functions. *Applied Measurement in Education, 7*, 171–186.

Harris, M. M. (1989). Reconsidering the employment interview: A review of recent literature and suggestions for future research. *Personnel Psychology, 42*, 691–726.

Lord, F. M. (1980). *Applications of Item Response Theory to practical testing problems*. Hillsdale, NJ: Lawrence Erlbaum Associates.

McHenry, J. J., Hough, L. M., Toquam, J. L., Hanson, M. A., & Ashworth, S. D. (1990). Project A validity results: Relationship between predictor and criterion domains. *Personnel Psychology, 43*, 335–354.

Mead, A. D., & Drasgow, F. (1993). Equivalence of computerized and paper-and-pencil cognitive ability tests: A meta-analysis. *Psychological Bulletin, 114*, 449–458.

Mislevy, R. J., & Bock, R. D. (1989). *PC-BILOG 3: Item analysis and test scoring with binary logistic models*. Mooresville, IN: Scientific Software Inc.

Overton, R. C., Harms, H. J., Taylor, L. R., & Zickar, M. J. (1997). Adapting to adaptive testing. *Personnel Psychology, 50*, 171–185.

Overton, R. C., Taylor, L. R., Zickar, M. J., & Harms H. J. (1996). The pen-based computer as an alternative platform for test administration. *Personnel Psychology, 49*, 455–464.

Reilly, R. R., & Chao, G. T. (1982). Validity and fairness of some alternative employee selection procedures. *Personnel Psychology, 35*, 1–62.

R. S. Wunder Corporation (1995). *Bell Atlantic Entry-Level Management Selection Procedure Benchmarking Study: Report to Participating Companies*. Kingwood, TX: Author.

Schmitt, N., Gilliland, S. W., Landis, R. S., & Devine, D. (1993). Computer-based testing applied to selection of secretarial applicants. *Personnel Psychology, 46*, 149–165.

Schmitt, N., Gooding, R. Z., Noe, R. A., & Kirsch, M. (1984). Meta-analysis of validity studies published between 1964 and 1982 and the investigation of study characteristics. *Personnel Psychology, 37*, 407–422.

Segall, D. O. (1994). CAT–GATB simulation studies. *NPRDC Technical Report*. San Diego, CA.

Zickar, M. J., Overton, R. C., Taylor, L. R. (1997). *Modeling response times to adaptive test items*. Poster presented at the annual meeting of the Society for Industrial and Organizational Psychology, St. Louis, MO.

3

Development of the Computerized Adaptive Testing Version of the Armed Services Vocational Aptitude Battery*

Daniel O. Segall
Kathleen E. Moreno
Defense Manpower Data Center, Monterey Bay, CA

The Computerized Adaptive Testing version of the Armed Services Vocational Aptitude Battery (CAT–ASVAB) is one of the most thoroughly researched tests of human proficiencies in modern history. Data from over 400,000 test-takers collected over a 20-year period have been used to address crucial research and development issues. In spite of its lengthy and thorough development cycle, CAT–ASVAB was the first large-scale adaptive battery to be administered in a high-stakes setting, influencing the qualification status of applicants for the U.S. Armed Forces. CAT–ASVAB was first used operationally in September 1990 at six locations. From 1990 to 1996, about 7% of all military applicants were administered the adaptive version. In 1996, implementation of a new CAT–ASVAB system began at 65 Military Entrance Processing Stations. CAT–ASVAB is currently used to test about two-thirds of all applicants, resulting in administration rates of over 400,000 adaptive tests annually. This chapter outlines the development of the battery and describes

---

*The views expressed are those of the authors and not necessarily those of the Department of Defense or the U.S. government.

some of the challenges and dilemmas faced in constructing a CAT version that is interchangeable with its preexisting paper-and-pencil (P&P) counterpart.

Since 1976, the P&P–ASVAB has been used for selection into the military, and classification into a number of occupational specialties. Because applicants tend to have little employment history, and because large numbers apply each year, scores on the ASVAB play an important role in determining an applicant's qualification status. The ASVAB has proven to be a good predictor of future training success. Because it can be administered to large groups of applicants and takes about 3 hours, it has proven to be an efficient means of obtaining information for predicting future success. In 1990, about one million applicants took the ASVAB. In recent years, the annual administration rate has dropped to about 600,000. The numbers fluctuate from year-to-year, depending on the economic conditions, and on military manpower needs.

In the years prior to 1976, the Army, Air Force, Navy, and Marine Corps each administered unique classification batteries to their respective applicants. Beginning in 1976, a joint service ASVAB was administered to all military applicants. The battery was formed primarily from a collection of service-specific tests. The use of a common battery among services facilitated manpower management, standardized reporting on accession quality to Congress, and enabled applicants to shop among the services without taking several test batteries.

Virtually from its inception, the ASVAB was believed susceptible to compromise and coaching (Maier, 1993). Historically, the ASVAB program has offered continuous *on-demand* scheduling opportunities, with nearly 1,000 testing sites located in geographically disperse areas. Both applicants and recruiters have strong incentives to exchange information on operational test questions. High scoring applicants can qualify for service, enlistment bonuses, educational benefits, and desirable job assignments. Performance standards for recruiters are based on the number of high-scoring applicants they enlist. Around the time of the ASVAB implementation in 1976, additional compromise pressures were brought to bear by the difficulty services had in meeting their goals in the all-volunteer service of the post-Vietnam era. In fact, Congressional hearings were held to explore alternative solutions to ASVAB compromise. Although other solutions were identified and later implemented (i.e., the introduction of additional test forms), one solution proposed during this era was implementation of a computerized adaptive testing (CAT) version of the ASVAB. The computerization of test questions was believed to make them less prone to physical loss than P&P test booklets. Additionally, the adaptive nature of the tests was believed to make sharing item content among test-takers and recruiters less profitable, because applicants receive items tailored to their specific ability level.

EARLY RESEARCH AND DEVELOPMENT

Just 1 year after the implementation of the ASVAB, concerns over test compromise and other practical issues led to the *Marine Corps Exploratory Development Project* (McBride, 1997). The purpose of the project was to answer practical questions related to computerized adaptive testing. First, could an adaptive-testing delivery system suitable for military personnel tests be developed? At the time, two classes of computers existed: mainframes and minicomputers. Mainframes were expensive to purchase, operate, and maintain. Previous attempts with CAT using mainframes were largely unsuccessful because of the unpredictable response times associated with time-sharing (Weiss, 1975). Similar concerns existed about minicomputers (which bear little resemblance to the personal computers of today). Minicomputers cost between $50,000 and $100,000, and there was some concern that they would not be powerful enough to handle the computations necessary to support multiple users in an adaptive testing environment.

A second question addressed the correspondence between empirical results (from live subjects) and those predicted on the basis of theoretical and simulation analyses. Specifically, would advantages claimed on the basis of theoretical studies be confirmed by empirical data obtained from military recruits? Although a great deal of theoretical work was suggestive of the relative advantages of CAT over P&P, empirical validation of these findings was largely absent from the testing literature.

These early practical questions were addressed by two studies. Both studies used CAT algorithms based on the three parameter logistic model (3PL) and Owen's (1969, 1975) Bayesian sequential procedure for item selection and scoring. The tests were administered on remote terminals controlled by a time-shared minicomputer system. The first study (McBride & Martin, 1983) compared the relative efficiency of experimental verbal tests administered in adaptive and conventional modes by computer. Data from 466 Marine Corps recruits were gathered and used to compute reliability and construct validity coefficients at different test lengths. The results corroborated the theoretical advantage of superior CAT efficiency manifested by reduced test lengths required to achieve a desired level of precision.

The second study (Moreno, Wetzel, McBride, & Weiss, 1984) expanded the investigation from one to three content areas: Word Knowledge, Paragraph Comprehension, and Arithmetic Reasoning.[1] Data from 356 Marine Corps recruits were gathered on three versions of each test: a CAT version, an opera-

---

[1] These content areas are included in the Armed Forces Qualification Test (AFQT) selection composite used by the services to qualify applicants for admission into the military.

tional P&P version taken prior to enlistment, and a second P&P version taken after enlistment. For each test, the CAT version administered roughly half the items as were contained in the P&P versions. Results were consistent with prior beliefs that a shorter CAT could measure the same constructs as a P&P test, with equivalent or higher precision.

Taken together, these two studies corroborated results between the empirical findings and those predicted from theory concerning CAT's increased efficiency. However, the suitability of computer hardware for the purpose of CAT was still questionable. Each minicomputer used in the study was only able to support a small number of users without distracting response time delays. Still other deficiencies, such as the inability to display graphics items and easily move computers between test sites, made them unsuitable for large-scale operational use.

Part way through the Marine Corps Exploratory Development Project, the Department of Defense initiated a Joint Service Project for development and further evaluation of the feasibility of implementing CAT (Martin & Hoshaw, 1997). A tasking memo was cosigned on January 5, 1979 by the Under Secretary of Defense for Research and Engineering, later Secretary of Defense, William J. Perry. By this time, there was a strong interest in CAT among the Services as a potential solution to several testing problems. This enthusiasm was partly generated by the possibility of addressing test-security concerns and partly by a litany of other possible benefits over P&P. These potential benefits included: shorter tests, greater precision, flexible start/stop times, online calibration, the possibility of administering new types of tests, standardized test administration (instructions/time limits), and reduced scoring errors (from hand- or scanner-scoring).

From the outset, the Joint Service CAT–ASVAB project had an ambitious and optimistic research and development schedule. Because of this compressed timeline, the effort was split into two parallel projects: contractor delivery system development (hardware and software to administer CAT–ASVAB), and psychometric development and evaluation of CAT–ASVAB. In 1979, microcomputing was in its infancy; no off-the-shelf system was capable of meeting the needs of CAT–ASVAB, including portability, high fidelity graphics, and fast processing capability to avoid distracting delays to test-taker input. Several contractors competed for the opportunity to develop the delivery system, and by 1984, three contractors had developed prototypes that met all critical needs. By this time, however, the microcomputer industry had advanced to the point where off-the-shelf equipment was less expensive and more suitable for CAT–ASVAB use. Consequently, the contractor delivery system was abandoned, and off-the-shelf computers were selected as a platform for CAT–ASVAB. During this same period, psychometric evaluation proceeded apace, with the development and validation of an experimental CAT–ASVAB version.

The Experimental CAT–ASVAB System

The experimental CAT–ASVAB system was developed to collect empirical data for studying the adequacy of proposed adaptive testing algorithms and test development procedures. The intent was to develop a full-battery CAT version that measured the same dimensions as the P&P–ASVAB that could be administered in experimental settings. Several substantial efforts were required to construct the system, including psychometric development, item pool development, and delivery system development.

Psychometric procedures (item selection, scoring, and item pool development) of the experimental system were based on item response theory (IRT). Earlier attempts at adaptive tests using Classical Test Theory did not appear promising (Lord, 1971; Weiss, 1974). The three-parameter logistic model was selected from among other alternatives (one and two parameter normal ogive and logistic models) primarily because of its mathematical tractability, and its superior accuracy in modeling response probabilities of multiple choice test questions.

By the early 1980s, two promising adaptive strategies had been proposed in the testing literature, one based on maximum likelihood (ML) estimation theory (Lord, 1980), and another based on Bayesian theory (Owen, 1969, 1975; Urry, 1983). The principle difference between the procedures involves the use of prior information—the ML procedure defines estimated ability in terms of the value that maximizes the likelihood of the observed response pattern. The Bayesian procedure incorporates both the likelihood and prior information about the distribution of ability. The two procedures also differ in their characterizations of uncertainty about the true ability value, and how the potential administration of candidate items might reduce this uncertainty.

Differences between the approaches had practical advantages and disadvantages in the context of CAT. The ML item selection and scoring procedure enables the use of precalculated information tables to improve the speed of item selection; however, provisional ability estimates required for item selection may be undefined or poorly defined early in the test (e.g., for all correct or incorrect patterns). Owen's Bayesian item selection and scoring procedure provides adequately defined and rapidly computed provisional ability estimates (regardless of the response pattern), but computations required for item selection taxed the capabilities of available processors at the time. The net result of these differences led to the development of a hybrid method (Wetzel & McBride, 1983) that combined the strengths of both procedures. The hybrid method uses Owen's Bayesian procedure to compute provisional and final ability estimates and bases item selection on ML information tables. In a simulation study of alternative methods, Wetzel and McBride found the hybrid procedure to compare favorably to the pure ML and Owen's Bayesian procedures in terms of precision and efficiency.

Large item pools were written and calibrated for the experimental system (Wolfe, McBride, & Sympson, 1997). Over 4,000 items were written (about 450 for each of nine content areas). These items were pretested on samples of military recruits (providing about 300 responses per item). Items with low discrimination were removed from the pools, and the remaining items were administered in paper-and-pencil booklets to over 100,000 military applicants (providing about 1,500 responses per item). IRT item parameter estimates were obtained using the joint ML procedure implemented by the computer program LOGIST (Wood, Wingersky, & Lord, 1976).

There was some concern about the calibration medium used to estimate the necessary item parameters. Specifically, would the IRT item parameters estimated from responses obtained on paper-and-pencil booklets be suitable for use of these same items administered in a computerized adaptive testing format? Given the large numbers of test-takers required, calibration of these items from computerized administration was not feasible. Some assurance concerning the suitability of P&P item parameters was given by the favorable results of other adaptive tests that had relied on P&P calibrations (McBride & Martin, 1983; Urry, 1974). A systematic treatment of this issue was conducted for the development of the operational CAT–ASVAB forms several years later by Hetter, Segall, and Bloxom (1994), who found that the medium of item calibration has no practical impact on the psychometric properties of adaptive test scores.

While the primary hardware–software system for nationwide implementation was under development by contractors, another delivery system was constructed in-house specifically for use in low-stakes experimental research (Wolfe, McBride, & Sympson, 1997). This experimental system had many important features, including the ability to present items with graphical content, capability of rapid interaction when processing examinee input, portability, and psychometric flexibility (in terms of item selection, scoring, and time-limits). By 1982, Apple III personal computers that could meet these requirements were commercially available. The experimental system consisted of up to eight Apple computers (with 256K of random access memory) networked with a single 10-megabyte hard disk drive.[2] The system included a modified keyboard, where all but six lettered keys (labeled A, B,C, D, E, and HELP) were covered. Additional keys were labeled "yes," "no," and "erase," which served to confirm and enter responses.

The experimental software, written in PASCAL, used the hybrid item-selection and scoring strategy, fixed-length adaptive tests (15 items for each power subtest except Paragraph Comprehension, which administered 10

---

[2]Individual computers had no internal hard drive because of the prohibitive expense. In 1982, a 20-megabyte hard drive cost about $5,500.

items), and incorporated two nonadaptive speed tests. The test lengths were about 40% to 50% shorter than their P&P counterparts and were consistent with both theoretical and empirical findings that demonstrated adaptive tests to be about twice as efficient as their P&P counterparts (McBride & Martin, 1983). To deal with potential delays to examinee input, it also incorporated a *look-ahead* procedure. While examinees were reading test questions, the system performed the necessary item-selection calculations to determine the most appropriate follow-up question for both correct and incorrect responses to the current item. Thus when the answer was input and scored, the next question appeared almost instantly on the computer monitor.

Joint-Service Validity Study

From 1982 to 1984, the experimental CAT–ASVAB system was used in a large-scale validity study to answer a fundamental question concerning the exchangeability of CAT and P&P versions of the ASVAB (Segall, Moreno, Kieckhaefer, Vicino, & McBride, 1997). Specifically, could a short adaptive version of the ASVAB have the same validity as its longer P&P counterpart for predicting success in training? Because the prediction of training success is a central function of the ASVAB, a direct answer to this issue was of primary importance. Previous studies had not examined criterion-related CAT validity, and only examined the construct validity of limited content areas. In addition, no empirical data were available on the performance of speeded (conventional) tests administered by computer and their equivalence with P&P versions.

Predictor data were gathered from 7,518 recruits scheduled for training in 1 of 23 military occupational specialties. There was some concern that the collection of predictor data from recruits (rather than applicants) would distort the outcome of the validity analysis. First, the time interval between the collection of predictor (ASVAB) and criterion (success in training) data was somewhat compressed for recruits. Thus, maturation in predictor-abilities may tend to inflate the validity estimates. Second, the nonoperational recruit testing environment is somewhat more variable and less motivating than the operational applicant testing environment; these factors would tend to lower validity estimates. However, applicant testing was not efficient or practical because only a small (unknown) portion of the applicant population would eventually be assigned to the 23 schools included in the study. To help control for the influence of these extraneous factors, recruits were tested on both CAT–ASVAB and P&P–ASVAB versions under similar experimental conditions. Consequently, three sets of predictors were available for analysis: the operational P&P–ASVAB taken prior to enlistment, the experimental CAT–ASVAB taken during basic training, and selected P&P–ASVAB subtests also taken during basic training.

Occupational specialties were chosen to ensure that (a) a broad spectrum of service training programs were represented, (b) all P&P–ASVAB tests were included in school predictor composites, and (c) within-specialty sample sizes would be large enough to make meaningful validity comparisons between CAT–ASVAB and P&P–ASVAB. Criteria data for study participants were collected several months later at the end of course instruction. These criteria consisted of final course grade, completion time, or a composite of midterm test scores. After removing subjects that did not complete course training, the average sample size for each school was about 327. (Actual sample sizes ranged from a low of 69, to a high of 456.)

For each of the 23 schools, multiple correlations (R's) were computed between criteria and optimally weighted subtests. Separate R's were computed for each of the three predictor sets (CAT–ASVAB, operational P&P–ASVAB, and nonoperational P&P–ASVAB). Multiple correlations based on optimally weighted subtests were used rather than the standard unit weighting because of scaling differences between the experimental CAT–ASVAB (which computed scores in the IRT θ-metric) and P&P–ASVAB (number-correct metric).[3] Significance tests comparing the validity of CAT–ASVAB to each of the two P&P–ASVAB versions were performed. Among the 56 comparisons, only one significant difference was found. This difference favored CAT–ASVAB. These results in general suggested that CAT–ASVAB and P&P–ASVAB predict school performance equally well.

In addition to the predictive validity analysis, the construct equivalences of the CAT and P&P versions were examined via factor analysis, based on correlations between the experimental CAT–ASVAB and the operational ASVAB test scores. Four factors spanning Verbal, Technical, Quantitative, and Speed dimensions were extracted. The pattern of factor loadings across CAT and P&P versions was very similar, and most CAT–ASVAB tests had equivalent or higher factor loadings (consistent with equivalent or higher measurement precision).

The results of the experimental validity study were very encouraging: Equivalent construct and predictive validity could be obtained by computerized adaptive tests that administered about 40% fewer items than their P&P counterparts. These results provided powerful evidence in support of the operational implementation of CAT–ASVAB.

OPERATIONAL CAT–ASVAB DEVELOPMENT

The 1984 decision to abandon customized hardware led to the selection of an off-the-shelf system of networked personal computer hardware, and software

---

[3]The P&P–ASVAB uses unit weighted composites computed from standardized subtest scores for predicting success in training. Because an equating between the CAT and P&P versions was unavailable at the time, CAT–ASVAB scores could not be placed on the same metric as the P&P–ASVAB.

was developed by project staff. With the resolution of hardware and software issues came a reevaluation and eventual resolution of psychometric aspects of the CAT–ASVAB system. Although the experimental CAT–ASVAB system was a useful research tool, in many respects it was ill-suited for operational use. Before CAT–ASVAB could be administered operationally to military applicants, substantial research and development efforts were needed in the areas of item pool development, psychometric procedures, and delivery system. The high-stakes nature and large volume of military applicant testing raised the burden of proof for the adequacy of CAT–ASVAB to an extraordinarily high level. Policy guidance from military leadership insisted that in spite of the promising outcomes of the previous empirical studies and many potential benefits of CAT, it was essential for CAT–ASVAB to match or exceed the high standards set by the P&P–ASVAB, and that there should be a very high degree of confidence among researchers and policymakers that these standards have been met. Work on the operational CAT–ASVAB system occurred from about 1985 to 1990.

Item Pool Development

Items for the first two operational forms of CAT–ASVAB were written and calibrated by Prestwood, Vale, Massey, and Welsh (1985). The P&P reference form (8A) was used to outline item content, but differences existed between the test specifications of the adaptive and conventional versions. The adaptive pools had an increased range of item difficulties and functionally independent items. For the Paragraph Comprehension subtest, this meant asking a single question per passage (for CAT), as opposed to multiple questions for P&P–ASVAB. This functional independence was necessary to help satisfy the IRT assumption of local independence.

About 3,600 items (400 for each of nine content areas) were written and pretested on a sample of recruits (providing about 300 responses per item). IRT item parameter estimates were obtained and used to select a subset of highly discriminating items (with an approximately rectangular distribution of difficulties) for more extensive calibration study. The surviving 2,118 items (about 235 items per content area) were assembled into 43 booklets and administered to about 137,000 military applicants. After editing, about 2,700 responses per item were available for item calibration. All items within a content area were calibrated jointly using the computer program ASCAL (Vale & Gialluca, 1985), along with operational P&P–ASVAB items taken for enlistment purposes. This design ensured that item parameter estimates were placed on the same scale across all experimental booklets.

One concern in the development of these pools was whether CAT items must be calibrated from data collected in a computerized administration, or if equally accurate results can be obtained by calibrating items from data collected in a P&P administration (Hetter, Segall, & Bloxom, 1994, 1997). If computer administration of CAT items is required for calibration purposes, then the item pool development effort would be increased substantially. Data from 2,955 military recruits were gathered to estimate two types of calibration-medium effects: (a) whether items calibrated by computer-produced adaptive test scores with greater precision than adaptive scores computed from a P&P-based calibration, and (b) whether calibration medium affects adaptive test scores in a systematic or nonsystematic way.

Examinees were randomly assigned to one of three groups. Shortened pools (for General Science, Arithmetic Reasoning, Word Knowledge, and Shop Information) were constructed from a subset of power test items with high expected usage rates. These pools were administered in fixed blocks by computer to two groups, and by P&P to the third group. Separate IRT calibrations were obtained using data from one computer group and the P&P group. Then, each calibration was used to estimate IRT adaptive scores for the remaining computer group. This was accomplished by applying the adaptive item selection and scoring algorithms post hoc to a subset of responses made by the second computer group. Calibration medium effects on the measured construct and on the reliability of the test scores were assessed by comparative analyses of the ability estimates using the alternative calibrations. Calibration medium effects on the score scale were assessed by comparing IRT difficulty parameters from computer-based and P&P-based calibrations. Results indicated that item parameter estimates obtained by P&P calibration produced adaptive test scores that have the same reliability and measured the same construct as scores produced from item parameters obtained by computer calibrations. The descriptive analyses of difficulty parameters suggested little or no effect of calibration medium on the score scale.

The IRT model used for CAT–ASVAB (i.e., the 3PL) assumes that each subtest is unidimensional (i.e., all items measure the same, single ability). Violations of this assumption may have serious implications for validity and test fairness. Three approaches were considered for dealing with this problem (Segall, Moreno, & Hetter, 1997): (a) unidimensional treatment (apply unidimensional adaptive item selection and scoring algorithms without special item-content constraints), (b) content balancing (place constraints on the numbers of items administered from targeted content areas), and (c) pool splitting (construct and calibrate separate item pools for targeted content areas and measure each from separately administered adaptive tests). For each item pool, a number of analyses were considered in determining the most suitable approach, including: factor analysis of items, the statistical significance of additional factors, factor interpretation, item difficulties, and factor intercorrelations. Several guidelines were developed to determine whether an item pool would be treated as unidimensional or multidimensional. If the factor structure of an item pool showed one significant factor, then the pool was treated as unidimensional. If the factor structure suggested that the item pool was multidimensional, but the factors were not interpretable or items loading on different factors did not overlap in item difficulty, then the pool was also treated as unidimensional. If the factor structure suggested multidimensionality, the factors were interpretable, and items loading on different factors did overlap in item difficulty, then the pool was treated as multidimensional. For multidimensional pools, content balancing was used when factor correlations were high and a split-pool approach was used when factor correlations were low. In accordance with these guidelines, six of the eight ASVAB power tests were treated as unidimensional, one (General Science) was content balanced, and another (Auto-Shop Information) was split into two pools, and measured by separately administered adaptive tests.

Available items were divided into two parallel item pools (Moreno, 1986). Pairs of items with similar measurement properties were assigned to alternate pools.[4] Through a series of simulation studies, the precision of CAT–ASVAB was compared to that of the P&P–ASVAB at a number of ability levels; it was desirable for CAT–ASVAB to have higher or equal precision at all ability levels. However, for two subtests (Arithmetic Reasoning and Word Knowledge), the precision of CAT–ASVAB fell below that of the P&P–ASVAB over the middle ability ranges. Item pools for these subtests were supplemented with additional items (from the experimental system), and the precision of supplemented pools matched or exceeded that of the P&P–ASVAB at all ability levels.

Psychometric Procedures

The development of the operational system provided an opportunity to review and revise psychometric procedures (Segall, Moreno, Bloxom, & Hetter, 1997). The success of the experimental CAT–ASVAB system made it a useful starting point. However, the high-stakes nature of applicant testing and the operational testing environment imposed additional requirements not specifically addressed in the experimental system development. These requirements dealt with item exposure, final scoring, time limits, scoring incomplete and speeded tests, collecting data on tryout items, and user interface issues.

Exposure Control.   After a review of data from the experimental CAT–ASVAB system, it became apparent that some items had an extremely high exposure rate. Many items were administered to a large portion of the sample. The experimental system used the *5–4–3–2–1* strategy (Wetzel &

---

[4] For test security and retesting purposes, it is necessary for CAT–ASVAB to have at least two forms consisting of unique (nonoverlapping) item pools.

McBride, 1985), which was intended to guard against one specific type of compromise: remembering response sequences. If item selection were based solely on the hybrid strategy (maximizing information at the provisional Bayesian ability estimate), then a given response pattern (e.g., ADECA) would lead to a deterministic set of presented items, and a predictable test score. Accordingly, once the correct pattern was known, a high score could be obtained by simply remembering the ideal response pattern. The *5–4–3–2–1* strategy guards against this strategy by randomly selecting the first item from among the five most informative, the second item from among the four most informative, and so forth. Item selection for the fifth and subsequent items is based solely on maximum information. This procedure was found to have little decrement in final score precision when compared to optimal (nonrandom) item selection. However, results from the experimental validity study indicated that the procedure may be susceptible to a different compromise strategy: sharing item-content among test-takers. Some highly informative items of moderate difficulty levels were administered to nearly all subjects. The *5–4–3–2–1* strategy guarded against one type of compromise strategy (remembering response sequences), but did not protect against another (sharing item-content among test-takers).

Recognizing this deficiency, Sympson and Hetter (1985) developed a procedure to guard against both types of strategies. Specifically, the exposure control algorithm was designed to: (a) place an upper limit on the exposure rate of the most informative items, and (b) reduce the predictability of item presentation. The algorithm is probabilistic, and controls item selection during adaptive testing through the use of previously computed parameters associated with each item (Hetter & Sympson, 1997). Items are selected on the basis of maximum information at the provisional ability level, but before an item is administered, a random uniform number is generated and compared to the item specific exposure control parameter. If the random number is less than the parameter, the item is administered. Otherwise, the item is set aside and not considered again for administration to the test-taker. Exposure control parameters are determined in advance through simulations. Highly informative items of moderate difficulty levels tend to have their usage restricted; items of extreme difficulty or lesser discrimination tend to have little or no usage restrictions. In simulation studies, Hetter and Sympson found the procedure resulted in only modest loss of precision (primarily over the middle ability ranges) when compared to optimal unrestricted item selection.

Stopping Rules. Both variable and fixed-length stopping rules were considered for use in the operational CAT–ASVAB. In variable length adaptive testing, additional test questions are administered until the examinee's standard error of measurement falls below some prespecified target level. In fixed-length adaptive testing, each test-taker receives a fixed number of items, regardless of the estimated precision of the test score. Fixed-length testing was selected for use in CAT–ASVAB primarily because of its increased efficiency over variable-length testing. The results of simulations showed that for examinees at the extreme ability ranges (where few informative items exist) the incremental value of each additional item quickly reaches the point of diminishing returns, leading to an inefficient use of the test-takers' time and effort.

Scoring. In the experimental CAT–ASVAB system, Owen's Bayesian ability estimate was used to update provisional scores after each administered item and at the end of the test to provide a final score. As a final score, it has one undesirable property: The score depends on the order in which the items are administered. It is possible for two examinees to receive the same items, provide the same responses, but receive different final Owen's ability estimates. This could occur if two examinees received the items in different sequences. To avoid this possibility, the Bayesian mode ability estimate was selected for use as a final score in the operational system. The Bayesian mode is unaffected by the order of item administration, and, as suggested by simulation studies, provides slightly greater precision than Owen's estimator. Other Bayesian ability estimates were also considered for final scores, but very little difference in precision among the methods was found. Among the alternatives studied, the Bayesian mode required the fewest numbers of computations.

Time Limits. Administrative requirements forced the imposition of time limits on each of the adaptive power tests for the operational CAT–ASVAB. There was some concern about the use of time limits as the standard IRT model does not make allowances for the effects of time pressure on item functioning. Much discussion ensued about the most desirable method for specification of time limits. One idea was to set the CAT–ASVAB subtest time limits from the per-item time allowed on the P&P–ASVAB.[5] Another proposal was to examine the distribution of subtest completion times from the untimed experimental version (using joint service validity data), and set time limits at the 95th percentile. These two methods produced very different time limits for the nine adaptive tests, and there was substantial pressure among policymakers to use the shorter (P&P–ASVAB based) limits, because they were likely to save additional testing time. However, data collected from an untimed pilot study (Vicino & Moreno, 1997) supported the use of the longer limits. Results indicated that (for reasoning tests) high-ability examinees generally took longer than low-ability examinees, indicating that these examinees would be most affected by shortened time limits. The explanation for this

---

[5]CAT–ASVAB time limits would be prorated to adjust for differences in test lengths.

finding was that high-ability examinees received more difficult questions, which required additional time to answer. This trend is exactly opposite of anticipated response times from traditional P&P tests. In traditional testing, motivated low-ability examinees are generally expected to take longer than high-ability examinees.

Ironically, even the longer time limits based on the untimed experimental pilot study were later found to be too short. The problem was noted during the early stages of data collection for an equating study (Segall, 1997a). For one subtest (Arithmetic Reasoning), fewer than 87% of the test-takers completed all 16 items. Other subtests also had completion rates lower than the 95% target. These early data were used to revise the time limits.

Penalty for Incomplete Tests.   The imposition of time-limits also led to a penalty procedure for incomplete tests. The Bayesian scoring procedure contains a bias: Generally, estimates are too close to the population mean, and this bias is inversely related to test length. A low-ability test-taker could use this property to his or her advantage. Below-average applicants could increase their score by answering the minimum number of items allowed.

To discourage this potential compromise strategy, a penalty procedure was developed for scoring incomplete adaptive tests (Segall, 1987). The procedure provides a final score that is equivalent (in expectation) to the score obtained by guessing at random on the unfinished items. In practice, penalty functions were determined through a series of simulations, and separate functions were determined for each subtest and each possible number of unanswered questions. The procedure has several desirable qualities: (a) the size of the penalty is related to the number of unfinished items, (b) applicants who have answered the same number of items and have the same provisional ability estimate will receive the same penalty, and (c) the penalty rule eliminates "coachable" test-taking strategies with respect to answering or not answering test items. Because the penalty procedure may punish high-ability test-takers disproportionately (especially when applied to reasoning tests) care was taken to ensure that very few test-takers were penalized. Accordingly, generous time limits were used, allowing sufficient time to permit over 98% of all test-takers to complete each adaptive subtest within the allotted time.

Seeding Tryout Items.   The operational CAT–ASVAB administers unscored experimental items for tryout and calibration purposes. Experimental items are administered as the 2nd, 3rd, or 4th item in the adaptive sequence. The experimental item is given early in the sequence where variation in item difficulty among successive items is high. Thus, the administration of an experimental item of inappropriate difficulty is likely to be less disruptive when administered toward the beginning of the test than toward the end where item difficulties tend to center tightly around the estimated ability. The position is randomly determined so that it is not apparent to the examinee specifically which item is nonoperational. This method of collecting data on new items has several advantages over traditional tryout methods, which collect data under nonoperational conditions, require special printing of test booklets, and typically require special data collection studies. By seeding new items among operational items in CAT–ASVAB, tryout data from highly motivated applicants can be obtained without additonal data collection efforts.

Speeded Subtests. The ASVAB contains two speeded tests: Numerical Operations and Coding Speed. Variation among scores on these tests is primarily attributed to variation in speed among examinees, rather than variation in response accuracy. (Nearly all attempted items are answered correctly, but examinees differ substantially in the number of reached items.) Consequently CAT–ASVAB speeded tests are not modeled by IRT. Like the P&P–ASVAB, the experimental CAT–ASVAB scored these tests by number-correct. Given equivalent time-limits across versions, it was found that CAT–ASVAB test-takers scored higher than P&P test-takers, primarily because pressing an answer key on computer was faster than marking an answer-sheet bubble with P&P. Thus, in the experimental system, an adjustment was made to the speeded-test time limits.

Partly to avoid time-limit specification issues, and partly due to other potential benefits (such as increased precision and desirable score-distribution properties), the operational CAT–ASVAB scores its speeded tests by rate score. One proposal (Greaud & Green, 1986) defined scores as proportion correct divided by the average response latency. Prior to operational use however, it was discovered that this score was susceptible to a possible compromise strategy: pressing answer keys rapidly, and at random. The positive numerator (about .25) and the small denominator produced very high scores, higher than was possible by reading and properly answering the question. Consequently, the operational system incorporates a correction for guessing in the numerator, so that the expected rate score is zero for random guessing.

Administrative Requirements. A number of administrative requirements were imposed on the system to make it suitable for operational use, including easy procedures for changing and confirming power test answers, implicit help calls (brought about by repeatedly pressing invalid keys, or not responding to an item), explicit help calls (to address questions raised by the examinee), and a clock (displayed on the lower right-hand corner of the screen showing the number of items and time remaining on the subtest). Because self-paced test-takers begin and end each timed section at different intervals, a standard wall clock or timer would be cumbersome. The computerized clock provides individualized information, allowing test-takers to pace themselves and use allotted time efficiently. Test-takers are not allowed to skip items, or to review previously answered items. The CAT–ASVAB branching feature requires a response to each item. If allowed, omitting would lead to less optimal scoring, and possibly to particular compromise strategies.

Operational Delivery System

In 1984, the contractor effort to develop a customized hardware platform was abandoned in favor of an off-the-shelf system consisting of networked personal computers (Rafacz & Hetter, 1997). At this time, microcomputing was still in its infancy, and only a few standards were available. The Hewlett Packard (HP) Integral Computer was selected primarily because of its superior portability (25 pounds), large random access memory (1.5 megabytes), fast CPU (8 MHz 6800 Motorola), and advanced graphics display capability (9-inch monitor with electroluminescent display and resolution of 512 by 255 pixels).[6] The HP operating system was UNIX-based, and supported the C programming language. Each station contained a floppy diskette drive, had no internal hard drive, and cost about $5,000.

The system design emphasized the use of RAM, and used a network to download software and items, and upload test-response data. To increase test security, no hard drive storage was used. All software and data were stored in RAM at each station. This allowed each station to operate independently of every other station so that network traffic did not slow system response. In the case of hardware failure, the test-taker response data was recorded on diskette, and could be transferred to any other station in the network for completion of the battery. Software was designed and written by in-house personnel to implement the psychometric procedures and item pools for operational use.

Although software development is an obviously important step in system development, an equal, but not so obviously important, step is acceptance testing. Here, we make a distinction between *software testing* (performed by software programmers) and *acceptance testing* (performed by an independent group, preferably those who are most familiar with the system requirements). In development of the operational CAT–ASVAB system, the time and effort dedicated to acceptance testing matched or exceeded that spent by programmers developing and debugging code.

Several useful refinements to acceptance testing procedures developed over the course of the project. First, it is useful to prioritize errors into level of

---

[6]Although these specifications seem pathetic by today's standards, they were advanced relative to other personal computers of the time.

severity, into those that affect: (I) what the examinee observes (item selection, familiarization, and practice screens), (II) final test scores, and (III) other software functions (networking, failure recovery, database accuracy, etc.). The severity of the error will often determine the necessary course of action, and the timing of this action. Almost without exception, Type I errors must be fixed because they have psychometric implications for test accuracy and validity. However, if the system is used nonoperationally for low-stakes research, then some Type II and III errors can be tolerated, because final scores can be computed after-the-fact, and not all data and networking functions are necessary. If the system is operational, then some Type III errors may be tolerated, because not all database fields and software functions are crucial. The course of action taken for each discovered error depends on the software use and the specific nature of the error.

Another useful acceptance-testing refinement included strict configuration management controls. To ensure that the proper software components were evaluated, all source code was compiled on a dedicated configuration management computer. The resulting computer program executable was compared to that provided by the software development group. This step was especially important when large numbers of individuals were involved in source code development, and changes were being made on a frequent basis.

A catalog of testing scenarios was developed over the course of the project to test important software functions. As errors were discovered and refinements made, additional scenarios were added to ensure software compliance. Two types of scenarios were developed: automated (where test-taker input was read from a file) and manual (where input was entered manually at the keyboard). Automated checks were used to verify item selection and scoring; manual scenarios were used to verify the accuracy of item presentation, system timing, database integrity, and failure-recovery procedures. Because of the complex interdependencies among software components, the entire catalog of scenarios was examined after a software modification, regardless of how small or trivial the change may have appeared.

KEY RESEARCH AND OUTCOMES

A number of studies played central roles in the eventual decision to implement CAT–ASVAB nationwide. These studies examined the comparability of the CAT and P&P versions of the ASVAB, the utility of adding new computerized predictors, and the economic benefits derived from CAT. This research provided policymakers with the reassurance necessary to make dramatic changes to the Armed Forces selection and classification system.

Human Factors

During the 1970s and early 1980s, the use of computers among young men and women was limited primarily to those with specialized interests. There was some concern that lack of computer experience among the majority of youth would be an impediment to accurate and valid CAT–ASVAB measurement. It was also believed that the favorable results obtained with the experimental CAT–ASVAB concerning clarity of instructions may not generalize to military applicants. First, the instructions for the operational CAT–ASVAB system had undergone extensive revisions to accommodate necessary changes for administration to applicants. Second, all previous studies had been conducted with recruits who had taken the ASVAB (P&P version) prior to enlistment, and who had scored in the middle or upper ranges. Consequently, it was important to evaluate instructions on a broad range of test-takers who did not have the benefit of prior ASVAB exposure.

Data were gathered from a sample of 231 military applicants and 73 high school students to address issues relating to computer familiarity, instruction clarity, and attitudes toward CAT–ASVAB. Data were collected during October and November of 1986. After completing CAT–ASVAB, each participant received a 42-item questionnaire. In addition, about 90 test-takers participated in structured interviews. In general, both computer-naive and experienced test-takers felt very comfortable using the HP-computer, exhibited positive attitudes toward CAT–ASVAB, and preferred a computerized test over P&P. Test-takers strongly agreed that the instructions were easy to understand, although some examinees did not understand particular words in the instructions (e.g., proctor). Based on the pilot study results, the reading grade level of some words and phrases was lowered to make the directions comprehensible to the target applicant population. The only negative outcome was the finding that many test-takers were bothered by not being able to review and modify previously answered questions. Because of the requirements of the adaptive testing algorithm, this aspect of CAT–ASVAB was not altered (Vicino & Moreno, 1997).

Reliability and Construct Validity

The constructs measured by an adaptive test, and the precision of scores depend on a number of factors, including content and quality of the item pool, item selection, scoring, and exposure algorithms, and the clarity of test instructions. Although IRT provides a basis for making theoretical predictions about these psychometric properties, most assumptions on which these predictions are based are violated, at least to some degree. Consequently before CAT–ASVAB scores were used operationally in high-stakes testing, an empirical verification of its precision and construct equivalence with the P&P–ASVAB was conducted. If CAT and P&P versions measured the same constructs, and the CAT–ASVAB version provided equal or greater precision, then the massive amount of predictive validity evidence accumulated on the P&P version would be directly applicable to CAT–ASVAB. Construct equivalence would also support the exchangeability of the two versions, allowing both versions to be used concurrently for selection and classification.

To study reliability and construct validity, military recruits were administered two alternate ASVAB forms (Moreno & Segall, 1997). One group ($N = 1,033$) received two P&P–ASVAB forms; another randomly equivalent group ($N = 1,057$) received two CAT–ASVAB forms. All participants' operational P&P–ASVAB scores taken prior to enlistment were also analyzed. Reliability coefficients for each medium were estimated from the correlations between like-named subtests of alternate forms. Evidence of construct equivalence was obtained from disattenuated correlations between CAT–ASVAB and operational P&P–ASVAB versions.

In comparison to the P&P–ASVAB, 7 of the 10 CAT–ASVAB tests displayed significantly higher alternate-forms reliability coefficients. The other three tests displayed nonsignificant differences. Nine of the 10 disattenuated correlations between CAT and the operational P&P were about 1.0 (with a very narrow confidence interval due to the large sample sizes). Only one speeded test (Coding Speed) displayed a disattenuated correlation substantially less than 1.0 (.86), which may be attributed to the differences in instruction clarity between the written (CAT) and oral (P&P) versions. The low disattenuated correlation for Coding Speed was not considered problematic because selection composites that contain this subtest had high disattenuated CAT–P&P correlations approaching 1.0. In general, these results confirmed the expectations based on theoretical IRT predictions: that CAT–ASVAB measured the same constructs as its P&P counterpart with equivalent or greater precision.

Equating CAT and P&P Versions

Equating is a psychometric analysis designed to place scores from two versions of a test (typically an older reference form and a new form) on the same scale. Equating CAT–ASVAB to the P&P scale was seen as a major psychometric hurdle to implementation. Historically, qualification standards for entrance into the military and into occupational specialties had been specified relative to the P&P–ASVAB number-correct score–scale. The CAT–ASVAB produces scores on the IRT ability metric. Before CAT–ASVAB could be used in high-stakes testing, an equating procedure for placing CAT scores on the P&P metric was required. The objective of the equating was to provide a transformation of the

CAT–ASVAB scale so that its score distribution would match the P&P version. This transformation, when applied to CAT–ASVAB, would allow scores on the versions to be used interchangeably, without disrupting applicant qualification rates.

The equating study (Segall, 1997a) addressed three concerns. First, how could qualification rates associated with the existing P&P–ASVAB cut-scores be preserved for CAT–ASVAB? Several equating procedures were considered and rejected. Ultimately, an equipercentile equating procedure based on observed test scores from test-takers was used to obtain the required transformations. Distribution smoothing procedures were used to increase the precision of the transformations and the equivalence of CAT–P&P composite distributions were verified to ensure that the use of CAT–ASVAB would not disrupt flow rates. (Although equating was performed at the subtest level, qualification scores are based on composites.)

A second concern dealt with disadvantaged subgroups: Subgroup members taking CAT–ASVAB should not be placed at a disadvantage relative to their subgroup counterparts taking the P&P–ASVAB. Although it is desirable to match distributions for subgroups as well as the entire group, this may not be possible for a variety of reasons. First, differences in precision between the CAT and P&P versions may magnify existing differences between subgroups. Second, small differences in dimensionality, such as the verbal loading of a test, may cause differential subgroup performance. The issue of subgroup differences was addressed by applying the equating transformation (based on the entire group) to subgroup members taking CAT–ASVAB, and comparing their distribution to their P&P counterparts. For specified subgroups (Blacks and women), the difference between CAT and P&P means was used to assess relative advantage/disadvantage among CAT–ASVAB test-takers. Although some statistically significant subgroup differences were observed from the equating study data, their practical significance on qualification rates was small.

The final concern addressed by the equating study dealt with the effects of motivation and other population characteristics on the equating transformation. Specifically, who should participate in the study, and under what conditions should they be tested? To eliminate the effects of motivation on the final equating transformation, the study was conducted in two phases. The first phase (Score Equating Development) was used to obtain a provisional equating based on data collected under nonoperationally motivated conditions. The second phase (Score Equating Verification) was used to obtain an equating transformation based on operationally motivated applicants, whose CAT–ASVAB scores were transformed to the P&P metric using the provisional equating. For P&P–ASVAB equating studies, the first phase is typically conducted on a sample of convenience—military recruits. However, for this first attempt at CAT–ASVAB equating, the provisional

equating was based on military applicants. Applicants were chosen over recruits primarily to provide the full range of scores necessary to obtain a precise
estimate of the transformation over the lower ranges. The choice of applicants
resulted in an especially burdensome data collection effort from both the applicant and recruiter perspective. It meant a full day of testing, rather than the
normal half-day. (In additional to taking a nonoperational CAT or P&P version,
each applicant was required to take an operational P&P version for enlistment
purposes.) The choice of applicants was especially fortuitous because a later
study conducted with recruits found the equating transformation to differ
across recruit and applicant populations (Segall, 1997c).

The equating data collection and analysis spanned a 4-year period from
1988 to 1992. For the Score Equating Development phase, data were gathered
from over 8,000 military applicants. Three randomly equivalent groups of
about 2,700 each were administered either a nonoperational P&P–ASVAB
form, or one of two nonoperational CAT–ASVAB forms. Scores on the
nonoperational CAT and P&P versions did not affect the applicant's eligibility
for enlistment, and were used to construct the provisional equating.[7] For the
second Score Equating Verification Phase, additional data were gathered from
about 10,400 applicants. Three randomly equivalent groups of about 3,500
each were administered either an operational P&P–ASVAB form, or one of
two operational CAT–ASVAB forms. In this phase, scores on the CAT and
P&P versions did affect the applicant's eligibility for enlistment and were used
to construct the final equating for CAT–ASVAB.

The results of the equating studies were noteworthy from several respects.
First, although some statistically significant subgroup differences were observed, their practical significance on qualification rates was small. Second,
the provisional and final transformations obtained from the nonoperational
and operational data collections were very similar, indicating that data collection and analytic procedures were consistent and reliable. Third, the beginning
of the Score Equating Verification phase in September 1990 marked a mile-
stone in the CAT–ASVAB project: For the first time, CAT–ASVAB was administered operationally in a high-stakes environment to qualify applicants for
military service.

Economic Analysis I: Enhancing ASVAB Content

Ironically, as data were collected to address the last major psychometric obsta-
cle (equating), the future prospects for CAT–ASVAB implementation had
reached an all time low. This pessimism was based primarily on a costs-benefits

---

[7]Nonoperational tests were administered first, followed by an operational P&P–ASVAB used
for selection and classification. By using only data from the first (nonoperational) test to develop
the equating, levels of fatigue and practice were expected to be equivalent across CAT and P&P
versions, and were expected to closely match those occurring under operational testing conditions.

analysis (Automated Sciences Group & CACI, 1988). This analysis weighed costs associated with CAT–ASVAB (e.g., computer hardware) against the potential savings accrued by improved selection and classification. The benefits of CAT–ASVAB were measured in terms of improved prediction of job success using a formulation developed by Cronbach and Gleser (1965). At the heart of this approach was the notion that the increased precision of CAT–ASVAB would lead to improved predictive validity. Unfortunately, at this point in the development cycle, the emphasis in efficiency led to a design that stressed time-savings (i.e., short tests), as opposed to increased precision. CAT–ASVAB was designed to be about half as long as its P&P counterpart, with equal or slightly greater precision. Consequently, the gain in predictive validity (correlation of test performance with training success) obtained by CAT–ASVAB was estimated to be a mere .005. Results indicated that the benefit based on the dollar value of improved person–job match was not great enough to offset the costs of computers. It was believed that a significant increase in predictive validity (above that provided by CAT–ASVAB) would be required to make CAT cost effective. Accordingly, the CAT–ASVAB program was redirected toward a joint service validation of new computerized cognitive and psychomotor tests. Support for this redirection came from a prediction made by Schmidt, Hunter, and Dunn (1987), who indicated that adding perceptual speed and psychomotor tests to the ASVAB could result in hundreds of millions of dollars' worth of personnel performance improvements annually.

The enhanced CAT (or ECAT) validity study (Wolfe, Alderton, Larson, Bloxom, & Wise, 1997) was intended to provide an empirical verification of the increased validity associated with new types of computerized tests. Specifically, the study was designed to identify the aptitude constructs that are likely to make the greatest contribution to increased validity and to provide estimates of their relative validity gains. Nine tests measuring four constructs were included in the experimental battery: nonverbal reasoning, spatial ability, psychomotor skill, and perceptual speed. Six of the nine tests required computer administration, whereas three tests had P&P counterparts.[8] These measures can be classified as tests of fluid intelligence, rather than as measures of crystallized intelligence assessed by most ASVAB tests. As measures of fluid intelligence, it was believed (and later confirmed with empirical data) that these measures were likely to display less adverse impact for educationally disadvantaged subgroups.

---

[8]CAT–ASVAB provided two practical opportunities for expanding ASVAB content. First, the computerized platform allowed types of measures not possible in P&P format. Second, the time savings resulting from the shortened adaptive power tests provided extra time for computerized versions of P&P assessments.

Predictor and criteria data were gathered from over 11,000 recruits attending 1 of 18 schools. Criteria included quizzes, homework assignments, and laboratory/shop exercises. Where possible, performance criteria were used in preference to written tests, because it was expected that the new tests would display the largest incremental validities with hands-on measures. The incremental validity of the new measures over ASVAB was estimated to be .031 using these performance-based criteria. According to the utility analysis, this gain should be sufficient to offset capital investment in computers. However, for several reasons, these results were not viewed as justification for CAT–ASVAB's benefits.

First, to obtain the full validity increment, the entire battery of nine tests (taking about 3 hours) would need to be added to the ASVAB. This was considered impractical from a recruiting and processing standpoint. With room to add only a small number of tests, the resulting incremental validity was not considered sufficiently large. Because of other practical constraints, tests were not considered for inclusion unless they could also be administered by P&P.[9] Among the remaining tests, Assembling Objects had the broadest application (in terms of incremental validity) and was tentatively added to the ASVAB, pending results of more extensive validity studies.

With ECAT validity data in hand, a second economic analysis was conducted to assess the feasibility of implementing CAT–ASVAB.

Economic Analysis II: Effects on Applicant Processing

In 1992, a confluence of events shaped the next economic analysis and the eventual decision to implement CAT–ASVAB. During this time frame, the ECAT validity study was nearing completion, and results were only moderately supportive of sufficient incremental validity. The equating study had just been completed, overcoming the last hurdle to operational use, and preparations were underway for an updated economic analysis. In framing the approach for the second economic analysis, it was apparent that the use of hypothetical utility dollars did not provide sufficiently compelling justification to policy makers who would be asked to divert real dollars from other sources to pay for computer hardware. Consequently, the revised utility analysis was expanded to include the economic effects of CAT–ASVAB on applicant processing.

The operational impact of CAT–ASVAB was examined in an Operational Test and Evaluation (OT&E) study conducted at five geographically disperse locations (Moreno, 1997). Together, these sites tested about 7% of all military applicants. Several types of data were collected, including CAT–ASVAB,

---

[9]The ASVAB concept of operation specified that the battery would be administered in both CAT and P&P formats and that the same constructs should be measured by both versions.

onsite observations, interviews (with testing personnel and recruiters), and questionnaires (recruiter and applicants). Several key findings with economic ramifications were identified. First, flexible start times (the ability for test-takers to start the test at individualized times) and the shorter CAT–ASVAB test length led to a reduction in the estimate of the number of required computers. Second, CAT–ASVAB enabled some sites to conduct 1-day processing, where the candidate could complete all processing and screening activities in a single day. Because of fewer meal and lodging expenditures, applicant processing costs were substantially reduced.

The limited implementation of the OT&E study also marked an important turning point in project support. Exceptional system design and performance led to the enthusiastic support of CAT–ASVAB by testing and recruiting personnel. It also eliminated any remaining concerns from Policy and Technical staff about the operational impact of the system. In fact, users of CAT–ASVAB were so enthusiastic that on completion of the study, all expressed an extreme reluctance to revert back to P&P testing. Consequently, CAT–ASVAB testing continued at these locations until the final system was implemented nationally several years later.

Armed with data from the OT&E study, a second economic analysis was conducted (Wise, Curran, & McBride, 1997). The primary objectives of the study were to determine how CAT–ASVAB would be used operationally and if its benefits justified hardware and other incremental costs. This study held the quality of selection and classification decisions constant across P&P and CAT versions, and rather focused on benefits relating to the reduction in recruiting and enlistment processing costs. The length (time) of the battery influenced these later costs. Thus the primary strength of CAT–ASVAB (shorter testing time) played a significant role in the outcome, unlike the first economic analysis, which did not consider operational savings. Based in large part on the feasibility of 1-day processing with CAT–ASVAB, the economic analysis indicated that savings in recruiting and processing costs would exceed the hardware costs after just 1 year. This outcome played a significant role in the decision to implement CAT–ASVAB at all high-volume locations nationwide, which together test about half of all applicants. Other applicants are tested at Mobile Examining Team Sites (METS), where it is impractical, for the most part, to use desktop computers. Studies are currently underway to examine the most cost effective strategy for testing at METS.

NATIONWIDE IMPLEMENTATION

Before CAT–ASVAB could be administered on a national scale, a new delivery system was required. The HP computers used previously were no longer manufactured. The use of new machines raised issues about the psychometric comparability of different hardware. Additional studies were conducted to address this and other issues concerning test compromise and the development of new forms.

Delivery System

The requirements of the nationwide delivery system were based on the capabilities of the HP and experiences from the OT&E study (Unpingco, Hom, & Rafacz, 1997). A number of factors were considered in hardware selection, including portability, microprocessor, random access memory, disk storage, monitor, networking capability, and input device. An attempt was made to select a system constructed from commonly used components. This would likely reduce maintenance costs, provide for future growth, and delay system obsolescence. Fortunately, nearly all performance standards of the HP system (designed in the mid-1980s) were met or exceeded by personal computers available in 1993. The selected system was an Intel-based compatible, with a 33Mhz or faster microprocessor. Only 4MB of RAM was required, with a 14-inch SVGA video monitor. Additional requirements included an 80MB hard drive, and an ethernet-networking card. Many of the psychometric routines for test administration and scoring were transported to the new system, although about 80% of the code was rewritten and designed specifically for the MS-DOS environment.

Hardware Effects

The use of a new delivery system led to concerns about the psychometric comparability of different hardware. It was conceivable that differences among computer hardware (monitor size and resolution, keyboard layout, physical dimensions) could influence item functioning. There was some evidence that speeded tests contained in the ASVAB were especially sensitive to small changes in test presentation format, more so than the adaptive power tests. A study was conducted to provide some insight into the exchangeability of different hardware—whether machines of different makes and models can be used interchangeably, and which hardware characteristics must remain constant among testing platforms to ensure adequate precision and score interpretation (Segall, 1997b). The study was designed to examine three psychometric characteristics, including score–scale, precision, and construct validity. Data were gathered from 3,062 subjects recruited from the San Diego area. Each subject was randomly assigned to one of 13 conditions. The effects of several hardware characteristics were studied, including input device, color scheme, monitor type, CPU speed, and portability. The outcome of the study indicated that adaptive power tests were robust to differences among computer hardware, whereas speeded tests are likely to be affected by several hardware characteristics.

Results of the hardware effects study demonstrated the sensitivity of speeded tests to hardware differences, supporting the need for an additional equating study using the new hardware. As in the previous study, this equating was conducted in two phases. The first phase used recruits to develop a provisional transformation; it used a random groups design with about 2,500 respondents per form. The second phase tested applicants using the provisional transformation to provide operational scores. This second data collection effort was also a random groups design with about 10,000 test-takers per form.

After completion of the first phase, there was suspicion that the provisional equating was flawed. This was based on a comparison of transformations (for the same forms) estimated from previous studies using the HP. It was hypothesized that for recruits there were different levels of motivation/fatigue between CAT and P&P groups, and this resulted in a biased estimate of the provisional equating transformation. The difference was in a direction that suggested that CAT examinees were more motivated than P&P examinees (possibly due to shorter test lengths or novel/interactive medium). Consequently, the prior equating based on the HP system was used provisionally (for power tests), and the equating based on the new hardware was used for the speed tests. A later analysis of operational applicant data confirmed suspicions that the recruit equating was flawed. Findings suggested that the results of a cross-medium equating may differ depending on whether the respondents are motivated or unmotivated. In future equatings, this problem may be circumvented by performing only within medium equatings when a sample's degree of motivation is in doubt.

Test Compromise

Several concerns about CAT–ASVAB test security led to a reevaluation of the effects of possible compromise. First, expected item usage rates resulting from the Sympson–Hetter algorithm are based on an assumed ability distribution, and may depart from those obtained with the actual ability distribution, especially for homogeneous subgroups. Second, each adaptively administered item may influence the final score more than an item on the P&P test, because CAT tests tend to be shorter than their P&P counterparts. Thus, knowledge of a single CAT item may result in a larger score gain than knowledge of a single item administered in a conventional P&P test. These concerns about the susceptibility of CAT to compromise motivated a simulation study (Segall, 1995) that examined the expected score gains resulting from six different compromise strategies. Strategies differed across three dimensions: the transmittal mechanism (sharing among friends or item banking), the correlation between the cheater and informant ability levels, and the method used by the informant to select items for disclosure. The dependent measure was score gain, which represented the mean gain for the group of cheaters over a group of noncheaters for the same fixed ability level. Score gains were computed for both CAT (assuming two forms), and for P&P (assuming six forms). The results indicated that the score gains for CAT were larger than those for the corresponding P&P conditions, with the largest CAT–P&P gain differences occurring for cheaters at the lowest ability ranges. Results suggested that more stringent item exposure controls should be imposed on the adaptive selection process. The effects of altering several characteristics of the adaptive test on potential score gains were also investigated. It was found that increasing the number of CAT forms (from two to three) had a substantial reduction in score-gain. Using three forms of CAT provided score gains equivalent to or less than those observed for six forms of the P&P–ASVAB under all compromise strategies. These results led to the decision to implement additional CAT–ASVAB forms.

Two additional CAT–ASVAB forms were subsequently developed (Thomasson, 1996), one for use in the operational testing program and another for use in a national norming study. The operational form (along with two other previously developed forms) will be used to help guard against compromise. The second form will become the new ASVAB reference form, to be administered to a nationally representative sample of young men and women. This form will be withheld from routine use and only administered in future equating studies. For these new forms, about 5,200 items were developed. About half the items were calibrated on a sample of over 100,000 military applicants, providing about 1,500 responses per item. Analyses found that dividing the item bank into two forms resulted in less precise ability estimates in some areas than the P&P–ASVAB. Consequently, some content areas were supplemented with highly informative items (originally intended for new P&P–ASVAB forms) to meet the precision criterion. These new forms will undergo equating studies similar in design to previous forms.

The implementation of CAT–ASVAB is expected to lead to additional challenges and refinements (Segall & Moreno, 1997). CAT–ASVAB data are being collected as part of the 1997 Profile of American Youth Study, which is a national norming study conducted jointly by the Department of Labor and the Department of Defense (DOD). It will serve two important purposes. First, it will provide information about the availability of high quality young men and women. This information can be used by force planners to determine the levels of advertising and enlistment incentives required to attract the necessary numbers of qualified applicants to fill jobs of increasing complexity. These data will also provide an opportunity to develop a new score–scale based on the natural IRT metric. This score–scale may have improved measurement properties over the existing number-right scale based on the P&P–ASVAB.

The implementation of CAT–ASVAB will also enable considerable stream-lining of new form development. DOD is considering the possibility of elimi-nating all special form-development, data-collection studies by replacing them with online calibration and equating. Currently, new item data are being col-lected by seeding experimental items among operational items. These data will be used to estimate IRT item parameters. These parameters can, in turn, be used to construct future forms, and possibly estimate provisional equating transformations. These provisional (theoretical) equatings could then be up-dated after they are used operationally to test randomly equivalent groups. Thus, the entire cycle of form development can, in principle, be seamlessly in-tegrated into operational test administrations.

SUMMARY

Over the last two decades, many benefits of computerized adaptive testing to the U.S. Armed Forces have been enumerated, studied, and placed into prac-tice. As the world's largest employer of young men and women, the DOD en-sured that the CAT–ASVAB matched or exceeded the high standards set by the P&P–ASVAB before making an implementation decision. This assurance was provided by numerous theoretical and empirical studies, and along the way to implementation, a number of important contributions to the field of psychometrics were made. In the years to come, inevitable ASVAB changes and refinements will likely add even greater efficiencies to this important component of the Armed Services selection and classification system.

REFERENCES

Automated Sciences Group & CACI. (1988). *CAT-ASVAB program: Concept of op-eration and cost/benefit analysis*. Fairfax, VA: Author.

Cronbach, L. J., & Gleser, G. C. (1965). *Psychological tests and personnel decisions* (2nd ed.). Urbana, IL: University of Illinois Press.

Greaud, V. A., & Green, B. G. (1986). Equivalence of conventional and computer presentation of speed tests. *Applied Psychological Measurement, 10*, 23–34.

Hetter, R. D., Segall, D. O., & Bloxom, B. M. (1994). A comparison of item calibra-tion media in computerized adaptive testing. *Applied Psychological Measurement, 18*, 197–204.

Hetter, R. D., Segall, D. O., & Bloxom, B. M. (1997). Evaluating item calibration medium in computerized adaptive testing. In W. A. Sands, B. K. Waters, & J. R. McBride (Eds.), *Computerized adaptive testing: From inquiry to operation* (pp. 161–167). Washington, DC: American Psychological Association.

Hetter, R. D., & Sympson, J. B. (1997). Item exposure control in CAT–ASVAB. In W. A. Sands, B. K. Waters, & J. R. McBride (Eds.), *Computerized adaptive testing: From inquiry to operation* (pp. 141–144). Washington, DC: American Psychological Association.

Lord, F. M. (1971). The self-scoring flexilevel test. *Journal of Educational Measurement, 8,* 147–151.

Lord, F. M. (1980). *Applications of item response theory to practical testing problems.* Hillsdale, NJ: Lawrence Erlbaum Associates.

Maier, M. H. (1993). *Military aptitude testing: The past fifty years.* (Report No. 93-007). Monterey, CA: Defense Manpower Data Center.

Martin, C. J., & Hoshaw, R. (1997). Policy and program management perspective. In W. A. Sands, B. K. Waters, & J. R. McBride (Eds.), *Computerized adaptive testing: From inquiry to operation* (pp. 11–20). Washington, DC: American Psychological Association.

McBride, J. R. (1997). The Marine Corps exploratory development project: 1977–1982. In W. A. Sands, B. K. Waters, & J. R. McBride (Eds.), *Computerized adaptive testing: From inquiry to operation* (pp. 59–67). Washington, DC: American Psychological Association.

McBride, J. R., & Martin, J. T. (1983). Reliability and validity of adaptive verbal ability tests in a military setting. In D. J. Weiss (Ed.), *New horizons in testing* (pp. 223–235). New York, NY: Academic Press.

Moreno, K. E. (1986). *A procedure for producing parallel item pools for computerized adaptive testing.* Unpublished manuscript, Navy Personnel Research and Development Center, San Diego, CA.

Moreno, K. E. (1997). CAT–ASVAB operational test and evaluation. In W. A. Sands, B. K. Waters, & J. R. McBride (Eds.), *Computerized adaptive testing: From inquiry to operation* (pp. 199–205). Washington, DC: American Psychological Association.

Moreno, K. E., & Segall, D. O. (1997). Reliability and construct validity of CAT–ASVAB. In W. A. Sands, B. K. Waters, & J. R. McBride (Eds.), *Computerized adaptive testing: From inquiry to operation* (pp. 169–174). Washington, DC: American Psychological Association.

Moreno, K. E., Wetzel, C. D., McBride, J. R., & Weiss, D. J. (1984). Relationship between corresponding Armed Services Vocational Aptitude Battery (ASVAB) and Computerized Adaptive Testing (CAT) subtests. *Applied Psychological Measurement, 8,* 155–163.

Owen, R. J. (1969). *A Bayesian approach to tailored testing* (RB-69-92). Princeton, NJ: Educational Testing Service.

Owen, R. J. (1975). A Bayesian sequential procedure for quantal response in the context of adaptive mental testing. *Journal of the American Statistical Association, 70,* 351–356.

Prestwood, J. S., Vale, C. D., Massey, R. H., & Welsh, J. R. (1985). *Armed Services Vocational Aptitude Battery: development of an adaptive item pool* (TR-85-19). San Antonio, TX: Air Force Systems Command, Brooks Air Force Base.

Rafacz, B., & Hetter, R. D. (1997). ACAP hardware selection, software development, and acceptance testing. In W. A. Sands, B. K. Waters, & J. R. McBride (Eds.), *Computerized adaptive testing: From inquiry to operation* (pp. 145–156). Washington, DC: American Psychological Association.

Schmidt, F. L., Hunter, J., & Dunn, W. (1987). *Potential utility increases from adding new tests to the Armed Services Vocational Aptitude Battery* (TN-95-5). San Diego, CA: Navy Personnel Research and Development Center.

Segall, D. O. (1987). *A procedure for scoring incomplete adaptive tests.* Unpublished manuscript, San Diego, CA: Navy Personnel Research and Development Center.

Segall, D. O. (1995, May). *The effects of item compromise on computerized adaptive test scores.* Paper presented at the meeting of the Society for Industrial and Organizational Psychology, Orlando, FL.

Segall, D. O. (1997a). Equating the CAT–ASVAB. In W. A. Sands, B. K. Waters, & J. R. McBride (Eds.), *Computerized adaptive testing: From inquiry to operation* (pp. 181–198). Washington, DC: American Psychological Association.

Segall, D. O. (1997b). The psychometric comparability of computer hardware. In W. A. Sands, B. K. Waters, & J. R. McBride (Eds.), *Computerized adaptive testing: From inquiry to operation* (pp. 219–226). Washington, DC: American Psychological Association.

Segall, D. O. (1997c, March). *The effects of motivation on equating adaptive and conventional tests.* Paper presented at the meeting of the National Council on Measurement in Education, Chicago, IL.

Segall, D. O., & Moreno, K. E. (1997). Current and future challenges. In W. A. Sands, B. K. Waters, & J. R. McBride (Eds.), *Computerized adaptive testing: From inquiry to operation* (pp. 257–269). Washington, DC: American Psychological Association.

Segall, D. O., Moreno, K. E., & Hetter, R. D. (1997). Item pool development and evaluation. In W. A. Sands, B. K. Waters, & J. R. McBride (Eds.), *Computerized adaptive testing: From inquiry to operation* (pp. 117–130). Washington, DC: American Psychological Association.

Segall, D. O., Moreno, K. E., Bloxom, B. M., & Hetter, R. D. (1997). Psychometric procedures for administering CAT–ASVAB. In W. A. Sands, B. K. Waters, & J. R. McBride (Eds.), *Computerized adaptive testing: From inquiry to operation* (pp. 131–140). Washington, DC: American Psychological Association.

Segall, D. O., Moreno, K. E., Kieckhaefer, W. F., Vicino, F. L., & McBride, J. R. (1997). Validation of the experimental CAT–ASVAB system. In W. A. Sands, B. K. Waters, & J. R. McBride (Eds.), *Computerized adaptive testing: From inquiry to operation* (pp. 103–114). Washington, DC: American Psychological Association.

Sympson, J. B., & Hetter, R. D. (1985). *Controlling item exposure rates in computerized adaptive tests.* Paper presented at the Annual Conference of the Military Testing Association, San Diego, CA.

Thomasson, G. L. (1996). *Item pool development for CAT–ASVAB Forms 3 and 4.* Unpublished manuscript, Defense Manpower Data Center, Monterey, CA.

Unpingco, V., Hom, I., & Rafacz, B. (1997). Development of a system for nationwide implementation. In W. A. Sands, B. K. Waters, & J. R. McBride (Eds.), *Computerized adaptive testing: From inquiry to operation* (pp. 209–218). Washington, DC: American Psychological Association.

Urry, V. W. (1974). Approximations to item parameters of mental test models and their uses. *Educational and Psychological Measurement, 34,* 253–269.

Urry, V. W. (1983). *Tailored testing and practice: A basic model, normal ogive models, and tailored testing algorithms* (NTIS No. AD-A133385). Washington, DC: Office of Personnel Management.

Vale, C. D., & Gialluca, K. A. (1985). *ASCAL: A microcomputer program for estimating logistic IRT item parameters* (RR ONR 85-4). St. Paul, MN: Assessment Systems Corp.

Vicino, F. L., & Moreno, K. E. (1997). Human factors in the CAT system: a pilot study. In W. A. Sands, B. K. Waters, & J. R. McBride (Eds.), *Computerized adaptive testing: From inquiry to operation* (pp. 157–160). Washington, DC: American Psychological Association.

Weiss, D. J. (1974). *Strategies of adaptive ability measurement* (RR 74-5). Minneapolis, MN: Psychometric Methods Program, Department of Psychology, University of Minnesota.

Weiss, D. J. (1975). *Computerized adaptive ability measurement.* Paper presented at the Annual Conference of the Military Testing Association, Fort Benjamin Harrison, IN.

Wetzel, C. D., & McBride, J. R. (1983). *The influence of fallible item parameters on test information during adaptive test* (TR 83-15). San Diego, CA: Navy Personnel Research and Development Center.

Wetzel, C. D., & McBride, J. R. (1985). Reducing the predictability of adaptive item sequences. *Proceedings of the Annual Conference of the Military Testing Association, 1,* 43–48.

Wise, L. L., Curran, L. T., & McBride, J. R. (1997). CAT–ASVAB cost and benefit analyses. In W. A. Sands, B. K. Waters, & J. R. McBride (Eds.), *Computerized adaptive testing: From inquiry to operation* (pp. 227–236). Washington, DC: American Psychological Association.

Wolfe, J. H., McBride, J. R., & Sympson, J. B. (1997). Development of the experimental CAT–ASVAB system. In W. A. Sands, B. K. Waters, & J. R. McBride (Eds.), *Computerized adaptive testing: From inquiry to operation* (pp. 97–101). Washington, DC: American Psychological Association.

Wolfe, J. H., Alderton, D. L., Larson, G. E., Bloxom, B. M., & Wise, L. L. (1997). Expanding the content of CAT–ASVAB: New tests and their validity. In W. A. Sands, B. K. Waters, & J. R. McBride (Eds.), *Computerized adaptive testing: From inquiry to operation* (pp. 239–249). Washington, DC: American Psychological Association.

Wood, R. L., Wingersky, M. S., & Lord, F. M. (1976). *LOGIST-A computer program for estimating examinee ability and item characteristic curve parameters* (Research Memorandum 76-6). Princeton, NJ: Educational Testing Service.

4

CAT for Certification and Licensure

Betty A. Bergstrom
Computer Adaptive Technologies, Inc., Chicago

Mary E. Lunz
American Society of Clinical Pathologists, Chicago

Computer based testing (CBT) has many advantages for examinees: convenience in scheduling, increased testing opportunities, automated data collection and prompt score reporting. This chapter presents information on one form of computer based testing, computerized adaptive testing or CAT. Although our experience and examples come from the certification and licensure arena, many aspects of this chapter will be useful to other test developers and users who are considering computerizing their assessment tools. The lessons we have learned are applicable across a wide range of domains.

The credentialing or licensing process is typically overseen by a certification or licensure board. Examinations are often part of the credentialing process and tests are developed by committees of subject matter experts from the particular field. Examples of professions that certify or license individuals include allied health, medicine, and architecture. This chapter discusses implementing CAT for high-stakes examinations that determine whether or not a particular candidate will be certified or licensed. The experience of several boards who have chosen to administer their licensure or certification examinations using the principles of CAT illustrates the process of moving into this mode of administration. Examples of the variety of options that can be utilized within a CAT administration are presented, the decisions that boards must make to implement CAT are discussed, and a timetable for completing the tasks that need to be accomplished is provided. In addition to the theoretical aspects of CAT, practical issues and problems are reviewed.

Computerized adaptive testing is a popular form of CBT because it enables shorter tests and provides licensure and credentialing boards with increased test security. CAT operates on the principle that items which are too easy or too difficult for a candidate contribute little information about that candidate's ability (Green, Bock, Humphreys, Linn, & Reckase, 1984). As a candidate takes a computerized adaptive test, the estimate of his or her ability is continually estimated based on all items presented to that point in the test. After each item, the current estimate of candidate ability is compared with the available items in the bank. The computer algorithm selects the best item available given all test specifications and the current estimate of examinee ability. In this way, items that are too hard or too easy for the candidate are not administered and the candidate takes an individualized examination. Competence is continually assessed online, and the difficulty of the test is targeted or tailored to the estimated ability of the candidate. Efficiency is gained because each candidate answers items appropriate to his or her ability, so test length can be shortened without sacrificing reliability.

REVIEWING THE PAPER-AND-PENCIL EXAMINATION PROCESS

Before an organization can move into CAT, the current paper-and-pencil examination process should be carefully reviewed. Boards must decide what components of the current process are essential to maintaining the validity of their examination. Issues such as protecting the public and serving their customer base (including candidates and educators) are factors for boards to consider. If an item bank and a test procedure are not already in place, the following information will also be useful for initial development of a computerized examination process.

In a typical paper-and-pencil licensure or certification examination process, committees of subject matter experts are asked to write and review items for inclusion in an item bank. They categorize the items according to test specifications, select items to be included on a particular test form, inspect the assembled test, and review item performance after the test is administered (Lunz & Deville, 1996). Tests are administered to large samples of candidates on specific dates one or more times per year. Weeks to months after the test is administered, results are mailed to candidates and programs. Because of computerized test administration and the use of adaptive algorithms, many of these processes change for CAT.

Reviewing Content Specifications and Currency of Items in the Bank

Maintaining content validity is essential for certification and licensure tests. Boards use well-defined content or "blueprint" specifications when constructing examinations to ensure that content validity is maintained (Knapp & Knapp, 1995). Prior to CAT implementation is a good time to redo job analyses and blueprint specifications. All of the items in the bank must be properly classified within content areas, a critical step for insuring that candidates are presented with valid CAT.

Once items are properly classified within the content blueprint, subject matter experts must review the entire item bank, item by item, to ensure that: (a) items are current and relevant to the field of practice; (b) duplicate and similar items are identified and flagged; and (c) item distribution within each content area is representative of the test blueprint (Bergstrom & Gershon, 1995). Because any item in the bank that meets difficulty and content criteria may be selected by the adaptive algorithm, outdated and duplicate items must be removed from the active bank. Adaptive test algorithms allow for content balancing so that the items administered to each candidate follow content percentage specifications (i.e., prespecified percentage of items are selected from each category). Adherence to the test blueprint ensures that the test's content validity, as defined by the job analysis and subject matter experts, is maintained.

In order for items to be utilized uniformly and to avoid overexposure, items in the bank should be distributed proportionally to the test blueprint. For example, if 10% of the adaptive test will be drawn from a specific content area, then approximately 10% of the items in the bank should cover that content area. If one content area in the bank has fewer than the blueprint-specified percentage of items, the items in that content area will be administered more frequently than other items in the bank (Lunz & Deville, 1996), which may lead to overexposure of these items.

Reviewing the Difficulty of Items in the Bank

If a test is adaptive, the range of item difficulty in the bank should reflect the range of ability of the candidate population. When a licensure or certification board initially reviews their item bank for the purpose of implementing CAT, they often find that the bank does not have enough difficult items or enough items near the pass point to construct tailored exams. For this reason, some organizations may need to spend several years building their item bank before CAT implementation. Because each candidate is administered a tailored test in which the difficulty of the items presented varies according to the estimated ability of the candidate, the range of items available for selection must adequately cover the anticipated distribution of candidate ability. Item difficulties should be adequately distributed within each content area as well as across the entire item bank. When the range of calibrated item difficulty is adequate, the bank can provide appropriately tailored examinations for each candidate, thus increasing examination precision and reliability.

The optimal item difficulty distribution depends on the test administration specifications. For example, if the test is variable length, candidates with ability estimates near the pass point will take more items than very highly qualified or very poorly qualified candidates who pass or fail in the minimum number of items. In this case, the distribution of item difficulty should be peaked at the pass point. If the test is fixed-length and scaled scores are reported at the subtest level, the bank will need to be more uniformly distributed.

Bergstrom and Stahl (1992) described a method for assessing the adequacy of the item bank under varying administration conditions that involves computing the information functions (and/or standard errors of measurement) for bank items. The difficulty of items within each subtest and across a range of candidate ability estimates are reviewed. Using the existing item bank, CAT is then simulated under varying content balancing schemes and with varying test lengths. Assessing the adequacy of the bank early in the process of transition provides focus for expanding and refining the item bank. Using this method, the American Society of Clinical Pathologists (ASCP) found that one of their item banks did not have sufficient items to gain maximum information about candidates at varying ability levels. An item writing and field testing campaign was undertaken to correct this deficiency 1 year prior to implementation of the CAT program.

Reviewing Item Bank Size

For security purposes, the more high-quality items in the bank the better, because large numbers of items limit the number of candidates who are presented with any one item (Stahl & Lunz, 1993). However, experience has shown if the bank is large and the candidate population small, items may not be exposed often enough to check the stability of item performance over time. Some items may also be underexposed if large item banks are inappropriately distributed across content and difficulty. For example, if the bank has too many easy items, only a few candidates per year may be administered each of the items.

The minimum number of items acceptable for a CAT item pool is controlled by several factors: test length; size of the candidate population; the percentage of candidates to whom an item may be administered (item exposure); and how individualized each computerized adaptive test should be (item overlap). The security of items that are administered too frequently may be compromised and, if the bank is inadequately distributed, candidates of similar abilities will be presented with many common items. Based on their experience with a number of different banks and varying candidate sample sizes, Stahl and Lunz (1993) suggested that for an annual sample of less than 1,000 candidates, the item bank should contain at least 500 items, optimally between 600 to 800 items, appropriately distributed within and across content areas.

Way (1997) proposed the following guidelines for licensure and certification tests:

1. The exam length to pool size ratio should be from 1 to 6–8. For example, if exam length is 100 items, an adequate bank size would be between 600 to 800 items.
2. On average, an item should only be presented to 10% to 15% of the candidate population.
3. On average, the overlap between items administered to any two candidates should not exceed 15% to 20%.
4. The maximum percentage of overlapping items two computerized adaptive tests should share is 40%, even between candidates of similar ability.

CALIBRATING THE ITEM BANK

In order for the computer algorithm to select items that are of appropriate difficulty for each candidate, the difficulty of the items must be known. Thus, one of the main requirements to implement computerized adaptive testing is a calibrated item bank. A calibrated bank refers to a collection of test items referenced by a common measurement system (Bergstrom & Gershon, 1995, 1997; Wright & Bell, 1984). Item Response Theory (IRT) provides a useful mathematical framework for the calibration and equating of items onto a common scale and is currently used by nationally administered CAT for licensure and certification.

Although some licensure and certification organizations have used IRT for analyzing their paper-and-pencil tests, many organizations are currently using "classical test theory." An essential difference between classical test theory and item response theory is the focus—in classical test theory, the unit of focus is the test; in IRT, the unit of focus is the item (see Bergstrom & Gershon, 1997). Next, we examine several consequences of analyzing data with IRT that make it useful for CAT.

Advantages of Using IRT

The IRT unit of measurement can be represented as a logit (natural log odds unit). Because the scale is logarithmic, logits are equal interval units. This property has important consequences when arithmetic computations are performed using test results. By contrast, classical test theory test results are based on number correct or raw scores. If raw scores are used to compare individuals or groups over time, the results may be misleading due to nonlinearity of the measurement unit (Wolfe & Chiu, 1997).

IRT represents candidates and items on the same scale. This facilitates the production of individualized test forms that are of appropriate difficulty for candidates. For example, when the test is targeted to ability, if the current on-line estimate of candidate ability is 1.00 logits, the CAT algorithm will search for an item that is close to 1.00 logits in difficulty.

IRT-based item calibrations are independent of the particular subpopulation of candidates used for calibration, and candidate ability parameters are independent of the particular set of items used for estimation (Wright & Stone, 1979). This is in contrast to the classical index of item difficulty (p-value) that is subpopulation-dependent and will vary based on the distribution of ability of the candidate sample. When a test is drawn from an IRT calibrated item bank, the estimate of the candidate's ability should be statistically equivalent regardless of whether he or she is administered easy items or hard items. Of course, the estimate will be more or less precise, depending on the number and targeting of the items the candidate is administered. This level of generality is essential for CAT because each candidate takes an individualized set of items. Differences in the difficulties of candidate's tailored tests are accounted for in the IRT estimation of ability and the same criterion standard (pass point) is implemented for all candidates, regardless of the particular items presented to them. This process of equating occurs across candidates, administration dates and scheduled testing times. Security is maintained because candidates are presented with different sets of items. Fairness is maintained because all items are anchored and equated to the bank scale on which the criterion standard has been established.

With classical test theory, the standard error of measurement is a function of test score reliability and variance and is often assumed (albeit incorrectly) to be the same for all candidates (Hambleton, Swaminathan & Rogers, 1991). Because the unit of analysis in IRT is the candidate–item interaction, a measure of precision is available for each item and each candidate. CAT algorithms target the difficulty of the test to the current ability estimate of the candidate by selecting appropriate items from the bank. Targeting maximizes the information from each item. When test information is maximized, the standard error of measure is minimized; when measurement contains less error, the examination can be shorter without loss of reliability.

Assumptions of IRT

IRT assumes that items on a test assess a single, unidimensional, underlying construct or latent trait. Test items define and quantify the underlying construct and provide an operational definition of the construct (Wright & Bell, 1984). Unidimensionality is always violated to some extent in practical applications (i.e., personality and/or test-taking factors may affect test performance). However, boards must ensure that the items on the test represent the underlying construct to such a degree that the ordering of candidates is the same regardless of the particular set of test items administered (Wainer, 1990). Thus, with CAT, any set of items administered to candidates by the computer must represent the underlying construct that was validated through the job analysis, content blueprint, and test specifications development process.

A second assumption of IRT is that items must function independently. When ability is held constant, candidates' responses to any pair of items must be statistically independent. In practical terms, this means that a candidate's response to one item cannot be influenced by cueing from another item. The most common example of cueing is when the text from one item gives away the correct answer to another item. Meeting the assumptions of unidimensionality and local independence becomes especially crucial when tests are administered adaptively from a calibrated bank. These assumptions must be reasonably satisfied in order for the estimation of candidate ability to be valid and stable.

IRT Models. The Rasch model, a member of the IRT family of models, has been used extensively in CAT for licensure and certification. If the item is more difficult than the candidate is able, the Rasch model predicts that the candidate will have less than 50% probability of correctly answering the item; if the candidate's proficiency exceeds the difficulty of the item, the Rasch model predicts that the candidate will have a greater than 50% probability of correctly answering the item (Wright & Stone, 1979).

Item banks for the examples of CAT for licensure and certification examinations presented in this chapter were calibrated with the Rasch model. Other IRT models that can be used for developing a calibrated bank include, but are not limited to, the 2 and 3 parameter logistic models (2PL & 3PL), rating scale models, and partial credit models for polytomous scoring. Calibrating items with the Rasch model requires a candidate population of at least 100 to 200 candidates (Linacre, 1994), although calibrating with other models usually requires a substantially larger sample.

Linking Items to Build a Bank

How do boards develop an IRT calibrated bank? One method for calibrating a core of items for an item bank begins with previously used paper-and-pencil test administration data and a procedure called *common item equating*. This procedure is appropriate when previously administered paper-and-pencil test forms contain common items, as is usually the case with certification and licensure tests. The most recently administered test is calibrated and is designated as the benchmark test. After other previously administered tests are calibrated, the common items are anchored to the benchmark calibration. Tests are linked through a network of common items and all items are equated to the benchmark scale, thus constructing the calibrated item bank (Wright & Stone, 1979). Common item linking is based on the assumption that, aside from estimation errors, the estimated difficulty for common items across test forms differs by only a linear transformation (Wainer, 1990). The common item link ensures that all items are linked to the item bank scale.

Banks can also be constructed with a method called "pooled equating." Using this method, candidate responses are pooled or combined from a number of previous test administrations (paper-and-pencil or computer based) and item difficulties are estimated from one large analysis. Common items link test administrations and all item parameters are estimated simultaneously in a single computer run. All item parameters are placed on the same scale without piecing together estimates from different sources. Missing data is not a problem because the procedure simply ignores items not administered to a particular candidate (Lord, 1980).

During their pilot phase, ASCP demonstrated that candidate ability estimates were highly correlated (.99) when item calibrations were derived from paper-and-pencil examinations and from item calibrations using CAT data (Bergstrom & Lunz, 1994). However, it is important to note that all items were multiple choice and fit on a single computer screen. Comparability of item difficulty from paper-and-pencil administration to computer administration should not be assumed, especially for items that contain graphics or scrollable text.

Sample CAT Bank

Figure 4.1 shows the distributions of candidate abilities and item difficulties for CAT administered by the ASCP. The left side of the figure shows the distribution of candidate ability estimated during one year of administration. The right side of the figure shows the distribution of item difficulties in the item bank. This bank was calibrated using data from previous paper-and-pencil test administrations. Note that the overall distribution of item difficulty is slightly easier (i.e., lower on the vertical axis) than the distribution of candidate ability. Very easy items were removed from the bank before CAT administration because, given the distribution of candidate abilities, they would have been administered infrequently, if at all.

```
                            MAP OF CANDIDATES AND ITEMS
MEASURE                                        |                              MEASURE
          ------------------CANDIDATES--+--ITEMS  --------------------
   4.0                                         +                                 4.0
                                          .    |
                                          .    |
                                               |
                                          .    |
   3.0                                    .    +                                 3.0
                                          .    | #.
                                        .#     | #
                                        .##    | #
                                        ###    | #
                                      .####    | ##
   2.0                                .#### +    ##                               2.0
                                   .#######  | ######
                                 .##########  | #########.
                               .############  | ###########.
                             .###############  | ###########
                          .######################  | ##################.
   1.0                 .########################  + ###############                1.0
               .##########################  | ##################.
              .##########################  | ######################
               .######################  | ####################.
                ####################  | #######################.
                 .###############  | ########################.
    .0              .############# + ########################.                   0.0
                     .##########  | ##########################.
                       .######## | ##########################.
                          .### | ##################.
PASS POINT = .42           .# | #################.
                           .  | ###############
  -1.0                     .  + ##########.                                      -1.0
                              | .
                              |
                              |
                              |
  -2.0                        +                                                  -2.0
          ------------------- PERSONS-+-  ITEMS --------------------
EACH '#' IN THE CANDIDATE COLUMN IS  15 CANDIDATES;
EACH '.' IS 1 TO  14 CANDIDATES
EACH '#' IN THE  ITEM  COLUMN IS   2 ITEMS  ; EACH '.' IS 1  ITEM
```

FIG. 4.1.   Item bank example. Bank is targeted at a 60% probability of correct response. Items easier than -1.50 logits were removed from the bank prior to administration.

Translating the Paper-and-Pencil Standard

A number of research studies, synthesized by Bergstrom (1992), found that candidates tested comparably across a variety of examinations regardless of whether the test was administered in the paper-and-pencil or CAT mode. However, when changing to CAT, boards would be wise to use the criterion standard (pass point) set on the paper-and-pencil exam for CAT. Maintaining the same standard enables comparisons of pass/fail decisions across modes of administration. It is especially reassuring to boards to have empirical data that indicates that the CAT is performing comparably to previously administered paper-and-pencil tests, even though candidates are tested year-round using the techniques of tailored testing.

Selecting CAT Administration Parameters

Once a board has made the decision to implement CAT and begins the process of calibrating and cleaning the item bank, a number of decisions about how CAT will be administered must be made. The CAT administration algorithm should be programmed to the specifications of the board. However, the specifications should be carefully considered prior to implementation.

Figure 4.2 provides a summary of the items administered to an actual candidate, the candidate's responses, the history of the estimation of the candidate's ability, and the 95% confidence interval about the estimate of ability. This graphical representation is called a "candidate map" (Gershon, 1990). As various administration issues are discussed, the candidate map will be referred to as an example. The criterion standard indicated as the "pass point," on the map was .42 logits; the candidate shown passed the examination.

Selecting the First Item

Conventional paper-and-pencil examinations often start with easy items as a warm-up for candidates. Data collected during a CAT pilot (Lunz & Bergstrom, 1994) indicated that candidates performed comparably on CAT regardless of whether their first item had a calibrated difficulty that was easy, medium, or hard. However, several considerations for choice of the first item should be weighed. As the purpose of certification and licensure examinations is to make pass/fail decisions, starting with items close to the pass point may be the best alternative (Lunz & Bergstrom, 1994). For example, the ASCP CAT begins with an item randomly selected from items within .10 logits of the pass point. The next nine items are constrained such that each item's difficulty is within .10 logits of the previously administered item's difficulty. This procedure effectively constrains the first 10 items to within one logit of the pass/fail point (Bergstrom, Gershon, & Lunz, 1994) and helps ensure that candidates with a final ability estimate near the pass point have appropriate items, even at the start of the test.

In Fig. 4.2, the first item administered has a calibrated difficulty of .48 logits. Note that the first 10 items are constrained near the pass point of .42 logits even though the candidate's ability is estimated to be higher.

Item exposure is another consideration in the choice of the first item. Candidates should be presented with different first items, so sufficient numbers of items at the specified start difficulty need to be available in the item bank.

COMPUTERIZED ADAPTIVE TEST OF A PASSING CANDIDATE

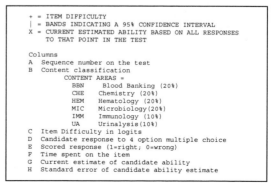

```
                                                      P
                                                      A
                            -3.0   -2.0   -1.0    0   S        2.0    3.0
                            |+++|++++|++++|++++|++++|++++|++S+|++++|++++|++++|++++|
 A   B     C   D E   F      G     H
 1  BBN  0.48  1 0  0'46                                     |+
 2  CHE  0.49  2 1  0'18   0.49  1.41                        |*
 3  HEM  0.48  4 1  0'47   1.18  1.22                        |+      X           >
 4  MIC  0.62  3 1  0'25   1.62  1.15                        |  +        X       >
 5  IMM  0.79  2 0  1'25   0.98  0.91    FIRST 10 ITEMS CLOSE|    + X
 6  UA   0.67  1 1  0'22   1.28  0.87       TO   PASS POINT  |   +     X
 7  BBN  0.74  1 1  1'16   1.53  0.84                        |   +       X
 8  CHE  0.85  2 0  0'58   1.15  0.73                        |     + X
 9  HEM  0.73  3 1  0'12   1.34  0.71                        |    +      X
10  MIC  0.79  2 0  0'34   1.07  0.65                        |     + X

11  BBN  0.62  4 1  0'22   1.22  0.63                       || +       X
12  CHE  0.83  3 1  0'38   1.37  0.61                        |   +       X
13  HEM  0.91  1 1  0'22   1.50  0.60                       ||   +         X
14  MIC  1.14  1 0  0'18   1.31  0.56                       ||    +       X
15  IMM  0.82  1 1  0'33   1.42  0.55                       ||    +       X
16  UA   0.94  1 1  0'26   1.53  0.54                       ||   +        X
17  BBN  1.10  4 1  0'34   1.64  0.53    AFTER ITEM 11 THE DIFFICULTY |  +       X
18  CHE  1.32  3 1  0'30   1.75  0.53      OF THE TEST IS TARGETED TO |   +        X
19  HEM  1.31  2 1  0'34   1.85  0.52    A 60% PROBABILITY OF CORRECT |   +         X
20  MIC  1.50  1 0  0'29   1.70  0.49      RESPONSE                   |       + X
21  BBN  1.33  1 0  1' 8   1.57  0.46                                 |     + X
22  CHE  1.23  1 1  0'55   1.66  0.46                                 |      +      X
23  HEM  1.23  1 0  0'30   1.54  0.44                                 |     + X
24  MIC  1.05  1 1  0'49   1.61  0.43                                 |+        X
25  IMM  1.29  1 0  0'13   1.51  0.42                                 |      + X
26  UA   1.09  1 0  0'36   1.41  0.40                                 |   + X
27  BBN  1.00  1 0  0'35   1.31  0.39                                 |  + X
28  CHE  0.88  2 1  0'39   1.37  0.39                                 |  +    X
29  HEM  1.01  1 0  1' 3   1.29  0.38                                 |  + X
*
40  MIC  0.88  4 0  0'46   1.21  0.32                                 | +  X
41  BBN  0.87  1 1  0'35   1.25  0.32                                 | +   X
42  CHE  0.75  2 0  0'24   1.19  0.31                                 |+   X
43  HEM  0.86  4 0  0'45   1.13  0.31                                 | + X
44  MIC  0.65  3 1  2' 0   1.17  0.30                                 +    X
45  IMM  0.82  4 1  0' 9   1.20  0.30                                 |+  X
46  UA   0.82  2 1  0'18   1.24  0.30                                 |+   X
47  BBN  0.91  2 0  0'40   1.19  0.30                                 | +  X
48  CHE  0.77  2 0  1'13   1.14  0.29                                 |+  X
49  HEM  0.74  2 1  1' 1   1.17  0.29                                 +    X
50  MIC  0.72  1 1  0'49   1.20  0.29                                 | +    X
*
80  MIC  0.81  4 1  0'20   1.25  0.23                                 |  +|   X
81  BBN  0.86  3 1  0'11   1.27  0.23                                 |   +   X
82  CHE  0.95  4 0  1' 0   1.24  0.23                                 |+ X
83  HEM  0.96  2 1  1'18   1.27  0.22    EVEN THOUGH THE CANDIDATE    |+   X
84  MIC  0.93  1 1  0'18   1.29  0.22    PASSED WITH 95% CONFIDENCE   | +   X
85  IMM  0.92  3 1  0'18   1.31  0.22    AFTER 15 ITEMS, TEST LENGTH  | +   X
86  UA   0.99  2 0  0'33   1.28  0.22    IS FIXED AT 90 ITEMS TO ENSURE|+  X
87  BBN  0.92  1 1  0'44   1.30  0.22    CONTENT COVERAGE             | +   X
88  CHE  0.99  4 0  0'13   1.27  0.22                                 |+  X
89  HEM  0.97  1 1  0'10   1.29  0.22                                 |+   X
90  MIC  0.98  1 0  0'14   1.26  0.22                                 |+   X
                            |+++|++++|++++|++++|++++|++++|+++P|++++|++++|++++|++++|++++|
                            -3.0   -2.0   -1.0    0   A        1.0    2.0    3.0
                            BANK SCALE                 S
                                                       S
```

*items 30 to 39 and 51 to 79 not shown

+ = ITEM DIFFICULTY
| = BANDS INDICATING A 95% CONFIDENCE INTERVAL
X = CURRENT ESTIMATED ABILITY BASED ON ALL RESPONSES
    TO THAT POINT IN THE TEST

Columns
A   Sequence number on the test
B   Content classification
        CONTENT AREAS =
            BBN   Blood Banking (20%)
            CHE   Chemistry (20%)
            HEM   Hematology (20%)
            MIC   Microbiology(20%)
            IMM   Immunology (10%)
            UA   Urinalysis(10%)
C   Item Difficulty in logits
D   Candidate response to 4 option multiple choice
E   Scored response (1=right; 0=wrong)
F   Time spent on the item
G   Current estimate of candidate ability
H   Standard error of candidate ability estimate

FIG. 4.2.   Candidate response map.

77

Pretesting New Items

The quality of any ongoing, operational CAT is dependent on the quality of the item bank. An adequate item bank must be in place when CAT is initiated; and provision for updating and adding new items is essential. All scored items in CAT must be calibrated. Once CAT is operational, pretest items can be seeded onto the computerized adaptive test. Pretest items are not used to estimate ability. Instead, after the seeded items have been administered often enough, the responses to the items are analyzed to determine the calibrated level of difficulty on the bank scale. Boards must decide the number and placement of pre-test items based on such considerations as the number of candidates who will test over a given period of time, the content areas for which additional items are needed, the distribution of candidate ability, the IRT model chosen to calibrate items, the stopping rule implemented, and the cost of test administration.

Stopping the Test

CATs can be fixed length or variable length. If the adaptive test is terminated after a specified number of items, it is a fixed length test. Two slightly different stopping rules result in variable length tests. The test can be stopped when a specified level of precision the standard error of measure for SEM is reached, or when a specified level of confidence in the pass/fail decision is achieved (Bergstrom & Lunz, 1992; Kingsbury & Weiss, 1983). Regardless of the stopping rule implemented, the number of items required to pass or fail a candidate with a specified degree of precision or confidence should be less for CAT than for a pencil-and-paper test. The adaptive test reduces the error of measurement and provides more information using fewer items.

Although ASCP piloted the use of a variable length test with a 95% confidence level stopping rule (Lunz & Bergstrom, 1994), the board ultimately decided to implement a fixed-length CAT. Their current test length is 90 scored items and 10 pretest items (American Society of Clinical Pathology, 1997; Fig. 4.2 shows the 90 scored items, but not the 10 pretest items). The ASCP pilot test experience indicated that variable length might be difficult to explain to candidates and, candidates who failed the exam with a relatively short test might feel that they did not have sufficient opportunity to prove their competence.

Several national licensure and certification examinations including the National Certification Examination (NCE) for registered nurse anesthetists administered by the Council on Certification of Nurse Anesthetists (CCNA) and the National Council Licensure Examination of Registered Nurses (NCLEX-RN™) administered by the National Council of State Boards of

Nursing, Inc. (NCSBN), give variable-length computerized adaptive tests. On the NCE, each candidate is administered a minimum of 90 items, 70 items drawn from the content outline and 20 pretest items; maximum test length is 160 items (Council on Certification of Nurse Anesthetists, 1996). On the NCLEX-RN, minimum test length is 60 items, maximum is 250 items plus 15 pretest items (National Council of State Boards of Nursing, 1995). The stopping rule on both the NCE and the NCLEX-RN is based on confidence in the pass or fail decision. Variable-length tests make optimal use of the item bank since many candidates take a minimum-length test.

Test length can be set to ensure that reliability is equal to or exceeds the reliability of the paper-and-pencil test or that confidence in pass/fail decisions is equivalent to, or exceeds, confidence obtained with paper-and-pencil tests.

Targeted Test Difficulty

If CAT is administered from an item bank that is calibrated with the Rasch model, the difficulty of the test can be easily specified. Maximum information from each item is obtained when the test is targeted to a 50% probability of correct response; however, there are several reasons why a board might want to consider giving an easier test.

1. Licensure and certification candidates are often not accustomed to taking tests on which they can answer only 50% of the items correctly and may find such a hard test frustrating.
2. The composition of existing item banks used to construct paper-and-pencil examinations may not include a sufficient number of difficult items to target all candidates at 50% probability of correct response.

When deciding whether to alter test difficulty, boards need to consider that the farther targeting moves from the optimal 50% probability of correct response, the longer the test must be to maintain comparable precision (Bergstrom & Lunz, 1992).

Starting with Item 11, the example test (see Fig. 4.2) is targeted at 60% probability of correct response. Note that the difficulty of the items presented is slightly easier than the current estimate of candidate ability. It is for this reason that the distribution of the item difficulty in the bank shown in Fig. 4.1 was constructed to be slightly easier than the distribution of candidate ability.

Boards moving to CAT must weigh the issues involved in test targeting. Easier tests may produce increased candidate comfort and make better use of the item bank but also may result in increased test length or decreased precision in ability estimation.

Option to Review Test Items

Boards must decide whether their version of CAT will allow candidates the opportunity to review previously answered items and to change their responses. This option may be important to candidates who fear that they may enter an incorrect response and not be able to change it, or who may have test taking strategies that include reviewing and checking their responses before they finish a test (Lunz, Bergstrom, & Wright, 1992; Stocking, 1997). Many studies have addressed the issue of review and changing answers on paper-and-pencil examinations. Benjamin, Cavell and Shallenburger (1984) reviewed 33 studies on changing answers on paper-and-pencil tests. They recount that, "after more than a half century of research on this topic" (p. 133), the evidence uniformly indicates that: (a) only a small percentage of answers are actually changed; (b) the majority of answers are changed from wrong to right; (c) most test-takers are answer-changers; and (d) most answer-changers are point-gainers.

Reviewing and changing answers has been extensively studied by the ASCP (Lunz et al., 1992; Lunz & Bergstrom, 1994). This research replicated findings from paper-and-pencil studies. Candidates were found to change few answers, more answers were changed from wrong to right than from wrong to wrong or from right to wrong, and candidates slightly improved their performance by changing answers. These studies also showed that the effect of changing answers on the precision of measurement was minimal. Under actual certification testing conditions, 70% of the candidates elected to change some responses and the mean increase in SEM was only .002 logits. This information loss could be recovered by increasing overall test length by just one item.

Opponents of allowing candidate review and answer changing on adaptive tests argue that altering responses compromises the efficiency of the adaptive algorithm and increases test-taking time (Wainer, 1993). Additional concerns have been raised that candidates might use the review process to manipulate their adaptive exam. On a paper-and-pencil test, all candidates receive a fixed set of questions. On a CAT, the items administered depend upon the performance of the candidate. Candidates who perform poorly will be administered easy items. The concern is that candidates will deliberately use this process to obtain a test comprised of easy items and then, during review, answer the items correctly. Although candidates attempting this strategy would still be measured comparably, the reliability of their test would be decreased because they took off-target items. If the test is very short (e.g., 20 items) and the range of item difficulty is wide, it is possible that candidates attempting this strategy would not be able to pass even if they answered all items correctly during review.

Allowing item review on CAT, although psychometrically feasible under controlled conditions and administratively possible if the bank is calibrated with the Rasch model, does increase administration time. In general, review has not been allowed on adaptive tests. For example, candidates are not allowed to review and change items on the CCNA NCE (Zaglaniczny, 1996). To our knowledge, the only currently administered large-scale computerized adaptive tests allowing review are the certification examinations delivered by the ASCP. All 100 items are administered, and candidates must respond to each item. At the end of the test, candidates can return to test items and change their answers. It is important to note that ASCP employs a computer algorithm to detect and prevent manipulation of the test. The percentage of items a candidate answers correctly is continuously monitored. Because tests are targeted to an expected 60% correct, if an unusual response pattern is detected (e.g., if percentage correct drops below 30% at any point after the first 10 items are administered), then items are targeted to the pass point rather than to the current estimate of ability. If review is allowed, candidates should be educated to answer items to the best of their ability when they are initially presented (Gershon & Bergstrom, 1996).

Content Balancing

Most certification and licensure paper-and-pencil tests are content-balanced to match blueprint specifications. Various methods of content balancing can be employed including administering content areas in blocks, administering a fixed order of items across content areas or randomly distributing items across content areas. Content balancing requires that the item bank be well-distributed within content areas, so that the most informative item within a specified content area can be selected for candidates of different abilities. ASCP, NCSBN, and CCNA employ a content-balancing algorithm of the type described by Kingsbury and Zara (1989) in which a constraint mechanism ensures that all candidates are administered a precisely content balanced examination. For an illustration of content balancing, note the distribution of items across content for the example test in Fig. 4.2.

Controlling for Item Exposure

A number of algorithms are available to control item exposure (Stocking & Lewis, 1995; Way, 1997). However, employing a randomization factor has proven to be a simple, effective way to control overexposure of items for CAT in licensure and certification settings, as long as the item bank is balanced to the content specifications. On the ASCP CATs, items are chosen at random from unused items within .10 logits of the targeted item difficulty within the specified content area. Figure 4.3 shows the usage of an item bank of 900 items for about 3,000 candidates. The items most frequently presented are close to

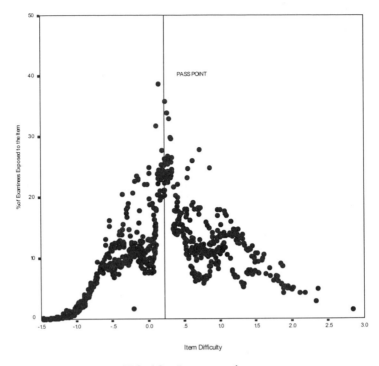

FIG. 4.3.   Item usage plot.

the pass point, but maximum exposure is generally less than 30%, with only a few items being administered to more than 30% of the candidates. These frequently presented items had a difficulty estimate near the pass point and were in content areas that contained proportionally fewer items.

CAT ADMINISTRATION

Software

CAT administration for licensure and certification tests requires a secure testing site, a computer to take the test, and computer software to store items, administer items, score candidates online, produce reports, and archive results. Boards must decide whether to develop custom software, purchase commercially available software or use software provided by a consultant or test administration vendor. The advantage to contracting for custom software development is that the board is not tied to a single vendor, but has the flexibility to change vendors or administer examinations independently. The advantage to using software provided by a consultant or test administration vendor is that the board is removed from the technical considerations that software purchase and maintenance requires.

Administration Sites

Boards must decide whether to use in-house staff to administer tests themselves or to use a testing organization that maintains multiple sites. Options for delivering CAT include, but are not necessarily limited to: (a) contracting with a national testing vendor who has multiple test sites, (b) setting up a single test site, or (c) setting up multiple temporary test sites at specified times during the year.

REPORTING CAT RESULTS

Before moving to CAT, boards need to review all existing reports to candidates and educational programs to identify those features that they wish to retain, change, or eliminate. With CAT, raw scores cannot be reported because candidates are administered items of varying difficulty. However, scaled scores with associated standard errors can be reported in text, table, or graphical format for candidates and programs.

Report Design

One result of adaptive or tailored testing is that all candidates, regardless of ability or pass/fail status, correctly answer similar percentages of items. For example, assuming an adequate item bank, if the test is targeted at a difficulty level of 60% expected correct response, all candidates will answer approximately 60% of the items correctly. Thus, raw scores or percent correct scores cannot be used to differentiate between candidates. IRT logit ability estimates that account for item difficulty can be converted to a more easily understood scaled score for reporting.

Due to the shorter test length of CAT, especially if the test is variable length, candidates who reliably pass or fail the total test in the minimum number of items may not have answered a sufficient number of items in all subsets to calculate reliable subtest scaled scores. Boards must decide what information they wish to report: only the pass/fail decision, scaled scores for the total test, or scaled scores for content areas. Scaled scores can be reported to all candidates or to failing candidates only. Reporting scaled scores for content areas may increase test length. The ASCP reports the pass/fail results and total test scaled score to passing candidates and the pass/fail results and total and content area scaled scores to failing candidates. The CAT specifications for these tests are designed to ensure an adequate number of items in each content area to reliably estimate a scaled score.

Report Distribution

Online estimation of candidate ability allows immediate score reporting, if desired; however, most licensure and certification boards do not report results at the test center. Candidate results are electronically transferred to the testing agencies, checked for accuracy and then mailed to candidates. This process results in candidates receiving scores much more rapidly than is possible with paper-and-pencil examinations but still allows for adequate quality control.

Timing of reports to educational programs may also change. Because candidates may be testing thoughout the year, summary reports must be aggregated over a reasonable period of time. Boards must decide how often to aggregate test results and how to summarize the information for educational programs and program directors. Factors that impact these decisions include annual candidate volume, the nature of the candidate's educational experience, and the amount of information reported to the candidate. Because all students take different tailored examinations, individual item performance summaries cannot be computed. However, reports based on content areas and total tests can be provided using some form of scaled scores, or graphic representation.

PILOT TESTING

After the CAT item bank is finalized and all decisions about the CAT delivery system have been made, the system should be pilot tested. This can be accomplished by setting up one or more temporary sites and enticing candidates to participate in the project. Initially, ASCP conducted pilot studies using medical technology students in the last year of their programs. These students participated in studies involving both paper-and-pencil and CAT administrations (Lunz & Bergstrom, 1994). Subsequent pilots were conducted with actual candidates who were given the option to retest with a paper-and-pencil examination if they failed the CAT exam. The purposes of the pilot test include, but are not limited to, assessing:

1. Efficiency and dependability of software for candidate registration, test administration, and reporting
2. Candidate comfort using the computer
3. Data transfer capabilities and efficiency
4. Accuracy of the computer algorithms

   5. Acceptability of item and graphic presentations on the screen
   6. Instructions to candidates
   7. Time requirements to complete the test
   8. Candidate test performance on CAT compared to paper-and-pencil
   9. Candidate registration efficiency
  10. Complexity and reliability of reporting procedures

The pilot study may be used to compare CAT and paper-and-pencil test performance and ensure that CAT does not make additional demands on the candidate that potentially interfere with the validity of the examination. It may be difficult for the board, committee members, and candidates to visualize exactly how CAT looks and works until they see it "working" on the computer monitor. Final revisions can be made after the pilot study.

Educational Materials

Preparing candidates for CAT requires the publication of fairly detailed explanations of what to expect. The black box nature of the computer algorithm makes some candidates and/or educators apprehensive about the test. Therefore, easily understood explanations of the number of items on the test, stopping rule, response entry method, and scoring procedures help alleviate some concerns. If possible, it is helpful to develop a demonstration disk so candidates can have the opportunity to practice taking a computerized adaptive test. The opportunity to learn the mechanics of taking the test seems to be very important to candidates.

The opportunity to monitor candidate reactions to CAT is facilitated by computer data entry. It is fairly easy to add an online survey to the examination that includes questions on candidate satisfaction with test instructions, screen readability, quality of graphics, and testing facilities. This information can be used to improve the quality of the tests.

ONGOING TESTING ISSUES

Examination Committees

The automated test construction of CAT changes the role of item writers and test developers. For written certification examinations, subject matter experts are often asked to write, review, and/or select items for a paper-and-pencil test form. Theoretically, this approach guarantees the face validity (how the examination appears to the candidate) and the content validity (the items test appropriate knowledge and skill and meet content specifications) of the test because each item is read and approved by the experts. This process is thought to ensure that the information tested is relevant and important and that test items do not duplicate or key each other.

For computerized adaptive examinations, the items presented to a particular candidate are selected by the computer algorithm. Thus, the work of the examination committee changes substantially, but is just as critical. Instead of selecting particular items for a paper-and-pencil form, the committee must review the entire item bank: (a) for overall quality with regard to item relevance and importance; (b) to identify duplicate items with similar calibrated difficulties, so that a candidate is not presented with two items that test the same knowledge; and (c) to verify the distribution of item difficulties within subtests, because the distribution of items within subtests must generally match the content specifications. Items testing the same concept must be written at different levels of difficulty (e.g., easy, moderate, hard) so that candidates at all ability levels can potentially be tested on an important concept. All work on the item bank must be completed prior to the examination, because the opportunity to delete items after a CAT is usually not available. This can be accomplished in one well-organized meeting per year. A study by Lunz and Deville (1996) found that CAT is perceived to be as valid as committee-selected paper-and-pencil exams with regard to face validity, adherence to test specifications, difficulty, item ordering, overall quality, and relevance.

Procedures for Exam Challenges

Due to the sophistication of computerized online scoring, errors in scoring are virtually nonexistent. However, candidates who receive a failing score may still wish to have their test results verified. It is essential that computerized archival records of all candidate information be maintained. Graphical "maps" of candidate performance, including each item administered and the online estimation of ability throughout the test, are useful for reviewing individual candidate performance and to verify pass/fail status. These maps (see Fig. 4.2) are not ordinarily released to candidates but instead are used for quality control procedures and to verify that candidates received a valid examination.

Test Maintenance

Item bank maintenance is especially crucial with adaptive testing. The estimated ability of the candidate is calculated online from the bank parameter values for the items. Thus items must be monitored to ensure relevance to the current field of practice and to assess the currency of the item calibration (i.e., the item may become easier or more difficult because of changes in practice).

Systematic reviews of all items in the bank for currency and relevance must be conducted annually. As shown in Fig. 4.3, some items will be used more frequently than others because items are tailored to candidates' abilities. This may make verification of the stability of very easy and very hard items difficult due to lack of usage.

Archiving Test Results

Archiving paper-and-pencil test results is relatively simple compared to archiving CAT results. Because each candidate is administered an individualized test, a test record must include a complete history of the individual test taken by each candidate including:

1. Candidate identification
2. Date of test administration
3. Identification of item bank
4. Record of each item administered including:

   A. Sequence number on the test
   B. Bank identification number of the item
   C. Content area classification
   D. Calibrated difficulty of the item
   E. Candidate's response
   F. Answer key
   G. Scored response (right or wrong)
   H. Time spent on the item

5. Total test and content area scores

SAMPLE PROJECT SCHEDULE

Tables 4.1 to 4.3 present a sample timeline for CAT implementation. It usually takes about 3 years for a board to change the entire examination process from paper-and-pencil administration to CAT, although timetables may vary greatly across boards and examinations. Because ASCP and the National Council State Boards of Nurses were among the first to switch modes of administration, they piloted extensively for years before actually implementing CAT. The Council on Certification of Nurse Anesthetists began reviewing their item bank adequacy several years before actually contracting for CAT development (Zaglaniczny, 1996). The Commission on Dietetic Registration, scheduled to implement in 1999, also spent several years improving their item bank and addressing administration issues in preparation for computer based testing (Ruiz, Fitz, Lewis, & Reidy, 1995).

TABLE 4.1
Sample Timetable: Year 1

1. Review existing paper-and-pencil test policies.
2. Calibrate the item bank (if not done).
3. Verify content specifications.
4. Assess bank deficiencies.
5. Write items to fill bank deficiencies.
6. Pretest new items on paper-and-pencil examinations.
7. Verify or set a criterion-referenced standard.
8. Research and identify CAT test specifications including starting rule, stopping rule, test length, estimation algorithms, randomization parameters, and content balancing algorithms.
9. Research CAT item banking and administration software.
10. Research test site alternatives.

TABLE 4.2
Sample Timetable: Year 2

1. Review all items in the bank for adequacy, currency, and redundancy. Check statistical performance. Retire items that do not meet the item bank criteria.
2. Write items to fill bank deficiencies.
3. Pretest new items on paper-and-pencil examinations.
4. Determine CAT test specifications.
5. Choose a test administration vendor or other alternate method for test administration.
6. Finalize test administration software.
7. Choose administration options for candidates: keyboard, mouse, arrow for data entry; front-end screens including logo, screen colors, and buttons.
8. Review items on the computer screen.
9. Design tutorial if needed.
10. Finalize test sites.
11. Develop educational materials for candidates, programs, and other interested persons.
12. Develop reports for candidates and programs.
13. Set up and implement a pilot study with sample of candidates. Review and compare results to pencil-and-paper examination.

TABLE 4.3
Sample Timetable: Year 3

1.   Promote the impending change in mode of test administration by providing educational materials for candidates and educators.
2.   Analyze pilot study results. Assuming they are satisfactory, proceed with plans or make revisions as needed.
3.   Finalize item banks.
4.   Finalize administration specifications.
5.   Contract with test administration vendor or set up and test temporary or permanent sites.
6.   Test all data transfer and other electronic communication methods.
7.   Finalize candidate and program performance report production and distribution.
8.   Verify successful operation of all aspects of CAT administration and reporting.
9.   Begin to administer computerized adaptive tests on a limited or national scale.

DISCUSSION

For certification and licensure examinations, changing to CAT entails a period of transition from "paper-and-pencil" ways of thinking about testing to a new, efficient, computerized mode of assessment. Items are selected and field-tested differently; abilities of candidates are estimated using different items; candidates take the test at different times and in different locations; reports look different. Boards willing to undertake the transition to CAT have found their candidates adjust to the changes and indicate a preference for computer based testing. However, it is essential that boards who decide to move their examination to CAT plan carefully to ensure that the transition will be acceptable, smooth, and successful. Boards must work through the political, educational and implementation dilemmas that are unique to their particular environment with careful and deliberate planning. Issues of validity, security, accessibility, and fairness must always be carefully considered. Although the magnitude of change should not be underestimated, rewards are realized in terms of increased security, efficiency, and availability.

The mathematical foundation and psychometric theory behind adaptive testing have been understood since the 1960s, but large-scale implementation in the certification and licensure arena became possible because of advances in computer hardware and software. However, computer-based testing is still in its infancy. Increased speed and graphical capability, new response mechanisms, multimedia and simulation capabilities are being developed even as you read this chapter. Boards moving into CAT today can look forward to additional computerized enhancements that will continue to improve the quality of the adaptive testing experience and the reliability of test results.

REFERENCES

Benjamin, L., Cavell, T., & Shallenburger, W. (1984). Staying with initial answers on objective tests: Is it a myth? *Teaching of Psychology, 11*(3), 133-141.

Bergstrom, B., & Gershon, R. (1997). *Advances in the use of item response theory in licensure and certification assessment*. Council on Licensure, Enforcement, and Regulation (CLEAR) Exam Review, Lexington, Kentucky.

Bergstrom, B., Gershon, R., & Lunz, M. (1994, April). *Computerized adaptive testing exploring examinee response time using hierarchical linear modeling*. Paper presented at the annual meeting of the National Council on Measurement in Education, New Orleans, Louisiana. Bergstrom, B. A. (1992). *Ability measure equivalence of computer adaptive and paper-and-pencil tests: A research synthesis* [ERIC Document Reproduction No. TM022402].

Bergstrom, B. A., & Gershon, R. C. (1995). Item banking. In J. C. Impara (Ed.), *Licensure testing* (pp. 187–204). Lincoln, Nebraska: Buros Institute of Mental Measurements.

Bergstrom, B. A., & Lunz, M. E. (1992). Confidence in pass/fail decisions for computer adaptive and paper-and-pencil examinations. *Evaluation and the Health Professions, 15*(4), 453–464.

Bergstrom, B. A., & Lunz, M. E. (1994). Equivalence of Rasch item calibrations across modes of administration. In M. Wilson (Ed.), *Objective theory into practice, Volume 2* (pp. 122–128). Norwood, NJ: Ablex.

Bergstrom, B. A., & Stahl, J. A. (1992). *Assessing existing item bank depth for computer adaptive testing* [ERIC Document Reproduction No. TM022404].

American Society of Clinical Pathologists, Board of Registry. (1997). *Procedures for examination and certification* [candidate handbook]. Chicago, IL: Author.

Council on Certification of Nurse Anesthetists. (1996). *Candidate handbook*. Park Ridge, IL: Author.

Gershon, R. C. (1990). *CATSoftware System™* [Computer program]. Chicago, IL: Computer Adaptive Technologies, Inc.

Gershon, R. C., & Bergstrom, B. A. (1996) *Does cheating on CAT pay: Not!* [ERIC Document Reproduction No. TM024692].

Green, B. F., Bock, R. D., Humphreys, L. G., Linn, R. L., & Reckase, M. D. (1984). Technical guidelines for assessing computerized adaptive tests. *Journal of Educational Measurement, 21*(4), 347–360.

Hambleton, R. K., Swaminathan, H., & Rogers, H. J. (1991). *Fundamentals of item response theory, Volume 2*. Newbury Park, CA: Sage.

Kingsbury, G., & Weiss, D. J. (1983). A comparison of IRT-Based adaptive mastery testing and a sequential mastery testing procedure. In D. J. Weiss (Ed.), *New horizons in testing* (pp. 257–283). New York: Academic Press.

Kingsbury, G., & Zara, A. R. (1989). Procedures for selecting items for computerized adaptive tests. *Applied Measurement in Education, 2*(4), 359–375.

Knapp, J. E., & Knapp, L. G. (1995). Practice analysis: Building the foundation for validity. In J. C. Impara (Ed.), *Licensure testing: Purposes, procedures, and practices* (pp. 93–116). University of Nebraska-Lincoln: Buros Institute of Mental Measurements.

Linacre, J. M. (1994, Winter). Sample size and item calibration stability. Rasch Measurement *Transactions, 7*(4), 328.

Lord, F. M. (1980). *Applications of item response theory to practical testing problems.* Hillsdale, NJ: Lawrence Erlbaum Associates.

Lunz, M. E., & Bergstrom, B. A. (1994). An empirical study of computer adaptive test administration formats. *Journal of Educational Measurement, 31*(3), 251–263.

Lunz, M. E., Bergstrom, B. A., & Wright, B. D. (1992). The effect of review on student ability and test efficiency in computer adaptive tests. *Applied Psychological Measurement, 16*(1), 33–40.

Lunz, M. E., & Deville, C. W. (1996). Validity of item selection: A comparison of automated computerized adaptive and manual paper-and-pencil. *Teaching and Learning in Medicine, 8*(3), 152–157.

National Council of State Boards of Nursing. (1995). *NCLEX using CAT.* [Pamphlet]. Chicago, IL: National Council of State Boards of Nursing, Inc.

Ruiz, B., Fitz, P. A., Lewis, C., & Reidy, C. (1995). Computer-adaptive testing: A new breed of assessment. *Journal of The American Dietetic Association, 95*(11), 1–2.

Stahl, J. A., & Lunz, M. E. (1993, April). *Assessing the extent of overlap of items among computerized adaptive tests.* Paper presented at the annual meeting of the National Council of Measurement in Education, Atlanta, GA.

Stocking, M., & Lewis, C. (1995). *Controlling item exposure conditional on ability in computerized adaptive testing* [RR-95-24]. Princeton, NJ: Educational Testing Service.

Stocking, M. L. (1997). Revising item responses in computerized adaptive tests: A comparison of three models. *Applied Psychological Measurement, 21*(2), 14.

Wainer, H. (1990). *Computerized adaptive testing: A primer.* Hillsdale, NJ: Lawrence Erlbaum Associates.

Wainer, H. (1993). Some practical considerations when converting a linearly administered test to an adaptive format. *Educational Measurement: Issues and Practice, 12*(1), 15–20.

Way, W. D. (1997, March). *Protecting the integrity of computerized testing item pools.* Paper presented at the annual meeting of the National Council on Measurement in Education, Chicago, Illinois.

Wolfe, E. W., & Chiu, C., W.T. (1997, March. *Measuring change over time with a Rasch rating scale model.* Paper presented at the International Objective Measurement Workshop 9, Chicago, Illinois.

Wright, B. D., & Bell, S. R. (1984). Item banks: What, why, how. *Journal of Educational Measurement, 21*(4), 331–345.

Wright, B. D., & Stone, M. H. (1979). *Best test design.* Chicago, IL: MESA Press.

Zaglaniczny, K. L. (1996). The transition of the national certification examination from paper-and-pencil to computer adaptive testing. *Journal of the American Association of Nurse Anesthetists, 64*(1), 9–14.

5

Developing Computerized Adaptive Tests for School Children

G. Gage Kingsbury
Ronald L. Houser
Portland Public Schools

Portland Public Schools (PPS) has a long heritage of trying to improve measurement for the students in the district. Since 1977, Portland has used tests drawn from large item pools calibrated to an item response (IRT) theory model (Hambleton & Swaminathan, 1985; Lord, 1980; Lord & Novick, 1968). These tests are designed as functional level tests (Hathaway, 1980), which match the difficulty of a test that a student takes to the student's past performance. This paper-and-pencil testing system allows students to take test questions that are challenging, but not frustrating.

From a testing system using IRT-calibrated item banks, it is a short step to a computerized adaptive testing (CAT) system. In 1984, PPS became the first school district to take this step. Since that time, PPS has tested over 50,000 students with four different types of adaptive tests in five different content areas. This chapter describes the details of the development of these adaptive tests, and suggests some procedures that may be used in the design of adaptive tests for young students. We focus here on the development of a survey test of mathematics achievement.

In particular, this chapter deals with the unique challenges that a test developer must face when developing adaptive tests to assess young students in a school setting. At the time PPS began development, much was known about adaptive testing (Weiss, 1978, 1983), but little was known about the use of such tests with young students. Developing these adaptive tests provided a unique challenge to the test developers for two reasons. First, the age of the test-takers brings with it unique requirements for the tests. Second, the nature of educational assessment makes unique demands on our measurement models. Together, these factors provide an opportunity for the development of unique adaptive tests and testing procedures, and we hope that the approaches that we have taken may be of use to test developers in a variety of settings.

A LITTLE HISTORY

In 1984, PPS decided to develop a set of computerized adaptive tests that would be used for special purpose testing in any given school building. Although there were many reasons for the decision to develop computerized adaptive tests, these were the primary ones:

- The adaptive nature of the tests would fit well into a districtwide testing system that already emphasized matching the difficulty of a test form to the achievement level of the student.
- The adaptive nature of the tests would make full use of the large, calibrated item banks that the school district had at its disposal.
- The computerized nature of the tests would enable schools to use tests as needed, rather than waiting for the districtwide paper-and-pencil tests that were given twice a year. At the same time, the amount of time that a student would spend engaged in the measurement process could be reduced.
- The introduction of the IBM PC computer and the development of less expensive local-area networks had made it much more technically feasible to distribute an adaptive testing system with a fairly modest cost.

Adaptive survey tests were initially designed in the areas of Reading, Mathematics, and Language Usage. These tests were implemented using the MicroCAT development system (Assessment Systems Corporation, 1984), and were put in place in six school buildings in the fall of 1985. These original tests were administered on IBM PC or IBM PC/XT computers, with each test selecting items from a pool of approximately 300 items. Tests were designed to allow no more than 1 second to elapse between successive items, to avoid having students lose their focus.

Following this initial development, the program expanded rapidly. By 1992, almost all of the 100 schools in Portland had adaptive testing available for use. In today's adaptive testing system (CARAT: Computerized Adaptive Reporting And Testing), schools can select from five content areas (Reading, Mathematics, Language Usage, General Science, and Concepts and Processes in Science). Students may be tested with four different types of adaptive tests (Survey Tests, Prediagnostic Tests, Graduation Standards Tests, and Special Program Candidacy Tests). Tests draw items from pools of over 1,500 items, with automatic content controls and longitudinal testing controls.

In addition, the system has grown to include a reporting package and database system that allows each school to produce custom reports concerning its own student population or particular groups from its population. Over 12,000 reports have been produced that detail student achievement in the individual schools.

A modified version of this system has been provided to other school districts through distribution by the Northwest Evaluation Association since 1990. Approximately 95 school districts throughout the United States have put this adaptive testing system into place. Although specific records of usage are not kept across districts, it is safe to say that over 200,000 students have been tested using this system nationwide.

The point of this historical overview is not to impress with the numbers of students tested, but rather to emphasize the nature of the developmental effort that has gone into these adaptive tests. In order to meet the needs of the students in Portland, the adaptive tests have been developed in an iterative fashion, changing incrementally each year. To allow these tests to be used with students in multiple districts, each with its own curricular emphasis and need for information, the development of the tests has moved from specific goals and test characteristics to a system that is extremely flexible and configurable. The procedures that have been used to make these tests usable and accessible to students in many different situations will be the focus of the remainder of this chapter.

USES FOR CAT IN THE SCHOOLS

A general computerized adaptive testing system causes a stir in a school district. When we announced our pilot project, teachers and principals had many ideas for the use of the system. Because it was our intent to build a system that would be used at the discretion of the schools, we collected a list of all the suggestions, and then tried to develop a system of tests that would be able to meet most of the schools' needs. In no particular order, then, here are the types of testing that interested the schools:

• *Entry Testing*: Because students move from school to school at all times of the year, it would be useful to have information concerning their achievement levels as quickly as possible. School transcripts from other districts may take a long time to arrive, and may not contain the achievement information that a school needs. As a result, a short test that provided a reasonably accurate score on the day of a student's registration or arrival would be very useful.

- *Diagnostic Testing*: Students have all sorts of different problems in keeping up with the curriculum, and it is sometimes very difficult for a teacher to determine content areas in which a student might be having problems. A test that would pinpoint areas of difficulty would be extremely useful for a teacher who wishes to individualize instruction in the classroom. This test would be a fairly long test and would interactively focus on areas in which students demonstrated performance problems.

- *Certification Testing*: Our district has a required test score that each student must achieve in order to receive a normal diploma. Students have several chances to demonstrate the desired achievement level on a paper-and-pencil test before they graduate, but an adaptive test that could be administered as needed could improve the existing system in two ways. First, it could reduce the anxiety associated with the test by allowing additional testing opportunities. Second, it could reduce the length of the test needed to make a confident decision, and therefore reduce fatigue as a factor in unsuccessful performance by students. This test would be a fairly long test, due to the importance of the decision, but could terminate once a confident decision could be made about the student.

- *Candidacy Testing*: Several programs in our district have special needs for determining a student's eligibility for services. For instance, our talented and gifted program (TAG) tries to target special services for students who are above the 97th percentile in Reading and Mathematics performance. It would be very useful for TAG and our other special programs to have a screening test that would identify students who should be considered as candidates for services. Such a test would be a fairly long test due to the importance of the decision, but could be terminated once a confident decision concerning candidacy could be made.

- *Growth Assessment*: We try to emphasize student growth over all else in our educational program. Toward that end, it would be very appropriate to have a test that allowed a teacher to test students at several times during the year and track the change in achievement for these students. This test could be used within a broad content area, such as mathematics, or in a more narrowly defined domain, such as geometry or problem solving. A short test would be appropriate here except that change is very tricky to measure at the individual level. As a result, a moderately long adaptive test would be needed to provide the accuracy needed in the individual scores to allow reasonable reliability of growth estimates.

- *Pretesting and Posttesting*: In our school district, there are many short-term changes in instruction that are made by building personnel, and also many short-duration special programs designed to help students learn specific subject matter. A test that could be used before and after the treatment would be of great benefit in determining whether these short changes have any impact on the curricular goals that are valued by the school district. A relatively short test providing a single score in a content area and using different items for the pretests and posttests would be ideal for this purpose.

As is evident from this partial list, the schools had an abundance of reasons for an adaptive testing system. Our task was to create a system that captured the needs of the schools without overwhelming them with a long list of tests. In addition, the tests had to be useful for students of many different ages, because we wanted to avoid developing a different test for each grade level. These two starting points led us to develop a short set of multipurpose tests that could be used by students in various grades, but which might respond differently to students in different grades. One of the first of these was the survey test of mathematical achievement.

THE SURVEY TEST OF MATHEMATICS ACHIEVEMENT

The Survey Test of Mathematics Achievement (Math Survey) was one of the first adaptive tests developed for use in Portland Public Schools. It was intended to serve as a quick, accurate measurement tool that would provide a single mathematics score for a student. It is only one facet of the overall CARAT system, but its development serves as a prototype for the development of all of the tests that we currently use.

In its current form, the Math Survey is used for several of the purposes suggested originally by the schools. In particular, it is used for entry testing, growth assessment, pretesting, and posttesting. In addition to these uses, the Math Survey is used as a gateway test into the certification tests. This use is described in more detail in the next section concerning the testing environment.

The Math Survey is the single most popular adaptive test in the CARAT system. In this system, the utility of a test can be tracked by its popularity, because there are no adaptive tests that are required to be given in our school district. Each adaptive test that is given represents a conscious decision on the part of the school to administer a test to a student. In an era in which students may be tested by the teacher, the district, the College Board, the state, and the federal government, among others, schools do not often recommend additional tests for a student. As a result, the tests that are given through the CARAT system normally represent the actual needs of the schools for additional assessment information about particular students.

As with any computerized adaptive test, the development of the Math Survey represents a series of decisions that were made concerning a number of test characteristics (and a number of revisions when the first decisions were wrong). Later, we describe the current features of the test, and then describe in much more detail some of the educational and psychometric decisions that went into the development of these features.

To describe the outcome of these decisions, we use an arbitrary sample of 1,793 student response records collected from PPS students. These records were collected in the 1991–1992 and 1992–1993 school years. This sample should be large enough to give us a picture of the performance of the adaptive test, but should not be considered complete or representative of all of the schools in the system.

Items

Current Status.   Each item is a five-alternative, multiple-choice question that was written and reviewed by a team of teachers, examined by a bias review committee, field-tested with a sample of 300 to 400 students, and examined for item fit. Approximately 66% of the original items survived to be used in the item banks.

Decision Process.   Before the development of the adaptive tests, the school district already had a large bank of mathematics items, calibrated to the one parameter logistic (1PL or Rasch, 1960) IRT model. In addition, the field testing processes, calibration procedures, and review policies were all in place.

A change in the item development process might suggest changes to all of the existing items, so any change in the process would not be made lightly. There was no particular reason to change from a five-alternative, multiple-choice format (as much as the folks promoting performance assessment might like it to be so) and so the format was not changed.

Our item review process consists of two portions. First, a panel of educators and community members reviews each item for curriculum appropriateness and for possible biasing factors. Second, during the calibration process, a number of statistical tests are performed to judge item performance. We had no reason to expect that changes in our test would induce biasing factors into the individual items, so there was little need to modify the human review policies and these remained the same.

One thing that might need to be altered with the development of the adaptive tests was the calibration procedure for the items, and the associated statistical tests. There has been enough speculation concerning the impact of the testing mode on the performance of test-takers (i.e., Green, Bock, Humphreys, Linn, & Reckase, 1984) that it was necessary to ascertain whether changing to CAT required a recalibration of the items in the banks. This is discussed in more detail in the "Measurement Scale" section that follows.

Item Pools

Current Status.   PPS has mathematics item banks containing approximately 6,500 calibrated items. From these item banks, we select the items that will be used in the item pools for the Math Survey. The item pool for the lower grades (2 through 5) contains 1,722 items and the one for the upper grades (6 through 12) contains 1,873 items. Two different, but overlapping item pools are used in the Math Survey for the lower and higher grades due to curriculum differences. About 40% of the items in active use appear in both item pools. At any time, only about half of the items that are available in the item banks are actually included in the item pools for the Math Survey.

Decision Process.   There are two primary decisions embedded in the current item pools. First, we only use about half of the items that are available for use in the item banks. Second, we use different item pools for upper and lower grades. One of these is a primarily practical decision, and one is a primarily psychometric decision.

The practical decision has to do with the size of the item pools we use at any one time for the test. We use less items than we have available (a) for security; (b) for convenience; and (c) to allow other item uses (such as our paper-and-pencil tests). In addition, we try to identify a pool of items that is adequate for measurement, without being overly large.

Concerning security, the use of only some of the items available allows us to create alternate item pools if we suspect that the current pool has been compromised. This is an unlikely event, given the low-stakes nature of this test. At the same time, using a large item pool provides us with security in numbers that is important in an adaptive test that will remain in place for a period of time. The larger the item pool is, the more unlikely it will be that best friends will see several common items. This reduces unintended or casual collusion between students. Therefore, using a large item pool that contains a fraction of the available items is to be preferred for security reasons.

Convenience was another governing factor in determining the item pool size. At the time the test was developed, hard disk space was very costly. Therefore, a test that used about three megabytes of space (as our current test does) was preferable to one that would require over 10 megabytes. In fact, our original tests were delivered on floppy disks, and used much smaller item pools.

Finally, the items in our item banks serve several purposes. To the extent possible, we try to avoid overlap in our different types of adaptive mathematics tests, and also try to avoid overlap with our paper-and-pencil tests. Life becomes much easier when we designate a unique subset of the available items for each of these purposes.

The psychometric decision concerned the use of two item pools in mathematics. Many research studies reinforce the concept that response dimensionality changes with training (e.g., Kingsbury & Weiss, 1979). Prior to exposure to material, factor structures tend to be less related to a consistent general mathematics achievement trait, and more related to group-specific factors. In a nutshell, our unidimensional IRT model does not fit well prior to instruction. In grade school mathematics, decimal notation and signed integer mathematics are not usually taught prior to the fourth or fifth grade. In Portland, these concepts are introduced in the fifth grade. As a result, we created the two item pools that we currently use in mathematics. They differ in content but both relate to the same underlying scale of mathematics achievement.

It is probably appropriate to make a distinction here between data collected for calibration, and data collected for measurement. In an educational setting, it is common to have a curriculum for use in the school district. It is not as common to see this curriculum followed in a school or classroom. Because factor structures change with instruction, we need to calibrate items with groups of students who have had an opportunity to learn the curriculum. After calibration, though, we may want to measure the achievement of students who come to us from other districts, with other curricula. We are therefore in the position of measuring students with unknown response dimensionality as if they were members of the group with known response dimensionality. To date, this has not caused obvious measurement problems, and scores before and after instruction seem to be well related. If we had not selected students based on the opportunity to learn for our calibration samples, our current scale might have developed substantial measurement problems. The distinction between calibration and measurement samples is an important one to make in an educational context, and is often overlooked by individuals creating a scale and scoring students with the same test administration.

Measurement Model

Current Status.   The 1PL model (Rasch, 1960) is used to calibrate the items on the test.

Decision Process.   The 1PL response model had been in use in Portland for approximately 8 years prior to the development of the Math Survey and the other adaptive tests. Although inertia is a major factor in using the 1PL with the adaptive test as well, it is not the only factor. Test scores, student reports, administrative reports, and all longitudinal data for the years prior to the development of the adaptive test were based on the 1PL model. Changing to a different response model would render new reports less comparable to older reports, and would have made it quite difficult to identify longitudinal change for individual students. The district was satisfied with the performance of the 1PL model for its paper tests, and therefore it seemed logical to use the same model for the adaptive tests.

The 1PL model has the advantages of being frugal in its use of data for item calibration, and its simplicity of application to an adaptive testing process. Beyond these ease-of-use arguments, and some specious arguments concerning the estimability of additional item parameters, there was no particular reason to choose the 1PL model over its more complex cousins. In fact, because we use multiple-choice items in our item pool, there are researchers who would say that we are sloppy in not accounting for guessing (at least) in our measurement model. In our setting, it appears that the correct question to ask is "How much measurement accuracy do we lose by not using a more complex model?"

Unfortunately, we do not have an answer to the question, but we do have some interesting suggestions concerning the 1PL model and its use with multiple-choice items in an adaptive test. One of the features of an adaptive test is that students take questions that are relatively close in difficulty to their achievement levels. This means that most of the interactions between students and items occur close to the difficulty parameter estimate for the item. The difficulty parameter is usually the most accurately estimated parameter, and tends to be close to the area of the item response function in which the 1PL model and the more complex models agree most closely. As a result, we may lose less accuracy in the adaptive test by using the less complex model than we would if we were developing a wide-range paper-and-pencil test.

Measurement Scale

Current Status. The measurement scale is a cross-graded IRT scale initially created using a set of 134 tests linked together and given to students in grades 3 to 8. The continuity of the scale is maintained through the use of fixed-parameter item calibration and drift studies to identify and correct scale changes.

Decision Process. Developing and maintaining a measurement scale for a large item bank is an arduous task, and goes well beyond the scope of this chapter. Among the issues involved are the need to maintain continuity within and across grades, and the handling of a distribution of student performance that is constantly changing. As a result, few calibration programs used today are designed or even able to maintain a consistent scale across test administrations and between grades. There are also some issues concerning the scale that relate directly to the Math Survey, and we discuss these. (For more information about the development and maintenance of a cross-grade scale of achievement, see Forster, Ingebo, & Wolmut, 1978, or Ingebo, 1997.)

A primary issue in moving from a paper-and-pencil testing procedure to an adaptive one is the continuity of the scale. Two relevant questions concerning this issue are whether the item calibrations remain invariant, and whether the scores from the two test media are comparable. We designed two studies to investigate these issues, one of which has been completed, and one of which is at the end of the data collection phase.

The study that has been completed (Kingsbury & Houser, 1988) compared achievement level estimates obtained from an adaptive test and from two paper-and-pencil tests. One of the paper-and-pencil tests was arbitrarily chosen as a criterion measure, and a regression analysis was conducted using the test results of over 700 students. The results of this study indicated that the achievement level estimates obtained from the CAT tests were as closely related to our criterion paper-and-pencil test as were the achievement level estimates from the other paper-and-pencil test. At the level of total test scores, this study provided strong evidence that our CAT test was as closely related to a paper-and-pencil test as the two paper-and-pencil tests were.

A second study was designed to identify whether individual item calibrations remain constant when the medium used for testing is changed. This study would be difficult to conduct during the developmental phase of an adaptive test, unless a wealth of resources is available, or the study is limited to checking the impact of computer presentation on item calibrations. We have now collected enough data to complete this study using a recently developed matrix calibration procedure (Kingsbury & Houser, 1998).

In the course of collecting data to compare item calibrations, a methodology was developed to test whether parameter estimates change more than expected when items are moved from paper-and-pencil administration to adaptive administration (Kingsbury & Houser, 1989). This methodology, the baseline-fit procedure, allows us to correct for the sampling variation in our calibration procedures while comparing item parameter estimates from adaptive and conventional tests. Preliminary investigations indicate that the procedure is able to identify items that are performing in an unusual manner.

Test Entry Procedure

Current Status.   A student who has no test history begins the test with a normal Bayesian prior distribution centered on the mean student performance in the grade and with a variance of 100. For these students, we offset item selection by a small random amount at the beginning of the test, to avoid having each student in a grade receive the same starting items. A student who has taken a test in the past begins the test with a similar prior distribution, but one centered on the regression estimate of current performance based on past performance(s). This information is tracked using the unique student identification number that is assigned when a student enrolls in the district.

Decision Process.   Many adaptive tests have each test-taker begin the test in the middle of the item pool, or the expected mean standing on the trait, and let the difficulty level change from this starting point on the basis of student performance. Although this approach is satisfactory when nothing is known about the test-taker, it is common in an educational setting to have useful prior information. We chose to use as much information as we have about a student to start the test with items of appropriate difficulty.

When we began development of the Math Survey, we used the grade level mean on the districtwide mathematics test established on the most recent paper-and-pencil administration as a starting point. To this procedure, we added a growth estimate adjustment, so that a person taking a test in the middle of the year would start the test midway between grade-level means. Finally, with the addition of the student database, we began using a student's test history to customize the starting point for each student.

Some Outcomes.   For students who are placed into the test at their grade-level mean, one would expect the students' final scores to be distributed around the entry point as the student achievement levels are distributed around the mean. To the extent that the scores are less widely distributed around the mean, we can assume that our entry point is more accurate than the grade-level mean would be for an entry point.

In our data set, the difference between final score and the entry point was distributed with a mean of 6.15 and a standard deviation of 21.06. The standard deviation of student scores in our data set was 22.64. Therefore, we improve our placement of students by approximately 7% by using the additional information to inform the entry point. Many of the students taking the Math Survey are entering students with no prior information so one would expect this improvement to be greater if all of the test-takers had useful prior information.

In the previous result, it is worth discussing that the entry point is, on average, 6.15 points below the final score. This was not done on purpose, originally. Rather, when we established the system, we noticed that students scored slightly higher on the adaptive test than expected on the basis of their paper-and-pencil test scores. As a result, the final score tends to be a little higher than the entry point. Teachers tend to like this feature, because it makes the first item seen somewhat easier for the student, so we have never adjusted the entry point to eliminate the difference. Adjusting the entry point to account for the difference in observed means between the two types of tests would also be expected to improve our student placement.

Although there is clearly a difference between the score that we expect a student to have based on paper-and-pencil test scores and the scores that we actually observe on the adaptive test, it is unclear what causes this difference. Because students are selected to take the math survey by their teachers and counselors, it is not uncommon for these students to be in special programs, or in other unusual circumstances. This may cause them to differ from their classmates enough that our regression equations are not accurate. Alternatively, the adaptive test may have a motivating effect on student performance that is not present in the paper-and-pencil test. Although this question is worthy of research, that research has not yet been carried out. One of the many difficulties of working in a system that involves voluntary testing is that some research questions are extremely difficult to answer.

Item Selection

Current Status.   Items are selected to maximize the expected information at the momentary achievement level estimate at any particular point in the test, subject to constraints.

Decision Process.   This decision was not overly complicated. Most of the evidence in the psychometric literature indicates that choosing items to maximize information at the momentary achievement level estimate produces the most reliable achievement level estimates. Unfortunately, what is simple in theory is often complex in practice.

In most classrooms, teachers tend to write exams so that knowledgeable students can correctly answer most of the questions. This expectation that high-performing students will answer almost all questions correctly does not mesh well with an adaptive test which selects items to maximize information. Maximizing item information tends to result in tests in which students answer approximately half of the questions correctly (somewhat more than half with models that include a parameter for guessing).

During the development of the system, we had ongoing discussions with teachers and school administrators about the impact of questions that were "too difficult" on the students taking the tests. Because PPS was already using a series of functional level tests, which try to match the difficulty of tests to the achievement of students, it was agreed to try the adaptive test with maximum information item selection. If students were unable to deal with the "difficult" test, we were prepared to lower the difficulty of the adaptive test.

When we administered the tests to our students, informal teacher observation and formal surveys responses indicated that students were challenged by the tests, not frustrated. As a result, we were able to maintain the psychometrically optimal item selection procedure, while establishing confidence in the testing program among our teachers. For those considering changing the difficulty of an adaptive test to please a client, it might be useful to collect some test-taker data first.

Item Selection Constraints

Current Status.   Eight goal areas exist in the Portland mathematics curriculum, and they are weighted equally in all tests. Therefore, item selection revolves through the eight goal areas, and the most informative item is selected from the specified goal. In addition, students who have been tested in the past do not see the same items again for a specified period of time. Items previously seen are locked out during item selection through the use of the student's test history attached to the student's district identification number.

Decision Process. The constraints that we use in item selection are fairly straightforward and are not nearly so complicated as those used by some other organizations. Even so, the constraints severely limit item selection. In an item pool of 1,700 items designed to measure students across three grade levels, there are probably about 400 items that are reasonably near to the achievement level of a particular student. The item difficulties in the eight content areas are not equally distributed, and as a result, one of these content areas may have only 20 items in the set of 400. Although this is fine for the first Math Survey, which will use only two or three items from any one content area, it may cause problems for repeat testing. After two or three tests, the items that are left in the thinnest content areas may not do a very good job of measuring the student's performance.

Some Outcomes. Because this test is a fairly low stakes test, we do not worry too much about item exposure, and do not have any specific procedure in place to control item exposure. In our data set, only 705 of the 1,722 items in the lower-grade item pool were used, with the most popular item being administered 274 times in 1,783 tests.

For higher-stakes adaptive tests, this would probably be unacceptable performance. High-stakes adaptive testing ordinarily requires additional constraints to implement exposure control procedures developed over the past 10 years. For our purposes, we do not feel a need to control exposure so explicitly. In fact, for us the most negative aspect of these results is that we are not using all of the items that we have available in our test and are thus wasting disk space and shortchanging the breadth of content that should be included in the tests.

This difficulty with item usage is probably related to the tabular approach that is used to identify the most informative item at any particular achievement level estimate. Because many items may have identical or similar difficulty parameter estimates in our pool, the tabularization creates an artificial ordering that affects item usage. For instance, if three items in the same goal area have the same difficulty, the one that appears first in the table will always be chosen first, while the other two will be chosen less often or not at all. We are currently considering a "randomesque" item selection procedure (Kingsbury & Zara, 1989) to correct this difficulty. This procedure would select an item at random for presentation from a set of items with similar characteristics.

Scoring for Item Selection

Current Status.   The momentary achievement level estimate used to identify the most informative item is a Bayesian score that starts with the prior distribution used for test entry and is modified by the item responses.

Decision Process.   When working with a mathematics scale that ranges from low third grade performance to middle fifth-grade performance, the difference in difficulties between the easiest items in the item pool and the hardest items in the item pool is quite noticeable. As a result, it is not desirable to move from an item of middle difficulty to the highest difficulty in the pool, unless you really want to make a third grader cry.

Because we have a strict dry-eye policy, we use a procedure that tries to pinpoint a student's achievement level well to begin with, and that moves through the difficulty range of the item pool in modest increments. Therefore, we choose the item that maximizes expected information at the Bayesian achievement level estimate. The achievement level estimate is based on the item responses and the prior distribution used for the entry procedure described previously. Because the standard deviation of student scores within a grade is approximately one-sixth of the range of the item difficulties in the pool, a student would have to answer four to six questions in a row correctly at the beginning of the test in order to move from items of middle difficulty level to the most difficult items in the item pool. For this type of item pool, with this population of test-takers, the Bayes achievement level estimate is more appropriate for item selection, and since it has been in use, student frustration (as reported by test proctors) has dropped dramatically.

Scoring for Reporting

Current Status.   The achievement level estimate used in score reporting and for test termination is the maximum likelihood score. This assures that student scores will not be biased toward the initial prior estimates and also assures that two students who respond in exactly the same manner to the same questions will receive the same score.

Decision Process.   Although the Bayesian scoring procedure using individualized prior distributions is quite useful for selecting items for an adaptive test, it may not be ideal for the score that will be reported to the student and teacher. If two students with exactly the same true achievement level and exactly the same test performance happen to start with different priors, they will end up with different Bayesian achievement level estimates. Although the true achievement level is unobservable, teachers and students can observe the responses to the test questions, and it would be very difficult to justify giving different scores to two students with the same set of item responses. Moreover, the use of a Bayesian scoring procedure will almost always result in achievement level estimates that are slightly regressed toward the mean of the prior distribution and this can have adverse impact on some of the people being tested (Samejima, 1980).

In addition, some Bayesian scoring procedures (i.e., Owen, 1969) are order dependent. Due to this dependency, two students taking the same items in two different orders (with identical responses to each item) will end up with somewhat different scores. This could result in one student being judged above a standard and another student being judged below a standard, even though they answered the same questions in the same way in the presence of the same prior distribution (but in a different order). Because many possible orderings of the same items might be seen in an adaptive test, a procedure for scoring that is order dependent is not acceptable.

The scoring procedure that we use to report student scores must only judge student performance on the day of the test, without regard to any prior information or the order of the questions on the test. As a result, we have chosen maximum-likelihood scoring for our reporting score. Because the score is not reported until the end of the test, we normally avoid the problem of dealing with the infinite maximum-likelihood estimates associated with perfect response vectors. The one exception to this occurs when a student manages to complete the entire test without answering a single question correctly (or a single question incorrectly).

Some Outcomes. Perfect response patterns are an uncommon occurrence for a wide range paper-and-pencil test, but they become even less likely in an adaptive test. In our data sample, no perfectly correct or perfectly incorrect response vectors were present in the 1,793 records. The longest string of incorrect responses found was 12 items, and the longest string of correct responses found was 13 items. Because the Math Survey is normally about 20 items in length, no student in the sample came close to completing the test with a perfect response vector, so the arbitrary scores that we assign to perfect correct and perfect incorrect response patterns were never used as reported scores in our data set.

Test Termination Procedure

Current Status. The test ends when the student has answered 22 questions (including 2 field test items) or when the standard error of the achievement level estimate drops below 5 points.

Decision Process. Students newly registered in a school often take two survey tests when they are first tested, so it is handy to have a relatively short test. The ideal, from a timing point of view, would be a test that was short enough to allow a third grade student to go through the instructions and take two tests in less than 50 minutes. Teachers were fairly confident that a young student could accomplish this if the tests were kept to about 20 items each. In addition, teachers at the lower grades were fairly certain that a test of 15 to 20 items would be short enough to maintain a student's interest and not diminish performance through fatigue.

Competing against the desire for a short test is the need for measurement accuracy in the student scores. The districtwide paper-and-pencil test that Portland uses each year has about 56 mathematics questions and results in an average standard error of measurement (SEM) of approximately 3.4 points across students and grades. This is a very good SEM because it is between .20 and .25 standard deviations, depending on the grade. The Math Survey does not need quite that much measurement accuracy, but in order to be useful, an average SEM of less than .50 standard deviations would be desirable. Our preliminary simulations indicated that an average SEM of slightly less than 5.0 points on our measurement scale could be obtained from our adaptive test with 20 scored items. This is equivalent to an SEM of approximately .35 to .40 standard deviations, depending on the grade of the student.

It seemed obvious that a 20-item Math Survey test would satisfy both needs, but we might be able to reduce this test length somewhat for very consistent students. As a result, we developed the stopping rule that allowed the test to terminate when the number of (scored) items administered reached 20, or when the SEM fell below 5.0 on our measurement scale, whichever occurred first. This rule has remained in place ever since.

Some Outcomes. In our data sample, the average number of scored items taken during a test was 17.3, with a minimum of 15 and a maximum of 20 items. The average SEM observed at the end of the test was 5.09, with a minimum of 4.78 and a maximum of 8.03. Given the design specifications, the SEM results are in keeping with our expectations.

Test Environment

Current Status. The test is given in a quiet environment in which the student is either alone (except for the proctor) or with several other students also taking tests on computers. A common environment is a counselor's office. All testing computers are located in locked rooms, or have removable storage devices that are kept in locked cabinets when testing is not in progress.

Decision Process. Finding a place for testing in a school building is not necessarily easy. The average school conducts large-scale testing in classrooms or in the cafeteria. It is not easy to find a quiet space to test one or two students. Some of our schools have found vacant rooms, but a more common occurrence is to use a small room located adjacent to the main office. Sometimes this can be the principal or vice-principal's office, or the nurse's office. In middle schools and high schools, the space most commonly used is a counselor's office. In general, we suggest a lockable room that does not have free student access. We will settle for a room with a teacher always present during school hours.

Finding appropriate space to secure the testing system and allow the student a reasonable testing environment is a difficult problem and an ongoing battle. Many schools would prefer to use computer labs for testing (as well as other activities), but this is normally not an appropriate setting for testing, if other activities are occurring while students are tested. We have found that labs can be useful if they are devoted to testing for a certain period of the day or set up with individual carrels and headphones so that students may work undisturbed. Obviously, in this type of setting, the need for proctor support is increased, not diminished, and the need for security procedures is also increased.

Moving toward individualized testing is a much greater logistic problem than a conceptual problem. Almost all teachers see the advantage in giving each student an individualized test, but testing one or two students at a time can be very disruptive to a classroom. A school environment is primarily a learning environment, and so we need to minimize the disturbance that testing causes. However, until we integrate assessment and instruction more closely, we will continue to have difficulties in scheduling tests.

Testing Interface

Current Status. Students enter all responses through the keyboard. In order to respond, students highlight the desired alternative, and press the enter key. Students can rotate the highlighting through the response alternatives by pressing the space bar.

Decision Process. The testing interface that we currently use has been changed several times, but we think it has finally been beaten into submission. The goal has been to make the interface very easy to learn and use, and the current version of the interface seems to work quite well. The current interface requires the test-taker to know only two keys (the space bar and the enter key). This is very simple to learn, and as a result, we only use two instructional screens and one example question to orient the test-taker.

In addition to the space bar, there are two other procedures to highlight alternatives that are built into the system. The up and down arrow keys on the number pad are active for moving the highlighting from one response alternative to another. In addition, typing the number or letter associated with a particular response alternative will highlight that alternative. These procedures are active for students, but they are not included in the training at the beginning of the test because they are not necessary to take the test.

The use of a mouse to enter responses was considered, implemented, and then rejected. Two factors worked against the acceptance of the mouse for the interface. First, field observation of young children indicated that they had a difficult time highlighting the correct response and then clicking the mouse button without accidentally moving the highlighting. Second, because the mouse cursor can be moved to any point on the screen, students seemed to take a fair amount of time to locate the cursor and move it to the desired alternative. The mouse seemed to be a distraction and a possible source of error, and thus it was eliminated.

We also investigated the use of a confirmation response, and rejected it. A confirmation response is a question that appears after the student has entered a response, and usually says something like "You have chosen A. Is this correct?" The confirmation response is designed to give the student a final chance to change a misentered response, before it becomes official. In observing a number of students using this type of response, one thing became very clear. The students did not use the confirmation response as a way to check their answers. Instead, they just chose the "yes" answer as quickly as possible and moved on. We did not conduct a serious study on this issue, but in observing about 10 students, it appeared that the "yes" response became an automatic part of answering the original question, rather than being a separate question. Insofar as it did not seem to be performing the task it was designed for, we removed the confirmation response from the testing interface.

Proctoring

Current Status.   All tests are proctored by a teacher, counselor, or school administrator. The proctor is available throughout the test, but they may work on other things in the office during the test.

Decision Process.   As difficult as it is to get testing space in a school building, it is even more difficult to get a test proctor. Most people in a school building have a job, and that job almost never involves testing. Therefore, our strategy was to enlist an individual in each school who had either a need for testing or an interest in testing. This individual, normally a counselor or a Title 1 teacher, became the primary proctor.

Because proctoring tests adds to their normal duties, we tried to arrange things so that the proctor could work on lesson plans or other paperwork during testing. We arranged for the testing area to have a desk for the proctor, and set up the testing system to beep at the end of the test. Because this is the only noise that the testing system makes, the proctors are alerted that the student is done. The proctor then records the test score on paper for immediate use and for school records.

Hardware and Software

Current Status. Tests are given on a PC compatible computer with at least an 80286 CPU and 640K memory. No mouse is required, and each computer has at least a CGA color monitor.

Decision Process. As in most school districts, our computer hardware is a mixture of old and new machines from various vendors. When this project began, the district had a policy that instructional PCs were to be Apple computers, and administrative computers were to be IBM computers. It appeared at the time that development for the IBM platform would be slightly easier and allowed for more expansion, so we called our computers "administrative computers" and moved on to software development.

At the beginning of the project, we needed four pieces of software: (a) an item banker, to allow us to enter thousands of test questions into electronic form; (b) an adaptive testing development system, to allow us to develop customized tests for different purposes; (c) a test presentation system, which would actually administer the tests we developed; and (d) a database system, which would allow us to collect information and produce useful individual and group reports for teachers and staff. We estimated that these four pieces of software would take approximately 2 person-years for development, and because we wanted to start our pilot project quickly, we looked for existing software to get us started. At that time, several systems were available for administering adaptive tests, but only one was available for the IBM PC that included an item banker and a test development system. The MicroCAT™ system (Assessment Systems Corporation, 1984) included an item banker, a development system, and a test administration system. We adopted the MicroCAT system with the expectation that we would either modify it or replace it with other software as it became possible.

The MicroCAT system proved to be very flexible, and a source license agreement that still allows us to make the changes that we needed to use the system for our purposes even today (Kingsbury, 1990). Although this system does not use fancy graphics, it does run on a wide variety of IBM PC-compatible computers with minimal memory and space requirements. It will run under Windows, but does not require it, which is extremely important in a school district that has many low-power computers.

Score Reporting

Current Status.   The student's score is displayed on the screen immediately following the end of the test. This screen remains on the display until the proctor enters a special code. At the end of the testing session, the results from all tests are fed into the school database. This database allows the school to generate various types of reports, including longitudinal reports for individuals and several different group reports.

Decision Process.   The Research and Evaluation Department at PPS has a set of guidelines for reporting that has been used for almost a decade. These guidelines include an emphasis on individual growth, an emphasis on graphically based reports, and an emphasis on providing error bands whenever feasible. These guidelines form the basis for the reporting system that has been built to work with the data collected by the adaptive testing system. This is the reporting portion of the Computerized Adaptive Reporting and Testing System (CARAT).

CARAT allows the scores from the Math Survey, and all of our other tests, to be immediately accessible in the schools by teachers and administrators. In its most basic reports, CARAT allows a teacher to call up a longitudinal record of a student's test performance going back 5 years. This record includes all adaptive tests and all paper-and-pencil districtwide tests. Each test score is shown in a graphic display, accompanied by the appropriate error band. The teacher may choose to display the district means, school means, and several other criterion levels of interest within the same graphic display.

The CARAT reporting system has approximately 10 different reports that may be generated for individual students, classes, grades, and predefined or ad hoc groups of students. In general, the purpose of the CARAT system is to empower teachers and school administrators. Reports that previously had to be requested from the Research and Evaluation Department can now be produced in-house, in a fraction of the time, to serve the school's particular reporting needs.

Data Flow

Current Status.   Student performance information flows from the individual testing station, to the school's database computer, to the Research and Evaluation department through a series of floppy disks and removable storage devices. Tests and information from the central district database flow to the schools and on to individual testing machines the same way.

Decision Process.   Space and time are difficult problems to solve in setting up an adaptive testing system in a school district, but the worst problem is communication. Most computers in our school district are not connected to a local area network, the internet, or even a modem. Adding any of these connections might involve opening up a wall in the school building, which could require asbestos abatement procedures, or a change in the telephone switching processes. Therefore, it is very difficult to set up an efficient communications system to move tests to the schools and to move student test information from the schools. As a result, the floppy disk transfer system that we use has been cobbled together. It works inadequately and is the weakest portion of the testing system.

To see how bad this system is, it helps to describe the transfer of data that might occur for a particular student's Math Survey.

> If Jason takes the Math Survey in March on a testing station that is not connected directly to the database server for the school, the data must be transferred to the server by floppy disk. Because the proctor makes a record of the test score for school use, there is not always an incentive for the school to transfer the data. This transfer may easily take several months, bringing us to the late spring.
>
> Once the data is on the server, it is immediately integrated into the school database, unless the student used a temporary identification number when taking the test (a common occurrence for newly registered students). The school must update the ID number with the student's actual number before the test record is included in the database or reported to central administration. This process should be fairly simple, but in practice may take several weeks, which will bring us to early summer, the end of the school year.
>
> Prior to leaving for summer vacation, the contact person for the adaptive testing system sends in a final floppy disk with the remaining test records for the year, unless he or she forgets, or is too busy during the last days of school. If Jason's test record is not sent in, it remains on the school computer for the summer. This means that the central administration will receive the score during the early to midfall (depending on how busy September is).
>
> Once Jason's test record is received by the Research and Evaluation Department, it usually moves quickly into the central database, unless something is wrong with the student name or ID number. If this happens, the school must be contacted to determine the correct ID and name, which may take several days. In all, the process to add the data to the central database can easily add a month to the process, bringing us to late October, when the results of Jason's test (in this worst case) finally appear in the central database.

Although this description is much worse than the average time for data to be moved to the central database, it is not as uncommon as it should be. To those developing an adaptive testing system, we cannot emphasize strongly enough the development of a data transfer system that is automatic and bidirectional. The development of such procedures helps reduce the possibility of human error, and also reduces the human workload, in the long run.

Computers are good at repetitive tasks such as data transfers at midnight, and an automated system would reduce frustration with the system dramatically.

SOME CONCLUSIONS

Although the features described in the previous section are fairly straightforward, some of the decisions made during the PPS CAT development were not. Some were an outgrowth of the adaptive testing development from the previous decade. Additional decisions were made relative to the educational needs of the students being tested. Finally, some decisions were made for reasons concerning the use of the data from testing. In the development of other tests within this system, the decisions have not been the same, and in the development of a different type of test, such as a test for licensure, it is very likely that many of the decisions will change.

It seems reasonable, though, to use the same general approach used by our development team. Whenever possible, we inform our decisions from data collected from our students. As a result, we did not rush into changing the difficulty of the test when teachers suggested that the students could not deal with these tests that were "too difficult." After student observation, we also decided to eliminate the confirmation response, and simplified the test interface by eliminating the mouse.

It is likely that we will continue to make changes to our testing system, but we are relatively pleased with the Math Survey the way it is currently configured. It is interesting that something as simple as a mathematics survey test gives us so many opportunities to practice our craft in turning the theory of adaptive testing into practice. The outcome of our attempt has been so positive that it is likely that we will be tuning that craft on many other tests in the future.

REFERENCES

Assessment Systems Corporation. (1984). *User's manual for the MICROCAT testing system.* St. Paul, MN: Assessment Systems Corporation.

Forster, F., Ingebo, I., & Wolmut, P. (1978). Rasch model monograph series. *North-West Evaluation Association Journal, 1,* 1–38.

Green, B. F., Bock, R. D., Humphreys, L. G., Linn, R. L., & Reckase, M. D. (1984). Technical guidelines for assessing computerized adaptive tests. *Journal of Educational Measurement, 21,* 347–360.

Hambleton, R. K., & Swaminathan, H. (1985). *Item response theory: Principles and applications.* Boston: Kluwer Nijhoff.

Hathaway, W. E. (1980). A school-district-developed, Rasch-based approach to minimum competency achievement testing. In R. M. Jaeger & C. K. Tittle (Eds.), *Min-*

imum competency achievement testing: Motives, models, measures, and consequences (pp. 113–137). Beverly Hills, CA: McCutchan.

Ingebo, G. S. (1997). *Probability in the measurement of achievement.* Chicago: MESA Press.

Kingsbury, G. G. (1990). Adapting adaptive testing: Using the MicroCAT testing system in a local school district. *Educational Measurement: Issues and Practice, 9,* 3–6.

Kingsbury, G. G., & Houser, R. L. (April, 1988). *A comparison of achievement level estimates from computerized adaptive testing and paper-and-pencil testing.* Paper presented at the annual meeting of the American Educational Research Association, New Orleans, LA.

Kingsbury, G. G., & Houser, R. L. (March, 1989). *Assessing the impact of using item parameter estimates obtained from paper-and-pencil testing for computerized adaptive tests.* Paper presented at the annual meeting of the American Educational Research Association, San Francisco, CA.

Kingsbury, G. G., & Houser, R. L. (1998). *A procedure for calibrating items to an existing measurement scale.* Manuscript in preparation.

Kingsbury, G. G., & Weiss, D. J. (1979). *Effect of point-of-time in instruction on the measurement of achievement* (ONR Research Report 79-4). Minneapolis: University of Minnesota, Psychometric Methods Program.

Kingsbury, G. G., & Zara, A. R. (1989). Procedures for selecting items for computerized adaptive tests. *Applied Measurement in Education, 2,* 359–375.

Lord, F. M. (1980). *Applications of item response theory to practical testing problems.* Hillsdale, NJ: Lawrence Erlbaum Associates.

Lord, F. M. (1983). Small n justifies the Rasch model. In D. J. Weiss (Ed.), *New horizons in testing: Latent trait test theory and computerized adaptive testing* (pp. 51–61). New York: Academic Press.

Lord, F. M., & Novick, M. R. (1968). *Statistical theories of mental test scores.* Reading, MA: Addison-Wesley.

Owen, R. J. (1969). *A Bayesian approach to tailored testing.* (Research Bulletin 69-92). Princeton, NJ: Educational Testing Services.

Rasch, G. O. (1960). *Probabilistic models for some intelligence and attainment tests.* Copenhagen: Danish Institute for Educational Research.

Samejima, F. (1980, October). *Is Bayesian estimation proper for estimating the individual's ability?* (Research Report 80-3). Knoxville: University of Tennessee, Department of Psychology.

Weiss, D. J. (Ed.) (1978). *Proceedings of the 1977 Computerized Adaptive Testing Conference.* Minneapolis: University of Minnesota, Department of Psychology, Psychometric Methods Program.

Weiss, D. J. (Ed.). (1983). *New horizons in testing: Latent trait test theory and computerized adaptive testing.* New York: Academic Press.

6

Development and Introduction of a Computer Adaptive Graduate Record Examinations General Test

Craig N. Mills
American Institute of Certified Public Accountants,
Jersey City, NJ

"Prospective graduate students, listen up ... " With these words, the introduction of a computer-adaptive version of the Graduate Record Examinations (GRE) General Test was announced (Cassone, 1993). The introduction of the GRE computer adaptive test (CAT) signaled both the culmination of years of research and development and the beginning of an extensive effort to develop and implement large-scale, high-stakes continuous testing using computers. The purposes of this chapter are to explain the rationale and process for the development of the GRE CAT, summarize the analyses conducted in its development and the decisions made during that process, discuss important issues associated with the ongoing maintenance of computer-delivered tests, and describe the new types of tests envisioned by the GRE Board as a result of the change to a computer-delivered assessment.

BACKGROUND AND RATIONALE
FOR THE DEVELOPMENT OF THE GRE CAT

The Graduate Record Examinations Program consists of the GRE General Test and a series of Subject Tests developed and administered by Educational Testing Service to aid in the graduate admissions process. The tests are administered to approximately 430,000 individuals throughout the world annually (Educational Testing Service, 1997). The tests have been shown to be a useful component in the prediction of graduate success and awarding of financial aid for graduate study (Educational Testing Service, 1997).

The GRE Tests are administered under the direction of the Graduate Record Examinations Board (GREB), an advisory board established in 1966. GRE Board members are typically deans of graduate schools. Two organizations, the Council of Graduate Schools and the Association of Graduate Schools, each appoint one Board member annually. The GRE Board also appoints two "at large" members each year. Board members serve a 4-year term. In addition to these 16 members, the past chair of the Board serves a 1-year term extension and the President of the Council of Graduate Schools is a permanent ex-officio member of the Board. Numerous committees (Services, Minority Graduate Education, Research, Subject Test Development, Technical Advisory, etc.) support the GRE Board and ETS in the development and administration of the GRE Program.

In the mid-1980s, the GRE Board began long-range planning for the future directions of the GRE Program. A paper (Ward, 1988) submitted to the GRE Board during the planning process proposed four objectives to be addressed in the revision of the Graduate Record Examinations tests:

1. Strengthen the tests as devices for use in graduate student selection;
2. Increase the ability of the tests to serve other assessment purposes;
3. Prepare to deal with changes in the graduate assessment context; and
4. Provide enhanced service to individuals and institutions.

Eighteen possibilities were discussed in relation to the four objectives and the effort required to develop them. One possibility, computerization of the tests, was described as an enabling activity that would allow the GRE Program to reduce its dependence on multiple-choice testing and facilitate enhancement of measurement within the program. Ward (1988) commented on the development of computer adaptive testing and constructed-response measurement, saying,

> The first set of possibilities, computerized adaptive testing and the introduction of constructed-response measurement, clearly should be high on any list of priorities. These technologies can broaden and strengthen measurement within the present examination program and will provide the enabling tools for many of the further changes that might be considered. (p. 19)

In response to this paper, the GRE Board approved development of a computer adaptive General Test as an "enabling technology" for the transition to new forms of assessment. The GRE Board also decided that the transition to computer delivery would be "evolutionary" rather than "revolutionary" (i.e., the transition would be implemented in phases).

DEVELOPMENT OF THE GRE ADAPTIVE TEST

Development of the GRE CAT began in the fall of 1988. In order to accommodate the Board's desire for a phased transition, the initial versions of the GRE CAT needed to produce results that were comparable to those derived from the paper-based program. Two potential sources of noncomparability were identified: the mode of delivery (computer or paper) and the testing model (adaptive or traditional/linear). Therefore, a two-phase plan for developing, evaluating, and introducing computer adaptive testing was adopted. In Phase 1, a linear computer-based test (CBT) was developed to assess comparability across modes of administration. Phase 2 was designed to assess comparability across testing models (traditional and adaptive) in a computer environment. Work on both phases proceeded concurrently. As the linear test comparability was being investigated, preliminary work on test specifications, administrative procedures, and adaptive testing simulations occurred.

Assessing the Comparability of the Linear CBT

In fall 1991, a sample of examinees who had taken the regularly scheduled October administration of the GRE General Test was invited to participate in a study to assess the comparability of the paper and computer versions of the test. Three different forms of the General Test had been administered during the October administration. Individuals in selected locations in the United States who had taken one of the forms were invited to take a second General Test during the period from mid-October to mid-December. In order to assess retest effects, some volunteers took a paper-based test and the remainder were administered a computer version of the test. The analysis sample consisted of 1,017 computer-based test records and 184 records from the paper-based test.

Analyses were conducted at both the item and test level. Schaeffer, Reese, Steffen, McKinley, and Mills (1993) reported that item level differences in performance were consistent with the variation that could be expected from instability in item parameter estimates. Test level results also supported comparability between modes of administration. Score distributions, section score intercorrelations, reliability, and standard errors of measurement were all comparable. There was some evidence of speededness in the computer test (i.e., examinees who took the computer-based test had more difficulty completing the test in the allotted time than those who took the paper-based version of the test), but the researchers concluded that the differences in speededness for the computer and paper tests did not affect performance.

These comparability results were the basis for a decision to introduce CBT in a traditional, linear format. Accordingly, on October 1, 1992, a CBT version of the GRE General Test was offered as a supplemental testing option.

Development of an Adaptive Version of the GRE General Test

Activities directed to the generation of an adaptive test design and field test of a CAT version of the GRE General Test occurred concurrently to the development and field testing of the linear version of the test. Among these activities were the establishment of test specifications and determination of numerous administrative policies and procedures.

Test Specifications.   Because the GRE Board had decided to introduce CBT gradually over a number of years, comparability of content and scores between the paper-based and computer-based test was important. However, one of the goals of the adaptive test was to reduce test length. As a result, there could not be an exact match between the test specifications for the traditional paper-based test and the computer adaptive version. Activities were undertaken to define adaptive test specifications that would yield comparable scores. A general assumption that guided this work was that the adaptive test would contain roughly half as many items as the traditional test and be of comparable psychometric quality.

Test development specialists constructed tables of test specifications for test lengths ranging from 10 items less than half of the traditional test length to 10 items more than half of the traditional test length. Construction of these tables was not a simple matter of reducing the content coverage allotted to a topic by, for example, 50%. Rather, it required a reasoned judgment based on both logical analysis and empirical results about the relative importance of different test specifications. Two examples are provided to illustrate this point.

The Verbal Reasoning component of the paper-based GRE General Test contains four reading passages, one each from the Humanities, Social Sciences, Physical Sciences, and Biological Sciences. Each test section contains two long and two short reading passages. Long passages are typically assessed by seven items. Four items are administered in association with each short passage. These items fall into seven content categories. In addition, at least one reading passage is classified as "culturally relevant" (i.e., it contains subject matter of particular relevance to females or members of ethnic minority groups). The adaptive version of the test, however, did not need four passages or the same number of items per passage as the traditional test. Thus, decisions

TABLE 6.1

Comparison of Traditional and Adaptive GRE General Test Content Specifications

Measure	Specification	Traditional	Adaptive
Verbal Reasoning			
	Time	60 Minutes	30 Minutes
	Antonyms	22	9
	Analogies	18	7
	Sentence completion	14	6
	Reading comprehension	22	8
Quantitative Reasoning			
	Time	60 Minutes	45 Minutes
	Quantitative comparison	30	14
	Discrete	20	10
	Data interpretation	10	4
Analytical Reasoning			
	Time	60 Minutes	60 Minutes
	Analytical reasoning	38	26
	Logical reasoning	12	9

were required regarding which categories of passages could be combined, how the content categories for items should be represented, how to reduce the number of items, and how to incorporate the requirement for culturally relevant material. A comparison of the specifications for the reading comprehension portion of the verbal measure in the traditional and adaptive modes is shown in Table 6.1.

In the Quantitative Reasoning portion of the traditional test, sections contain a fixed number of an item type called *quantitative comparisons* as the first items in the section. Quantitative comparison items are unique among the item types in the GRE General Test in that they contain only four answer options (all other items are five-option questions). Furthermore, the options are identical for all quantitative comparison items.

A common answer sheet containing five response positions for all items is used for the traditional test. This is necessary because the order of sections varies among test editions and because some test forms contain two quantitative sections and others contain three (one of which is a nonoperational pretest section). By grouping the quantitative comparison items together at the beginning of the test, it was presumed that examinees would be less likely to make erroneous marks on their answer sheets than if the items were interspersed with other, five-option items. Also, in the traditional test, the four answer options were presented once at the top of the page of the test book. All quantitative comparison items were then printed on that page to reduce the number of pages in the test books.

None of these concerns is relevant when the test is administered via computer because all relevant information (stem and appropriately labeled answer options) is presented on a single screen. Thus, some of the paper-based test specifications were eliminated in the computer adaptive version of the test. As a result, it was possible to intersperse quantitative comparison items with other item types, greatly increasing the flexibility available to the item selection algorithm.

Following the development of alternate test specifications, simulations were conducted to evaluate the extent to which the initial pools of items to be used in the CAT could fulfill both content and statistical constraints at each test length. Based on these simulations, final specifications and test lengths were established. A comparison of the paper-based and adaptive test lengths as defined through the process described here is shown in Table 6.1. Adaptive test lengths are approximately half the length of the paper-based tests for the verbal and quantitative tests. For the analytical measure, the adaptive test is 70% as long as the paper-based test. The analytical test contains only two item types: analytical and logical reasoning. Roughly three-quarters of the traditional test consists of analytical reasoning items that are presented in sets. The use of item sets results in a less optimal test design (from a psychometric view) and, as a result, requires more items than tests that contain mostly discrete items.

Selection of Initial Items.   A specification was required regarding the selection of the initial test questions. In the traditional GRE General Test, items appear in approximate order of difficulty (from easiest to hardest) within item type. It is commonly presumed that this ordering provides most examinees an opportunity for an initial "success experience" on the test and that test anxiety may be reduced as a result. In developing the specifications for the adaptive test, many test developers desired to approximate this initial success experience. From a purely psychometric view, however, it is preferable to begin the test with an item of middle difficulty. To balance these competing factors, a decision was made to begin the adaptive test with a moderately easy test question. In this way, an acceptable compromise between the efficiency of the test and the desire to ensure that most examinees were successful on the first item was accomplished. Once this decision was made, the next decision required was how different the second item should be from the first in terms of difficulty.

Because an adaptive test uses information about past performance to estimate ability and that ability estimate is then used, among other things, to select items for administration, it is not possible to order test questions by difficulty. However, examinee ability cannot be estimated until at least one item has been answered correctly and at least one item has been answered incorrectly. Therefore, arbitrary decisions are required governing the increase (decrease) in difficulty between items following correct (incorrect) answers until ability can be estimated. Simulations were used to investigate the effect of a specification to select the hardest (easiest) possible items until ability could be estimated. The results of these simulations indicated that the specification to select the hardest (easiest) possible item in the pool actually did not result in the selection of an extremely hard (easy) item as the second item. Rather, the effect of other constraints on item selection (content, item types, etc.) moderated item selection such that a moderately difficult (easy) item was typically selected. This result was considered acceptable, so simulations of other alternatives were not conducted.

Selecting Items Within Sets. All three measures that comprise the GRE General Test (verbal, analytical, and quantitative) contain at least some sets of items based on a common stimulus. Decisions were required regarding the administration of items associated with sets. From a psychometric perspective, it would have been desirable to select individual items throughout the test. However, this could result in presenting the same stimulus material to an examinee on multiple occasions during the administration. As a result, examinees would have to read the stimulus multiple times. For reasons of efficiency and fairness to examinees, a decision was made to select a given stimulus only once during the test. The adaptive item selection algorithm was then constrained to select only items associated with that stimulus until the required number of items had been administered.

Item Exposure. Item exposure refers to the frequency of item administration in the examinee population. Items that are selected frequently may become known to examinees in advance of the test administration and, as a result, fail to perform as expected. Several factors need to be considered when evaluating item exposure controls. These include frequency of administration, the proportion of the examinee population exposed to the item, and the length of time over which the exposure occurs. For example, one might decide that item security will not be threatened even with very high exposure rates if the exposure occurs within a very short period of time or if the examinee population is small and widely dispersed. However, as the population becomes large and the length of time an item is used is extended, the likelihood that examinees will remember the item and communicate it to future examinees is increased. Two designs were considered to control item exposure.

An exposure control procedure (Kingsbury & Zara, 1984) that introduces a random element to the administration of the first 10 items was evaluated first.

This random procedure identifies a defined number of "candidate" items for administration based on the examinee's current ability estimate and other test constraints. Ten candidate items are identified for the first item to be administered. One of them is selected at random. Following the examinee's response, nine candidate items are identified for the second item to be administered and one is selected at random. The number of candidate items is decreased by one following the administration of each additional item until, by the time the 10th item is administered, only a single candidate item is identified. This method assumes that the variation in items selected by the procedure for the first nine items will be sufficient to allow a single candidate item to be identified for the remainder of the test without increasing item exposure to unacceptable levels.

A second item exposure method, the Sympson–Hetter method (cited in Wainer et al., 1990) was also evaluated. The Sympson–Hetter method requires simulations to determine the likelihood of administration for each item. Controls are then established to prohibit overadministration of a single item. That is, an exposure control parameter is developed for each item in the pool. When the algorithm selects an item, a random number is generated and compared to exposure control parameter. Based on this comparison, the item is either administered or rejected and replaced by another item. Modifications to the Sympson–Hetter method were developed to extend it to item sets and the associated stimulus material (Stocking, 1992).

Maximum exposure limits specified that no item in the pool be administered to more than 20% of the examinees. The simulations showed that the modified Sympson–Hetter method produced results that more closely complied with the 20% exposure ceiling than the random method. Therefore, the modified Sympson–Hetter method was selected for exposure control.

Subsequently, following operational implementation of the adaptive tests, the need was identified to expand exposure control to a conditional exposure control methodology. Conditional exposure control refers to the establishment of exposure controls not only for the entire examinee population, but also within ability levels. Thus, for example, one might desire to limit item exposure not only for the total population but also, for example, for examinees of high ability. Conditional item exposure was implemented for the GRE adaptive test in the fall of 1997.

Omitting Items.   In traditional tests, examinees may take questions in any order. For example, a common test-taking strategy is to review the entire test, identify and answer those items or kinds of items the examinee feels most comfortable answering and then return to omitted items to complete them as time permits. Consideration was given to allowing examinees to omit the items on the adaptive test. However, there are drawbacks to allowing this strategy.

Omitting items degrades the quality of the tests. That is, the testing algorithm has identified a particular item as the best item to be administered given content constraints and the examinee's prior performance. If the examinee is allowed to omit the item, a less appropriate item will be selected. Were there no negative consequences to omitting items (i.e., the item is not scored), examinees could construct easy tests for themselves. That is, if an examinee did not know the answer to a question, he or she could omit that question and be presented with a new question. If he or she also did not know the answer to the second question, it could be omitted as well. Eventually the algorithm would be likely to select an item that the examinee could answer correctly. By continuing this strategy, an examinee could select only items for which he or she was certain of the correct answer. In this case, the resulting ability estimate would not be an accurate reflection of the examinee's ability, since he or she has had the opportunity to ignore all difficult questions.

Alternately, the omitted item could be treated as incorrect. This would reduce the estimate of the examinee's ability even though the examinee had not actually provided additional information about performance, a decision that would likely be perceived as unfair.

Another alternative would have been to allow examinees to indicate that they do not know the answer to a question through the addition of a "Do Not Know" or "Mark Me Wrong" option. This feature has not been implemented for the GRE adaptive test because it is known that examinees differ in their propensity to guess and, as a result, examinees who guess may be unfairly advantaged or disadvantaged relative to those who choose not to guess.

In sum, concerns that the test administration be as fair as possible to all test-takers drove the decision regarding the omission of items. Test-takers may not omit questions on the GRE CAT, but must provide an answer to each question at the time it is presented to them.

Item Review. A more controversial decision that was made in the design of the adaptive test was the decision not to allow item review. In traditional testing, examinees are routinely advised to review their answers. Also, some test-takers report that they will occasionally recognize that they have answered an item incorrectly later in the test. In this case, examinees desire the opportunity to return to the earlier test question and change the response. However, some test-takers could use item review to inappropriately tailor the test to their advantage.

To understand how item review might be used to build an inappropriate test, consider the possibility that a relatively bright test-taker begins to take the adaptive test. The first test question, a relatively easy one, is presented and the examinee knows the correct answer. However, rather than provide the correct answer, the examinee deliberately misses the question. The item selection algorithm, recognizing an incorrect answer, searches for an easier test question. When this question is presented, the examinee again deliberately provides an incorrect answer. In theory, an examinee could continue to deliberately miss test questions until all items have been administered. Then, the examinee could review the test and change all incorrect responses to correct ones and obtain a perfect but nonetheless inaccurate score.

The decision to prohibit item review has been controversial. Many people believe that examinees should have the option to return to test questions. Furthermore, research has been conducted that would seem to indicate that item review can be permitted on an adaptive test (Lunz, Bergstrom, & Wright, 1992; Stone & Lunz, 1994). However, these studies have typically been conducted in a low-stakes environment, and examinees have not been coached on how they might use item review to improve their scores. Thus, concerns about possible inappropriate use of item review in high-stakes situations persist.

In order to evaluate the extent to which examinees use and benefit from item review, data would be needed that show how often examinees return to test questions, how often responses are changed, and whether the changes result in improvements to scores. Because a traditional form of the GRE General Test had been administered on computer, an appropriate dataset was available. Analysis of this dataset indicated that item review is not widely used. The average number of items reviewed in each section of the test was less than 10% (Stocking, 1996). When omitted items were excluded from the analyses, the percentage dropped even further. Analysis of item review and changes to items for which a response had initially been provided indicated that the lack of item review was not a significant factor in test performance. When initial omits are excluded (because omitting is not permitted on the adaptive test), three kinds of changes are possible: wrong to wrong, wrong to right, and right to wrong. Table 6.2 provides a summary of these changes for the traditional CBT. These results (comparing wrong to right to the sum of right to wrong and wrong to wrong) make it clear that item review results in approximately the same number of items being revised to correct responses as are revised incorrectly. Thus, it does not appear prohibiting item review materially affects scores.

Although the data indicated that item review is not widely used, when it was used, review occurred most frequently in items associated with sets. Therefore, a study was conducted to determine whether or not it was possible to allow item review (Stocking, 1996). Simulations were conducted in which examinees were allowed to review a portion of their adaptive test. For purposes of the simulation, it was assumed that examinees always revised their answers to be correct. Score gains under this condition were compared to score gains from a simple test–retest simulation. The results indicated that, if the adaptive test is administered as several sections rather than as a single test and item review is permitted within section, the gains realized from item review

TABLE 6.2

Summary of Item Revisions in the Traditional GRE Computer-Based General Test

Type of Revision	Verbal	Quantitative	Analytical
Number of items	76	60	50
Average number answered	75.34	59.23	48.54
Average number reviewed	17.73	8.09	6.84
Average number revised	8.21	3.52	4.85
Right to wrong	0.43	0.13	0.09
Wrong to wrong	0.73	0.27	0.21
Wrong to right	1.02	0.44	0.43
Omit to wrong	2.68	1.31	1.98
Omit to right	3.35	1.37	2.22

are small compared to those realized from retesting. However, to date, item review has not been incorporated in the GRE adaptive test because implementing item review would require introducing numerous administrative and design changes to the test and the effects of these changes on score comparability are unknown.

Scoring Incomplete Adaptive Tests.   The initial design of the adaptive test was intended to provide sufficient time to allow virtually all examinees to complete the test. However, it was recognized that regardless of how generous the time limits were, some examinees would not finish. Several options were evaluated for scoring the incomplete tests. Among the options considered were (a) not providing a score for any incomplete test, (b) scoring only the items answered, and (c) scoring all unanswered and unadministered items as incorrect or generating responses to those items based on the examinee's prior performance. The first and third options were rejected as unfair. The second option, with modification, seemed to provide a feasible solution. Even if an examinee was unable to complete the test, the GRE Program decided to provide a score based on the examinee's demonstrated performance if it was psychometrically feasible to do so. The fairest option was to provide a score if the examinee completed enough of the test that sufficient content coverage was provided and minimal psychometric stability could be assured.

Controls were needed to meet these conditions. For example, if examinees were not required to respond to at least some minimal number of questions, some test-takers might decide to answer the first question and, if they were confident that they had answered it correctly, stop testing. In this case, a score would be generated on the basis of a single item. Clearly, this is unacceptable. Therefore, analyses were conducted to determine at what point in the test there was reasonable stability in the ability estimate and sufficient coverage of the various elements of the test specifications that a score could responsibly be reported. Based on these analyses, a decision was made to report scores for examinees who answered at least 80% of the questions on the test.

This 80%-rule appeared to work well initially. However, beginning in the fall of 1995, statisticians noted that an increasing percentage of test-takers were not completing the adaptive test. Furthermore, analyses indicated that these students seemed to be obtaining higher scores than test-takers who completed the exam. It appeared that some test-takers were adopting a strategy of allowing themselves more time to answer each question without attempting to complete the entire test. These examinees were, in effect, taking a shorter test with less stringent time limits than those who attempted to complete the full test, a potentially unfair practice. Thus, a scoring method was needed that would both encourage examinees to complete the test and provide a fair estimate of ability for those who were truly unable to complete the test in the time allotted.

A new treatment was developed for scoring incomplete adaptive tests. This method, proportional scoring (Steffen & Schaefer, 1996), adjusts the test score based on the proportion of the test completed by an examinee. To understand proportional scoring, it is important to understand how scaled scores are generated for the GRE adaptive tests. Following completion of the test, an ability estimate is derived for the examinee based on the items answered. This ability estimate is translated into a number correct score on a traditional linear test via a carefully developed conversion table. That number correct score is then transformed into a scale score using the previously established conversion parameters associated with that form of the test. The translation of an ability estimate into a number correct score is independent of the number of items on either the adaptive test or the traditional test. Of course, on the traditional test, the number of items answered is incorporated into the score.

Consider, for example, two examinees who answer all the items they attempt correctly. The first examinee in this example completes the entire test. The second examinee, however, completes only half the items on the test. If these two examinees were taking a traditional paper version of the test, they would not receive the same score. The first examinee would likely receive the highest possible scaled score while the second would receive the scaled score associated with answering half the test correctly. Under the original scoring model used for the GRE adaptive test, these two examinees would have received the same score. Proportional adjustment corrects this problem by adjusting for the proportion of items answered. In the previous example, the second examinee would receive credit for correctly answering half the items on the traditional test form.

Proportional scoring was evaluated against several other options: random responses to all remaining questions, correct responses, incorrect responses, and completion of the test based on the ability estimate derived after the last item answered (Steffen & Schaeffer, 1996). Simulations were run comparing performance across these various options. The results of these analyses indicated that, in the vast majority of the cases, proportional scoring generated a lower score than the other methods. Thus, the decision to implement proportional scoring would serve to encourage test-takers to complete the test. For these reasons, proportional scoring appears to be an acceptable method of scoring incomplete adaptive tests. However, additional study is required to determine how it works in practice and how characteristics of the item pool, the test selection algorithm, and test-taking strategy affect scores. For example, a question that arises is whether it is better for an examinee to work slowly, but comfortably and then guess toward the end of the test or to work slightly less optimally on each item, but at a pace that ensures completion of all items.

EVALUATING THE ADAPTIVE TEST

Once test design and administration specifications for the adaptive test were completed, it was necessary to determine whether or not the simulation results would be duplicated in practice in order to proceed with Phase 2 of the GRE CAT introduction. To evaluate the adaptive test, a comparability study was conducted during the 1993–1994 testing year (Schaeffer, Steffen, Golub-Smith, Mills, & Durso, 1995). The design of the study called for the last section of each operational test to be an adaptive section. Thus, examinees took two verbal sections, two quantitative sections, two analytical sections, and one adaptive section (verbal, quantitative, or analytical). Prior to the beginning of the last section of the test, information appeared on the computer screen explaining to examinees that they were going to be administered an adaptive test. To ensure motivation, examinees were informed that their score report would include either the traditional or the adaptive test score, whichever was higher.

In this study, 3,856 examinees participated. Summary statistics are shown in Table 6.3. The results indicated that there was clear comparability between the verbal sections in the adaptive and traditional tests. Differences were found between the traditional and adaptive quantitative sections, but these differences were not considered to be large enough to prohibit introduction of the adaptive test. The results for the analytical measure, however, were not comparable. An equating study was performed to adjust for this lack of comparability.

TABLE 6.3
Summary Statistics for Comparison of Traditional
and Adaptive GRE General Tests

Measure	Sample Size	Test	Mean	SD
Verbal	1,507	CBT	502	115
		CAT	504	109
Quantitative	1,354	CBT	522	131
		CAT	535	132
Analytical	995	CBT	538	125
		CAT	555	135

ITEM AND POOL ROTATION

When the GRE adaptive test was introduced in the fall, 1993, one item pool was available for use. The second item pool was introduced in October 1994, at the beginning of a new testing year. Initial plans called for the introduction of new pools at a rate commensurate with increases in test-taker volume. In addition, analyses were underway to identify ways to optimally use test questions across multiple item pools, consistent with concerns of item exposure and pool security.[1]

Initial analyses were conducted to explore a pool development procedure referred to as "children pools." Children pools are derivative item pools consisting of items drawn from multiple independent pools. That is, independent pools have no test questions in common. Children pools contain items drawn from their independent "parent" pools and might have items in common with one another.

Children pools require a large collection of items (equal to at least several independent pools) from which children pools can be developed. However, it is not typically the case that such a large number of test questions becomes available at a single point in time. Rather, items become available in smaller batches based on the results of pretesting. Development of children pools must, as a result, wait until enough pretested items are available to form several independent pools. When a testing program has an extremely large inven-

---

[1]The security of the GRE adaptive test became a matter of public concern when, in December 1994, Kaplan Educational Centers alleged to have uncovered a serious security flaw in the GRE adaptive test. "Kaplan" had instructed over 20 of its employees to take the GRE CAT and memorize as many items as possible. The incident is not discussed in this chapter because, as of this writing, the incident is still under litigation.

tory of test questions, this periodic development of pools may be feasible. If, however, the supply of items is limited, a technique that allows continuous pool development, using new items as they become available, is desirable.

In order to use newly available items as quickly as possible, to remove the items that had been administered to a large number of candidates, and to reduce security risks, the GRE Program investigated and implemented a pool rotation strategy based on "item vats." Vats consist of all items currently available. This collection of items includes items that are currently in use in operational testing, items that have previously been used but are not in use at the present time, and newly acquired items that have not been administered operationally. On a more or less continuous basis, item pools are drawn from the vat. A set of rules has been developed for use in the GRE program regarding the eligibility of the items for inclusion in operational pools. Although specifics are not public information, the rules fall into three general categories of those that:

- Govern the use of items that have been administered in the past 2 months,
- Govern the use of items that have been administered more than a specified number of times in the last 4 months, and
- Require the retirement of an item once the number of administrations of the item exceeds a critical value.

In this way, pools are formed that contain both new and previously used questions. Any given pool will overlap with other pools; however, limits are also placed on the amount of overlap permitted.

The procedures described previously control the use and exposure of *items* over time. Another issue concerns the exposure a single pool can have without risking a security breach. As noted previously, the first GRE pool was used for a full year. However, at that time, the number of examinees taking the adaptive test was quite small. In the first year, for example, fewer than 20,000 people took the computerized test. As volume increased, a concomitant increase in the number of pools was required. Today, when any pool is used by itself (i.e., it is the only pool being administered worldwide), it is used for an extremely short period of time, typically on the order of a week or two. When multiple pools are used simultaneously, of course, the period of time they are used can be extended.

THE FUTURE OF THE GRE GENERAL TEST

The move to CBT for the GRE does not represent a goal in and of itself. Rather, the rationale for moving to computer is to enable new tests that measure different skills and abilities and that measure existing constructs in improved ways. At the time the GRE Board approved CBT, it also approved an ambitious agenda to redefine the verbal, quantitative, and analytical measures. Plans were developed to research and introduce new item types in all three measures. In addition, research was undertaken to develop two new measures. These measures are a writing test and a new test of mathematical reasoning.

The desire to measure writing is based on concerns about the lack of sufficient emphasis on the development of writing skills during undergraduate study. If students do not have sufficiently well developed general writing skills, it is likely that they will have difficulty developing the discipline-specific skills required to complete graduate study and a dissertation. Although a writing test does not, in and of itself, require the technology associated with CBT, introducing the writing test as a computer-based test makes sense given the pervasive use of computers for writing and the potential of technology to reduce the expense associated with scoring essays.

Current plans call for the introduction of a writing test in 1999. This test is expected to include two writing tasks. One essay will be allotted 30 minutes for response, and the other will be allowed 45 minutes. At the time the GRE writing test is introduced, it is expected that students will be given the option of typing or handwriting their response. This option is provided in recognition of the fact that not all students are familiar with the use of computers for composition purposes. However, there are plans to require essays to be written on the computer within a few years.

The desire to assess productive tasks such as writing an essay is long-standing. The ability to develop and reliably score such tests is well established. The major barrier to the widespread use of essay tests has been the time and expense required to score them. This is an area in which technology will provide enormous advantages to the assessment process. At the time the GRE writing test is introduced, the essays will be scored via a national online scoring network first developed in 1997 for scoring essays from the computer version of the Graduate Management Admissions Test. Through this network, essays will be distributed throughout the country to scoring centers or individual locations. In these locations, scorers will be able to receive training, to display the essays on their screen, and to provide scores. Real-time monitoring of performance will provide not only the same level of quality of scoring as current procedures, but also a level of monitoring of individual scorer performance that has been unattainable in the past.

In addition, research in the area of natural language processing holds great promise. Natural language processing software developed at ETS, for example, has recently successfully matched the scores assigned by human raters in over 90% of the cases (Burstein et al., 1997). Although the technology has not progressed to the point where it is possible to assign scores to essays in a high-stakes environment without human participation, it is reasonable to assume that in the very near future automatically generated scores may serve as an initial indicator of the expected score. In the event a human rater provides the same score as that predicted by natural language processing software, a second human rating may not be required. The potential of automated scoring to reduce the number of people, time, and expense of scoring essays may make large-scale assessment of the essay performance more feasible in large-scale testing programs.

Mathematical Reasoning

Performance of GRE test-takers with highly quantitative backgrounds (e.g., engineering, physics, economics) on the existing quantitative measure has been very high. As a result, the ability of the current quantitative measure to distinguish effectively among these high-performing students is limited. There has long been a desire to develop a test that would provide admissions committees with useful distinctions among these students. The introduction of a CBT provides an opportunity for the development of such a test.

The mathematical reasoning test is expected to measure a higher level of mathematical reasoning than the current quantitative test and take advantage of types of questions that can only be delivered effectively on a computer. The initial specifications for the mathematical reasoning test included the administration of test questions requiring manipulation of graphs and other figural responses. This test will also allow examinees to use an on-screen scientific calculator to calculate and record their response.

The development of a new mathematical reasoning test raises some concerns. As tests become more selective and are administered to highly selected groups of examinees, differences in performance among subgroups may become more pronounced (Willingham & Cole, 1997). The mathematical reasoning test will be administered to a highly selective group of examinees. That is, students taking this test will not only have completed 4 years of undergraduate study, but also will represent disciplines with a rigorous mathematical curriculum. Care will need to be taken in the design and implementation of this test to ensure that it does not inappropriately produce group differences.

This latter point is especially important to the GRE Board. At the time the CBT was introduced, many board members expressed both reservations about the potential negative impact of computer administration of tests on subgroups and optimism that computer administration would provide opportunities to address issues of performance differences in the existing test. Early research provided evidence that the first concern was likely not to be of substance. Performance on both the traditional and the adaptive versions of the GRE on computer did not show any increase in the differences between scores for members of different subgroups.

In order to ensure that the board's emphasis on the use of the GRE General Test to increase access and opportunity for graduate study in the United States for members of all groups, the GRE Board launched an initiative known as

F.A.M.E. (fairness, access, multiculturalism, and equity). The F.A.M.E. initiative does not represent a change in policy emphasis or procedure for the GRE Board. Rather, it is a coordinating concept by which current processes and procedures are unified to increase their potential to affect the development and operation of the testing program to the benefit of all qualified students regardless of their background.

SUMMARY

The Graduate Record Examinations introduced a CBT in 1992. Following a year in which a traditional version of the test was administered on computer, an adaptive version was introduced in 1993. This chapter explained several decisions made during the development of the adaptive test, research conducted to ensure the comparability of the adaptive and traditional versions of the test, the development of numerous administrative procedures, and the maintenance of the item pools. The computer adaptive test is a first step in the evolution of the Graduate Record Examinations Program. Additional measures are being developed that take advantage of the technology provided by a computer testing environment to provide more appropriate measurement for graduate admissions purposes. Technology is also being developed to improve the scoring of constructed response tasks.

Introduction of a computer based and computer adaptive GRE General Test marks the beginning of revolution in large-scale admissions testing generally and in the Graduate Record Examinations Program specifically. Substantial research was conducted prior to the introduction of the adaptive GRE General test, but much remains to be done. Among the topics worthy of additional research are alternate algorithms for item selection, the role of content constraints, development of mechanisms to monitor the quality of the items, tests, and item pools over time, additional methods for scoring incomplete tests, and the impact of administrative conditions (e.g., omitting items and prohibiting item review). In addition, the movement to computer-delivered tests provides opportunities for dramatic revisions in the tests, items, and test development and scoring procedures.

REFERENCES

Burstein, J., Braden-Harder, L., Chodrow, M., Hua, S., Kaplan, B., Kukich, K., Lu, C., Nolan, J., Rock, D., & Wolff, S. (1997, June 27). *Computer analysis of essay content for automated score prediction.* Unpublished manuscript.

Cassone, J. (Producer). (1993, October 15). *World News Tonight.* New York: American Broadcasting Corporation.

Educational Testing Service. (1997). *Guidelines for the use of GRE scores.* Princeton, NJ: Author.

Kingsbury, G. G., & Zara, A. R. (1984). Procedures for selecting items for computerized adaptive tests. *Applied Measurement in Education, 2,* 359–375.

Lunz, M. E., Bergstrom, B. A. & Wright, B. D. (1992). The effect of review on student ability and test efficiency for computer adaptive tests. *Applied Psychological Measurement, 16,* 33–40.

Schaefer, G. A., Reese, C. M., Steffen, M., McKinley, R. L., & Mills, C. N. (1993, April). *Field test of a computer-based GRE General Test* (Research Rep. No. RR-93-07). Princeton, NJ: Educational Testing Service.

Schaefer, G. A., Steffen, M., Golub-Smith, M. L., Mills, C. N., & Durso, R. (1995, August). *The introduction and comparability of the Computer Adaptive GRE General Test* (Research Rep. No. 95-20). Princeton, NJ: Educational Testing Service.

Steffen, M., & Schaefer, G. A. (1996, June). *Comparison of scoring models for incomplete adaptive tests.* Presentation to the Graduate Record Examinations Technical Advisory Committee for the GRE General Test.

Stocking, M. L. (1992). *Controlling item exposure rates in a realistic adaptive testing paradigm.* (Research Report No. 92-2.). Princeton, NJ: Educational Testing Service.

Stocking, M. L. (1996, April). *Revising answers to items in computerized adaptive tests: A comparison of three models.* (Research Rep. No. RR 96-12). Princeton, NJ: Educational Testing Service.

Stone, G. E., & Lunz, M. E. (1994). The effect of review on the psychometric characteristics of computerized adaptive tests. *Applied Measurement in Education, 7,* 211–222.

Wainer, H., Dorans, N. J., Flaugher, R., Green, B. F., Mislevy, R. J., Steinberg, L., & Thissen, D. (1990). *Computerized adaptive testing: A primer.* Hillsdale, NJ: Lawrence Erlbaum Associates.

Ward, W. C. (1988). *A framework for research and development for a potential new Graduate Record Examination.* Princeton, NJ: Educational Testing Service.

Willingham, W. W., & Cole, N. S. (1997). *Gender and fair assessment.* Mahwah, NJ: Lawrence Erlbaum Associates.

7

Computer Assessment Using Visual Stimuli: A Test of Dermatological Skin Disorders

Terry A. Ackerman
John Evans
Kwang-Seon Park
Claudia Tamassia
Ronna Turner
University of Illinois, Urbana-Champaign

One of the advantages afforded by computerized software is the ability to present on screen the photographic-like images of objects, people, or scenes. Over the past several years, testing practitioners have taken advantage of this capability and started to create computerized tests containing images embedded within the items. The potential for the use of such images spans many disciplines. For example, art instructors could use computerized tests with images to test students' ability to identify certain works or artists; instructors of dendrology could have students identify different types or parts of trees; and geology instructors could have their students classify different types of rocks or rock formations. To provide an in-depth example of such an assessment, this chapter focuses on a computerized test that was developed in the medical field of dermatology. It was a joint effort between the University of Illinois Educational Psychology Department and the Medical College of Wisconsin Dermatology Department. To date, the development of the test has spanned more than 2 years.

137

The computerized dermatological exam is an extended matching test in which examinees are presented items that consist of a brief history of the patient and a digitized image of the patient's skin disorder and must select the correct name of the disorder from a list of possible diseases. Before it was computerized, a group administration format was used to present individual items via a slide projector. Images were projected onto a screen while the patient history was read aloud, and students were allowed 45 seconds to identify the condition and write their response on an answer sheet. In this format, items were selected for the test by the examiner in a pseudo-random fashion. The student's ability to examine the projected picture of the "disorder" was partly a function of the student's location in the classroom relative to the screen. Students were not allowed to change seats or move closer to inspect the image. The examiner presented each slide and monitored the test. All of the exam answer sheets were hand-scored.

As with other tests involving visual material, there were several reasons for converting this test to a computerized format. Many of the problems associated with administering the exam via the slide projector were eliminated. One important problem—difficulty in seeing the image displayed by the classroom slide projector—was rectified. Because students use their own computers, no one is disadvantaged by his or her seating arrangement in relation to the image being projected. Computerized testing also allows for individualized student evaluation; the instructor was not required to be present during the testing period. Another advantage of putting the exam on the computer is that it could easily be downloaded to multiple sites, which in turn increases the number of students able to take the exam. Moreover, students and faculty can receive immediate and detailed feedback including individual scores, item statistics, and test analyses. Finally, as in the case of the dermatology test, images that are expensive and difficult to obtain can be shared world wide (e.g., via World Wide Web) and used simultaneously.

THE TEST CONTENT

Developing a test of knowledge or achievement first involves specifying the content and/or skill domains that are to be assessed. Practitioners need to articulate the goals or purposes of the test (e.g., how are the test results intended to be used?). For example, if the goal of the test was to assess students' achievement relative to various levels of curriculum, skills that characterize each level should be identified. A table of specifications would then be constructed indicating the number of items per skill and content, the format of the items, and the visual stimuli associated with each item that would be required to accurately assess students' proficiency at each curriculum level. If the test was to be used as a certification test, the skills that the certified practitioner should possess would need to be outlined. Specification would then describe the items that would be required to measure the complete domain of requisite proficiencies. For the types of tests described here, the key is to use visual stimuli to reliably assess the skills identified in the table of specifications.

Consider the dermatological test, which is designed to measure students' abilities to recognize and accurately identify different skin disorders. With the computerized version, an instructor can randomly generate a test that is a representative subset of 110 conditions across eight dermatological domains. The content domains are:

- Dermatitis, urticaria, and drug eruptions;
- Acne, photodermatoses, pigment alterations, and related diseases;
- Papulosquamous and benign tumors;
- Infections, infestations, STDs, and AIDS;
- Bullous diseases, connective tissue diseases, and vasculitis;
- Cutaneous manifestations of internal diseases, hair diseases, and nail diseases;
- Pediatric dermatoses;
- Skin cancers.

The order of the domains presented by a generated test can be randomized. The instructor also has the option of keeping a particular sequential item order or randomizing the items within each domain. Care was given to present the visual stimuli illustrating each disorder with the same degree of clarity and color-correctness on the computer that is available from observing the patient in the examination room.

Software Requirements

The software that was used to develop the test is called Authorware® 3.0 and is distributed by Macromedia™. Authorware provides the means for creating multimedia pieces that use digital movies, sound, animations, text, and graphics to engage the user. Currently, this software requires a 486/66Mhz or more powerful computer that has at least 16MB of RAM. The program can be run in the Windows™ 3.1 and Windows 95 environments. The computer should have at least a 16-bit VGA graphics adapter and a monitor capable of SVGA resolution. The Authorware libraries take up about 40MB of hard disk space. Compiling the main program and subprograms may require 100MB of hard disk space. To edit and paste scanned images into Authorware programs, we used both Quicktime for Windows and Adobe Photoshop™.

Test Administration

Students are first required to log into the computer system. This process requires students to enter their student site identification number, their first and last name and middle initial, and their social security number. After each piece of information has been entered the examinee is asked if the information entered, is correct. If a mistake has been made, the examinee is given the opportunity to correct it. For security purposes, there is a site ID file that contains the social security numbers of all students at that site. Should an examinee enter a number that is not in the site ID file, access is denied and testing is terminated. The computer automatically notes the time, date, site ID, and name of each individual, even in cases where access has been denied. Because the test is intended to serve as a study aid, students can take the test as often as they choose. The time, date, and responses are appended to both the student's and instructor's file. Test information for each administration is recorded; details about the information saved are provided in Fig. 7.1.

After a student has logged in successfully, he or she is presented with pretest items to provide familiarization with the item format, the response process, the zoom feature, and the time limit to respond to an item. An example of the pretest process is illustrated sequentially in Figs. 7.2–7.5.

In Fig. 7.2, the examinee is given explicit directions about "zooming in" or enlarging the sample slide should greater clarity be required to make the correct identification of the disorder. Figure 7.3 describes the process of scrolling through the list of alphabetized disorders to select the correct one. Figure 7.4 depicts the timing process. Examinees have only 75 seconds to respond to each item. A clock in the lower left-hand corner shows the time remaining. Finally, when the examinee is familiar with the type of items and the response process and has reviewed the pretest items, he or she would begin the real examination.

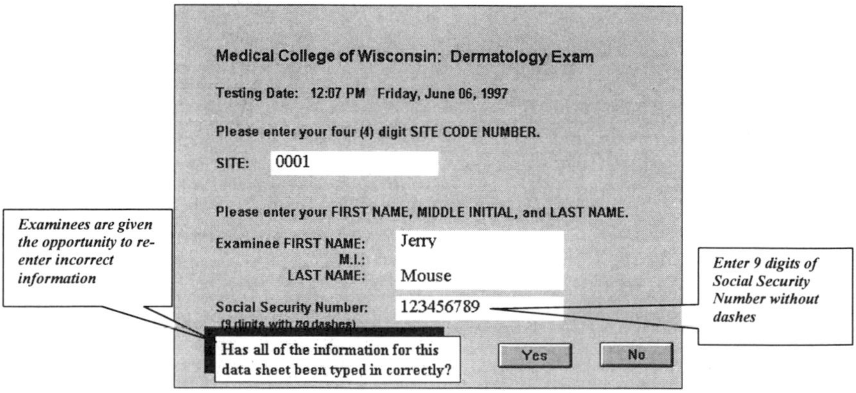

FIG. 7.1. Login screen.

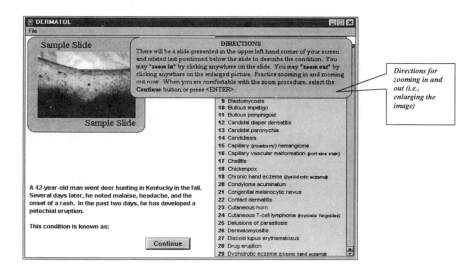

FIG. 7.2. Pretest screen 1.

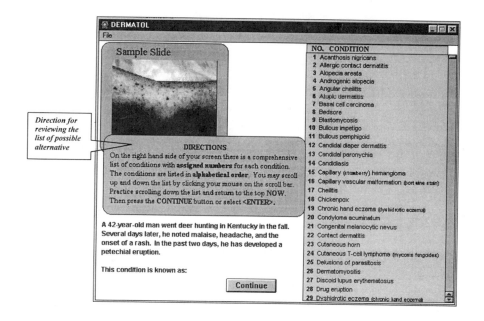

FIG. 7.3. Pretest screen 2.

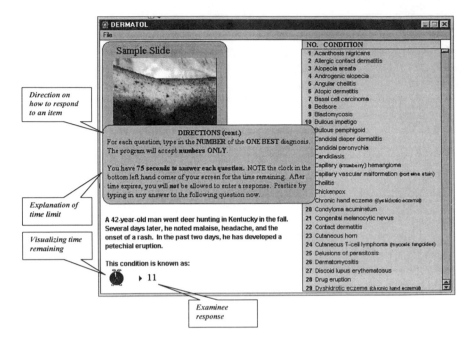

FIG. 7.4.   Pretest screen 3.

Item Format

Once a student has logged in and practiced with a sample item, the test begins (see Fig. 7.5). A typical item screen is shown in Fig. 7.6. The item format is identical to that described in the pretest. Currently, an examinee is given up to 75 seconds to respond. This length is predetermined by the instructor and is the same for all items. A clock below the patient's description indicates the time remaining to respond. Students are not allowed to enter a response after the time expires and must proceed to the next item. Unlike a paper-and-pencil version, this computerized test does not permit the student to return to previously administered items.

The extended matching format of the exam approximates a free-response format. Students select their answer from a list of 110 possible alphabetized disorders that are presented as a column on the right side of the screen (see Fig. 7.6). The response process involves examining the slide, identifying the correct alternative, identifying the number of the disorder, and entering that number. Students can scan through the list of alternatives by using a mouse or page-up and page-down keys. Once a student has selected an answer, he or she responds by typing in the number corresponding to this selection. After the number is entered,

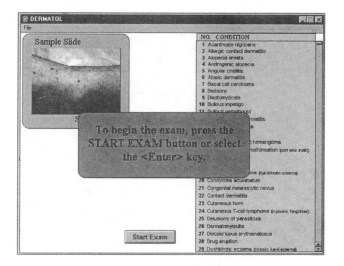

FIG. 7.5. Pretest screen 4.

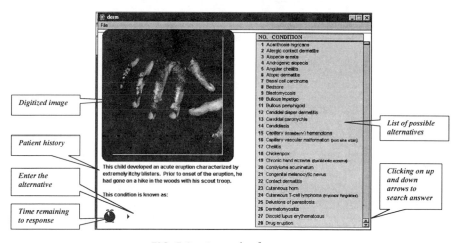

FIG. 7.6. A sample of test item.

the student is given a chance to check the response and change it if necessary. For some cases, there may be several possible correct answers for the disease.

We had thought about simply having the cursor "highlight" each response as the student scanned the list and then have the student hit "enter" when the correct answer was highlighted. The extended memory allocation needed in conjunction with the Authorware programming software did not make this alternative feasible.

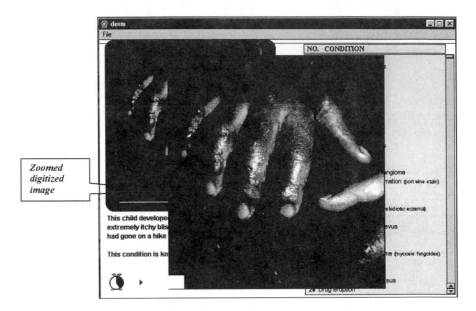

FIG. 7.7. A sample of test item with zoomed picture.

The use of four alternatives with one correct answer for each item was dismissed by the test developers because they felt that guessing would be too strong a possibility. Moreover, the test developers wanted the test to emulate the cognitive diagnosis process that a dermatologist would go through when identifying a skin disorder. The goal was to make the item format as close to a free response format or a clinical diagnosis as possible.

For each item, a brief patient history is shown accompanied by a digitized image of the patient's disorder. Students may view an enlarged image of the disorder by "clicking" the mouse anywhere on the original image. The zoomed slide (Fig. 7.7) can then be returned to its initial size by "clicking" the mouse anywhere on the enlarged image. This process can be repeated as many times as desired.

Scanning and Saving Images From Slides

To scan slides of the various skin disorders we used Adobe Photoshop 3.0 software and a slide (film) scanner, ScanMaker™, by Microtek. The Photoshop software allows the instructor to scan slides in black and white or color, set the dots per square inch (dpi; we usually used between 1,005 and 1,023 dpi), set the scaling requirements, and modify features such as degree of brightness, hue, and clarity.

The Program Files

Authorware uses icons instead of scripting. Programs are written by concatenating icons into a living flowchart. Figure 7.8 displays a living flowchart for one of the eight *.app files. There are three types of program files, described in Table 7.1. The first two types of files, the *.exe and the *.app, are compiled/packed and are executable. The file dermatol.exe functions as the main controlling program. It interacts with the other eight *.app files. The *.app files contain the individual items for each of the eight dermatologic domains.

When new items are added or original items need to be edited or deleted, one must work with the *.a3w files. If, for example, one needs to edit an "acne" item, the acne.a3w file would be edited. In the case of an addition or deletion of a dermatitis case, the derm.a3w file would also have to be updated and then packed.

Figure 7.9 illustrates the complete relationship between the subprograms source files (*.a3w) and their compiled versions (*.app).

Figure 7.10 shows how the two kinds of compiled/packed subprograms (*.app) and the main controlling program, Dermatol.exe, interact with one another. Dermatol.exe controls accesses one subtest at a time. After retrieving and displaying items from one subprogram, say Acne.app, the main program will randomly or sequentially retrieve and administer items from one of the remaining unused domains.

Results

Currently, the test administration program, Dermatol.exe, stores examinee ID information, the date and time of the administration, the number of the

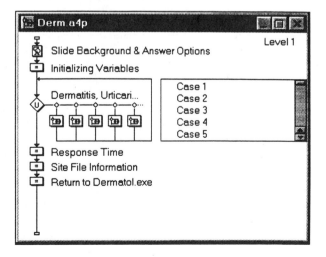

FIG. 7.8. An example of subprogram concatenating icons into a living flowchart.

TABLE 7.1
Types of Files Used in the Test

File Type	File	Content
exe	dermatol.exe	• Executable file • Accesses eight subprograms. • Produced with compiling command *With RunA3W*
app	acne.app bull.app cutan.app derm.app infec.app papul.app ped.app skin.app	• Executable but serve as subprograms for the main controlling program (the main controlling program, *dermatol.exe*, these eight subprograms) • Produced with compiling command *Without RunA3W.*
a3w	acne.a3w bull.a3w cutan.a3w derm.a3w dermatol.a3w papul.a3w ped.a3w ped.a3w skin.a3w	• Original program/code files before packing/compiling. • Use these files when changing (adding/deleting) the content(s) of a subprogram.

Note. acne = acne, photodermatoses, pigment alterations, and other; bull = bullous diseases, connective diseases, and vasculitis; cutan = cutaneous manifestations of internal diseases, hair diseases; derm = dermatitis, urticaria, and drug eruptions; infec = infections, infestations, STDs, and AIDS; papul = papulosquamous and benign tumors; ped = pediatric dermatoses; skin = skin cancers.

items that were administered in each of the eight domains, the examinee response, and, if the response is incorrect, the correct alternative. Students can obtain the test results immediately after finishing the test and receive a print-out similar to the one shown in Fig. 7.11. The output consists of the time and the place where the exam was taken along with the number right and percent correct scores for each of the eight dermatological domains.

The test administrator would receive more detailed output containing both group and individual test summary statistics as displayed in Fig. 7.12. This output file contains the same information the student receives in addition to a detailed report of the item number given to each subject, his or her response, and the correct answer if different from the student's response. These data can be aggregated across a class or school to identify items most often missed and the most commonly selected distractor. Such information could be used to identify student misconceptions and ultimately improve classroom instruction.

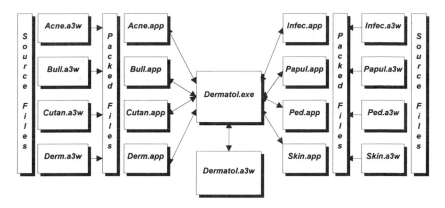

FIG. 7.9. Interaction between the main controlling program and eight subprograms.

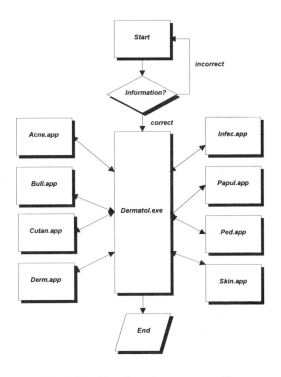

FIG. 7.10. Flowchart illustrating item files.

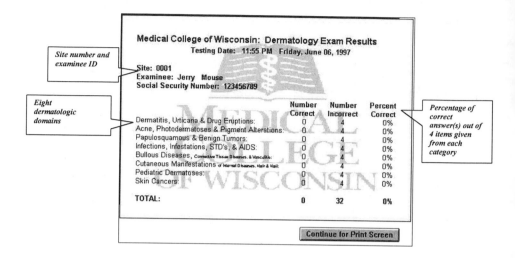

FIG. 7.11.   An example of student output.

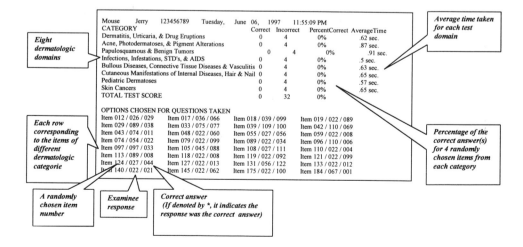

FIG. 7.12.   An example of instructor output.

FUTURE ENHANCEMENTS

There are several modifications that we have considered for future work. Currently, the test is designed for assessment only; it could be revised to supplement instruction and serve as a means to study or review in-class content. To this end, immediate instructive or remedial feedback could be provided to the student after the test was administered. For each incorrect answer, the correct answer could be given as well as an annotated image of the patient, highlighting features that the student should have recognized in making the correct diagnosis.

Information about the incorrect item responses could also be summarized so that this diagnostic information could be provided to an instructor for review. Clearly, the pattern of incorrect responses suggests directions for remedial instruction. Within a particular class, disorders that were often missed could subsequently be reviewed. The summary of incorrect responses would also help the instructor identify the confusion that led to incorrect diagnoses. A review panel examining results from different medical schools could note particular weaknesses in individual schools or instructors.

Another feature that is being considered for future versions of the software would permit students to type in questions they would like to ask the patient or tests they would like to run to confirm their diagnosis. These could then be reviewed by the classroom instructor and possibly some type of scoring procedure could be established.

Currently, the item responses are scored dichotomously. However, in the future it might be helpful if the student could provide a rationale for his or her choice. In addition to a written description explaining why a particular selection was made, the student might highlight and annotate areas on the displayed image that led to the particular diagnosis. Currently, a student may select the right answer, but not understand all the features that would lead to a conclusive answer. Or, a wrong answer may not mean that all the necessary features were overlooked. Such an annotated history provided by the examinee would be more realistic and could be scored with partial credit. Moreover, this information would be helpful for medical faculty to distinguish examination errors and highlight areas that need to be reinforced pedagogically. One challenge for this approach would be the development of software that could score each student's annotated results.

This software could also be used to assess general practitioners' knowledge of dermatological disorders. Frequently, the primary care physician is the first to see the patient and subsequently is the one responsible for initial treatment. It would be interesting to administer the dermatology test to general practitioners and see how well they do—can they do as well as individuals specifically trained in dermatology?

ACKNOWLEDGMENT

This work was conducted under the direction of David Crosby, MD, at the Medical College of Wisconsin. Dr. Crosby obtained a research grant from the Sulzberger Institute for Dermatologic Education.

8

Creating Computerized Adaptive Tests of Music Aptitude: Problems, Solutions, and Future Directions

Walter P. Vispoel
The University of Iowa

Standardized listening tests for assessing music aptitude have been available for almost as long as have standardized written tests of verbal and quantitative skills. Carl Seashore published his classic *Measures of Musical Talent* in 1919, and new tests have continued to emerge with each passing decade (see, e.g., Bentley, 1966; Davies, 1970; Drake, 1957; Gordon, 1965, 1979, 1982, 1989; Karma, 1985; Kwalwasser & Dykema, 1939; Long, 1965; Seashore, Lewis, & Saetveit, 1960; Stankov & Horn, 1980; Webster, 1992; Wing, 1948, 1961, 1970). One important lesson that we have learned from such tests over the years is that it is very difficult to measure music listening skill accurately in an efficient manner. There are several factors that account for this problem. One factor is an inherent limitation of any fixed-item test. To measure a broad range of skill accurately with such a test, there must be items targeted at all relevant ability levels. To accomplish this, the test must be reasonably long and therefore time consuming. The problem of test length is exacerbated further in many music aptitude tests because answers frequently focus on only two response alternatives (e.g., whether two musical excerpts are the same or different). Because the probability of guessing correct answers is high for items with only two choices, test lengths have to be longer than those for items with more alternatives to achieve comparable levels of reliability.

Another factor hindering efficient measurement of music aptitude is fatigue. Performing well on music aptitude tests requires special concentration because each item is played only once with no opportunity for replay and little opportunity for answer change. The high level of concentration required on such tests is difficult to maintain over a long period of time and can quickly tire examinees, especially when the tests are long. The need to maintain constant attention is less crucial in paper-and-pencil tests of verbal and quantitative skills because examinees can reread items, skip and return to them later, and change answers at any time.

A third factor affecting accurate measurement of music listening skill is the repetitious and monotonous nature of many tests. The Pitch subtest from the current form of the *Seashore Measures of Music Talents* (Seashore et al., 1960), for example, consists of 50 pairs of pitches in which the examinee must indicate which of the two pitches in each pair is higher. With so many repetitious items, examinees easily can become bored, apathetic, tired, inattentive, or careless when responding.

To address inefficiency, fatigue and other related problems, developers of music aptitude tests have tried to strike a balance between administrative efficiency and measurement accuracy by shortening test lengths, catering item difficulty predominantly to average levels of ability, and limiting testing time to 1 hour or less on a given day. Unfortunately, such compromises often result in music aptitude tests that yield inadequate levels of score reliability. To illustrate these problems, reliability coefficients for several music aptitude tests are reported in Table 8.1. Subtests from the Kwalwasser Dykema Music Tests, a battery seldom used today, yields the lowest reliability, but even among the other batteries, reliability coefficients in the .30s, .40s, .50s, and .60s are common. Further inspection of Table 8.1 suggests that many of the lower reported subtest reliability coefficients may be due to the small number of items or answer options employed. Reliability coefficients tend to be lower for subtests with 25 or fewer items and/or three or fewer answer options such as those from the Bentley and Davies batteries and higher for subtests containing more items and/or answer choices such as those from the Drake, Seashore, and Gordon batteries.

The ways to improve the reliability of music test scores would seem obvious; simply increase the number of response options or the number of items or both. Yet, there are reasons that test developers have shied away from these seemingly quick and easy solutions. One reason is the desire to keep the test as simple as possible. This usually translates into employing only two response options to minimize the role of specialized knowledge about music in selecting an answer. Items requiring same/different discriminations are ideal for these purposes; they are easily understood by children and individuals with no prior training in music. A second reason for using a minimum number of answer options is that some ways of increasing the num-

TABLE 8.1
Characteristics of Selected
Music Aptitude Test Batteries

Subtest	*Seashore "Measures of Musical Talents" (1960 Edition)*		
	Number of Items	*Number of Options*	*Reliability Range*
Pitch	50	2	.82–.92
Loudness	50	2	.74–.85
Rhythm	30	2	.64–.88
Time	50	2	.63–.78
Timbre	50	2	.55–.79
Tonal Memory	30	3–5	.81–.88

Subtest	*Kwalwasser-Dykema "Music Tests"*		
	Number of Items	*Number of Options*	*Reliability Range*
Pitch	40	2	-.05–.63
Quality	30	2	.10–.66
Intensity	30	2-	.10–.60
Tonal Movement	30	2.	37–.85
Time	25	2	.00–.63
Rhythm	25	2	.04–.48
Tonal Memory	25	2	.43–.73
Melodic Taste	10	2	.06–.61
Pitch Imagery	25	2	.14–.45
Rhythm Imagery	25	2	.20–.40

Subtest	*Drake "Musical Aptitude Tests"*		
	Number of Items	*Number of Options*	*Reliability Range*
Musical Memory	54	4	.85–.93
Rhythm A	50	Open-ended	.56–.95
Rhythm B	50	Open-ended	.69–.96

(Continues)

TABLE 8.1 (Continued)

Subtest	Wing "Standardised Tests of Musical Intelligence"		
	Number of Items	Number of Options	Reliability Range
Chord Analysis	20	6	*
Pitch Change	30	3	*
Tonal Memory	30	3–10	*
Rhythm	14	3	*
Harmony	14	3	*
Intensity	14	3	*
Phrasing	14	3	*

Subtest	Bentley "Measures of Musical Abilities"		
	Number of Items	Number of Options	Reliability Range
Pitch Discrimination	20	3	.65–.74
Tonal Memory	10	6	.53–.83
Chord Analysis	10	3	.71–.74
Rhythmic Memory	10	5	.57–.61

Subtest	Gordon "Musical Aptitude Profile"		
	Number of Items	Number of Options	Reliability Range
Melody	40	3	.67–.88
Harmony	40	3	.66–.89
Tempo	40	3	.60–.85
Metre	40	3	.60–.85
Phrasing	30	3	.60–.78
Balance	30	3	.60–.79
Style	30	3	.60–.80

Subtest	Gordon "Primary Measures of Music Audiation"		
	Number of Items	Number of Options	Reliability Range
Tonal	40	2	.68–.89
Rhythm	40	2	.60–.86

TABLE 8.1 (Continued)

Subtest	Gordon "Intermediate Measures of Music Audiation"		
	Number of Items	Number of Options	Reliability Range
Tonal	40	2	.72–.88
Rhythm	40	2	.70–.84

Subtest	Gordon "Advanced Measures of Music Audiation"		
	Number of Items	Number of Options	Reliability Range
Tonal	30	3	.81–.86
Rhythm	30	3	.80–.87

Subtest	Davies "New Tests of Musical Aptitude"		
	Number of Items	Number of Options	Reliability Range
Melody	15	3–7	.73–.76
Pitch	15	3	.41–.58
Intervals	15	3	.37–.54
Rhythm	15	2	.46–.63

Note. The reliability coefficients presented in this table are intended to be illustrative, not exhaustive. The data were adapted from Shuter-Dyson and Gabriel (1981, pp. 274–287) and Gordon (1982, 1989). It also should be noted that the reliability coefficients for composite scores from the cited batteries are higher than the reliability of individual subtests.

*The present author was unable to find reliability coefficients for the Wing subtests in the battery's test manual. Omission of subtest reliability coefficients is consistent with Wing's view that musical ability consists of one general rather than several specific factors. Reviews in Buros (1966) indicate that subtest reliability coefficients range from .65 to .85. In research studies by Vispoel and Coffman (1992, 1994) and Vispoel, Wang, and Bleiler (1997), reliability coefficients for the Wing Tonal Memory subtest have ranged from .65 to .89.

ber of options may jeopardize the construct validity of test scores. Most subtests from the *Musical Aptitude Profile* (Gordon, 1965), for example, employ a same/different answer format with an additional "in doubt" option to be used by examinees if they are unsure about the correct answer. The use of this controversial answer option may reduce construct validity because individuals who are inclined to use this option receive systematically lower scores (i.e., "in doubt" responses are scored as incorrect). Consequently, a score on these tests may measure both music aptitude and a personality-related risk taking factor. A final and perhaps most obvious reason for restricting the number of answer options and the number of items is that both tend to increase testing time and thus make the test less efficient.

Creators of music listening and other fixed-item tests inevitably face a dilemma in choosing between measurement precision and administrative efficiency. Long tests are needed to provide accurate measurement precision over a broad range of skill levels, but such tests are very time consuming. Short tests are less time consuming, but they cannot provide high levels of measurement precision over a broad range of skill levels. With music aptitude tests, the typical compromises made between measurement precision and administrative efficiency often result in tests that have serious deficiencies.

IMPROVING THE ASSESSMENT OF MUSIC
SKILLS WITH COMPUTERIZED ADAPTIVE TESTS

Computerized adaptive testing represents one possible solution to the problems of inefficiency, fatigue, and low measurement precision that have hindered the measurement of music listening skills. Computerized adaptive tests (CATs) can reduce test length and testing time but maintain high measurement precision by dynamically tailoring the administration of items to examinees' ability levels based on their responses to previously answered items. Items are selected successively from a large, carefully designed pool that contains many items targeted to each ability level in the population of interest. A common algorithm for administering a CAT is shown in Fig. 8.1. The CAT begins with the most discriminating available item of medium difficulty. The response to that item is scored and the examinee's ability and its associated error are estimated. The next item administered is the one remaining in the pool that most reduces the measurement error associated with that ability estimate. This item also will be the one remaining in the pool that best discriminates among examinees at the examinee's current level of estimated ability. This process continues, item by item, until a test termination criterion is reached, which typically occurs when either a fixed number of items have been administered or when a prespecified level of measurement precision has been reached. The net result of this procedure is that examinees receive only those items that are in line with their abilities, thereby avoiding items that are either too easy or too difficult. As a result, test efficiency is improved and problems of fatigue, inattention, boredom, apathy, and carelessness are reduced.

To implement the CAT algorithm in Fig 8.1 successfully, it must be possible to estimate ability and measurement error from responses to any items in the CAT pool. This is generally accomplished by using item response theory-based measurement models that reference ability estimates and item parameters (difficulty, discrimination, guessing) to common scales (see Hambleton, Swaminathan, & Rogers, 1991 for a reasonably complete and mostly nontechnical introduction to item response theory measurement models). Once the

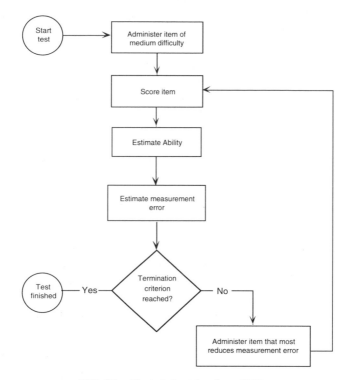

FIG. 8.1. Typical algorithm for a CAT.

item parameters and ability scale are established for the target population through a norming (or calibration) study, ability estimates and their errors can be derived for new examinees from their responses to any items in the CAT pool. Ability estimates and their associated errors are computed from equations that take into account the parameters of the items taken (i.e., difficulty, discrimination, and guessing values) and the examinee's responses to those items (i.e., which items the examinee answered correctly and incorrectly). The complexity involved in deriving the ability estimates and their errors on an item-by-item basis is one of the reasons why adaptive testing procedures were not implemented on a widespread basis until the development of current generations of high-speed microcomputers (see Wang & Vispoel, 1998, for an in-depth discussion of the properties of ability estimation methods and measurement precision indices in computerized adaptive testing).

The use of CATs for large-scale standardized testing has increased dramatically over the last decade. There currently are operational CAT versions of the Graduate Records Examination (GRE; Reese, 1992), the Armed Services Vocational Aptitude Battery (ASVAB; Segall, 1995), the General Aptitude Test battery (GATB; Segall & Carter, 1995), the Differential Aptitude Test (DAT; McBride, Corpe, & Wing, 1995), certification exams for the Board of Registry of the American Society of Clinical Pathologists (Gershon, 1994; Lunz, Bergstrom, & Wright, 1992), course placement tests for colleges and universities (American College Testing, 1995; Doucette, 1988; Legg & Burr, 1987), and survey and diagnostic tests for high schools and elementary schools (Bahgi, Gabrys, & Ferrara, 1991; Kingsbury, 1990). Research into the effectiveness of such tests generally shows that CATs require about half as many items to match the measurement precision of conventional tests and that CATs exceed the precision of conventional tests when test length is held constant (Wainer, 1990; Ward, 1984; Weiss, 1982).

DEVELOPMENT OF COMPUTERIZED ADAPTIVE MUSIC TESTS

One of my small contributions to research in music aptitude testing was to develop and evaluate the first item response theory-based CATs for measuring music aptitude. I began this work in 1982 as a graduate student at the University of Illinois at Urbana-Champaign. The development and evaluation of a tonal memory CAT eventually became my doctoral dissertation project (Vispoel, 1987a; also see Vispoel, 1987b, 1990, 1993b). My original tonal memory CAT was developed for the PLATO™ mainframe system, but since that time I have developed versions of the test for both IBM-compatible and Macintosh microcomputers (see Vispoel, 1990, 1997; Vispoel & Coffman, 1992, 1994; Vispoel & Twing, 1990; Vispoel, Wang, & Bleiler, 1997).

The development of each version of the CAT required a tremendous investment of time and effort. Some of the problems encountered were (a) choosing a suitable construct to measure, (b) choosing appropriate types of items to measure the construct, (c) developing a large and broad-ranging bank of items to assess the construct, (d) recording the test items, (e) piloting the items, (f) selecting an appropriate item response theory-based model to represent the data, (g) deriving parameters for the items based on that model, (h) choosing items for the final adaptive test pool, (i) evaluating the fit of the model to the data, (j) choosing a computer system to administer and score the CAT, and (k) developing software to administer and score the CAT. In most cases, practical constraints had a heavy influence on how I handled each of the problems was addressed.

I began my CAT development project by reviewing the literature on music aptitude testing and aptitude testing in general. An important study that guided selection of constructs to measure was conducted by Stankov and Horn (1980). Their work was derived from the theory of fluid and crystallized intelligence proposed by Cattell (1971) and Horn (1976) and from the meta-theory of simple structure factor analysis (Thurstone, 1947). The goal of the Stankov and Horn study was to provide indications of how auditory abilities are organized within the framework of the theory of fluid and crystallized intelligence. The researchers administered 44 auditory tests, including 22 music tests to 241 adult males, and they factor analyzed the results at the test level. The music tests consisted of 11 subtests from the *Seashore Measures of Music Talents* (Seashore et al., 1960), *Drake Musical Aptitude Tests* (Drake, 1957), *Wing Measures of Musical Intelligence* (Wing, 1961), and 11 original tests developed by the researchers. The factor analysis results highlighted seven primary factors indicative of capabilities for Auditory Verbal Comprehension (Va), Auditory Immediate Memory (Msa), Speech Perception Under Distraction/Distortion (SPUD), Discrimination Among Sound Patterns (DASP), Temporal Tracking (Tc), Auditory Cognition of Relationships (ACoR), and Maintaining and Judging Rhythm (MaJR). The music tests were correlated most highly with the last four factors: DASP, Tc, ACoR, and MaJR.

My initial long-term goal was to develop four CATs, with one designed to tap each of the primary factors related to music listening skill. Such tests might be used for a variety of purposes including predicting success in learning music, identifying potential talent for music, evaluating growth and change in music listening skill over time, adapting music instruction to individual needs and abilities of students, evaluating the effectiveness of programs designed to improve music listening skill, and diagnosing strengths and weaknesses in music listening skills. Creating a battery of four tests, however, was well beyond my resources at the time. As a result, I focused my attention on one factor; namely, Discrimination Among Sound Patterns.

In a related factor analytic study involving 26 auditory tests in which many of the speech tests used in Stankov and Horn (1980) were omitted, Stankov and Spilsbury (1978) found that the Discrimination Among Sound Patterns factor reduced to a Tonal Memory factor. Tonal memory seemed like a good basis for a music CAT for several reasons: (a) tonal memory tests have a long tradition in the music testing field (Seashore, 1917, 1919); (b) tonal memory-related factors have emerged more frequently than any other factor when subtests from commercially available music aptitude test batteries are factor analyzed (Stankov & Horn, 1980; Whellams, 1971); (c) tonal memory tests provide a conservative benchmark for evaluating music CATs because they often provide the most reliable and concurrently valid subtest scores within commercially available test batteries (Shuter-Dyson & Gabriel, 1981; also see Table 8.1); and (d) prior research provided some evidence that scores from tonal memory tests are sufficiently unidimensional to justify the use of item response theory-based procedures (Whellams, 1971).

Having decided on tonal memory as the construct to measure, there remained the task of selecting suitable test content. I began by analyzing the content of the most widely used tonal memory tests, which included those from the *Seashore Measures of Music Talents* (Seashore et al., 1960), the *Measures of Musical Abilities* (Bentley, 1966), and the *Wing Standardised Tests of Musi-*

cal Intelligence (Wing, 1961). Items from each of these tests consist of the playing and replaying of short melodies. The examinee's task is to identify the tone that changes when a melody is replayed. The tests differ from one another along three dimensions: *instrumental timbre* (electronically produced vs. piano-produced), *rhythmic complexity* (constant vs. varied note values), and *tonality/atonality* (tonal vs. atonal melodies) that affect the extent to which the test items resemble conventional music. Items with an electronically produced sound, constant note values, and atonal melodies such as those from the Seashore test would be considered the least musical, whereas items with a traditional instrument's sound, varied note values, and tonal melodies such as those from the Wing test would be considered the most musical.

Using musical versus nonmusical items in a tonal memory test has been a controversial issue in the music literature, and the choice of item content has depended more on the test developer's philosophy than on empirical data. Seashore (1919, 1939) advocated using nonmusical (or culture fair) items to reduce potential experiential biases on test performance (familiarity with instrumental timbre, scale structures, styles of music, etc.). Wing (1970) and Bentley (1966), however, favored musical sounding items because such items resemble melodies that musicians would encounter more often in practice. Prior to building my music CAT, I found no study that systematically varied the timbre, rhythmic complexity, and tonality/atonality of tonal memory test items to determine how these dimensions might affect empirical indicators of test score validity.

To address this issue, I created four forms of a 60-item tonal memory test that differed in instrumental timbre and rhythmic complexity: (a) piano with tones of equal rhythmic duration, (b) synthesizer with tones of equal rhythmic duration, (c) piano with tones of varied rhythmic duration, and (d) synthesizer with tones of varied rhythmic duration. Each test form included both tonal and atonal melodies ranging in length from 4 to 9 tones. The four test forms were administered in counterbalanced orders to 125 college student volunteers. Scores from these tests were evaluated in a series of factor analytic, ANOVA, correlation, and regression analyses to determine the most suitable types of items to include in the CAT item pool.

Confirmatory factor analyses of item cluster scores from the four tests were used to evaluate test dimensionality. The results indicated that a one-factor model fit the data well and that model fit did not improve when more complex models were considered (models with separate factors for tonal and atonal melodies, models with separate factors for piano-produced and synthesizer-produced melodies, etc.). To evaluate possible instrument familiarity biases on test performance, total scores for the four tests and subtest scores for tonal and atonal items were analyzed in separate split-plot ANOVAs with two within-subject factors: instrumental timbre (piano and synthesizer) and rhythmic complexity (notes of equal and varied duration) and one between-subjects factor: piano-playing experience. Each ANOVA yielded significant main effects for piano experience but no significant interactions involving piano experience. That is, individuals with more piano-playing experience consistently outperformed individuals with less experience on all tests, but they did not have an unfair advantage over less experienced individuals on the piano timbre tests. Concurrent validity indices based on correlations of test scores with music experience indexes and self-ratings of musical ability revealed that tests with melodies of varied rhythmic duration provided better results than did tests with melodies of equal rhythmic duration. A final set of correlation and regression analyses showed that item difficulty had essentially no relation with instrumental timbre, but strong relations with melody length (i.e., number of tones) and tonality/atonality.

On the basis of these results, I decided to include varied-rhythm tonal and atonal melodies of 4 to 9 tones in the CAT pool, anticipating that these items would provide reliable and concurrently valid results over a wide range of ability levels. I also decided to use synthesizer rather than piano primarily because synthesizer-generated items could be reproduced more easily on the mainframe and microcomputer computer systems on which I could implement the CAT (see Vispoel, 1987a and 1993b, for further details about the analyses used to select adaptive test items).

After completing these preliminary analyses, I assembled a pool of 312 items for the CAT pool. Items were recorded in a studio in the university's music building using a mini-Moog synthesizer. All items were played at constant volume with a tempo of 100 quarter notes per minute. Each item consisted of a pair of melodies. Examinees would indicate whether each pair of melodies was the same or different; if different, they would indicate the number of the single altered tone. Figure 8.2 shows examples of two such items in which the correct answers are 4 and 2, respectively.

In an ideal situation, all items within the CAT pool would have been administered on computers to a large and nationally representative sample of individuals from ages 7 to adult. These age groups span those for which the Seashore, Bentley, and Wing tonal memory tests were originally normed. Unfortunately, I had to rely on an accessible sample of 467 high school and college student volunteers. Also, it was not possible to administer all items from the pool to these examinees on a computer. Instead, I created several shorter test forms and administered them in group settings using high quality audio equipment. The forms were linked to each other through a common set of anchor items, with most examinees responding to over 100 items. In creating the forms, items of different lengths and difficulty levels were mixed to anticipate how those items might be administered on a CAT. Rest periods also were incorporated into item administration to reduce fatigue and other problems related to music aptitude testing discussed earlier.

FIG. 8.2.   Examples of tonal memory CAT items.

Before items for the CAT could be calibrated, it was necessary to select an appropriate item response model. Initially a 2-parameter model was used because the examinee calibration sample size seemed too small to justify the use of a 3-parameter model, and the variability among the item-total score biserial correlations within each test form seemed too great to justify the use of the 1-parameter model.[1] Once the item response data were collected and the

---

[1]In typical applications of item response theory, measurement models are selected according to the size of the examinee calibration sample and the degree to which the probability of correct answers to items are affected by differences in item difficulty, discrimination, and pseudo-guessing. Desired sample size increases as the number of parameters increase. The 1-parameter model allows items to vary only in difficulty, the 2-parameter model in both difficulty and discrimination, and the 3-parameter model in difficulty, discrimination, and pseudo-guessing.

2-parameter model was selected, it was a simple matter to calibrate the item parameters using the LOGIST mainframe computer package (Wingersky, Barton, & Lord, 1982). Because all examinees had responded to a common set of anchor items, LOGIST was able to place the parameters of items from all test forms on a common metric. Space limitations on the computer system that eventually was used to implement the CAT restricted the size of the final item pool to 180 items. Items for the final pool were chosen to provide the highest possible discrimination at each difficulty level.

Assumptions governing the use of the item response model used to represent the data were evaluated using several methods suggested by Hambleton (1989) and Hambleton, Swaminathan, and Rogers (1991). Unidimensionality was checked by examining Eigenvalues for the interitem tetrachoric correlation for each test form. In each case, a dominant first factor was found. The invariance of ability parameters across different samples of items was checked by correlating ability estimates derived from easy and hard items. In support of invariance, a strong linear relationship between ability estimates was found. Finally, the invariance of item difficulty parameter across different examinee samples was checked by correlating difficulty parameters derived from high- and low-ability samples. Again, a strong linear trend was observed.

The next step was to choose a computer system on which to implement the CAT. The crucial factors considered were: ability to produce music, ability to implement software to administer and score CAT items, and accessibility to test takers. I was fortunate at the time to have the PLATO mainframe computer system at my disposal, because it included an interactive music production and programming system (Haken & Schmid, 1984). PLATO, which stands for Programmed Logic for Automatic Teaching Operations, was developed at the University of Illinois for Control Data computers. The PLATO system along with the IBM 1500 system at Stanford University (Allvin, 1967; Kuhn & Allvin, 1967) and Pennsylvania State University (Deihl & Radocy, 1969) were the platforms on which most early research into computer-based music instruction was conducted. Early work into uses of computers in music instruction is chronicled by Kostka (1974) and Boody (1975) and later work is summarized by Higgins (1992). The most extensive and up-to-date information about current applications of technology in music instruction is available in annual directories published by the Association for Technology in Music In-

---

Difficulty or "b" parameter values represent the point on the ability scale where an item is most discriminating. These values generally vary from -3 to +3 with higher values representing greater difficulty. Discrimination or "a" parameter values represent the extent to which an item discriminates between examinee ability levels at the item's difficulty level. These values typically vary from 0 to 2, with higher values indicating greater discrimination. Pseudo-guessing or "c" parameter values indicate the probability of an examinee of lowest possible ability getting the item correct. These values are generally less than or equal to the probability of answering an item correctly through random guessing. Guidelines for selecting an appropriate item response model are provided in Hambleton (1989) and Hambleton, Swaminathan, and Rogers (1991).

struction (ATMI). The 1997–98 directory (Murphy, 1997), for example, has descriptions of 1,083 products, including 249 microcomputer-based programs for computer-assisted instruction. (See the ATMI home page at http://www.music.org/ for further information.)

At the University of Illinois, I also had the good fortune of having worked as a research assistant for Kumi and Maurice Tatsuoka when they were developing computerized adaptive diagnostic testing systems on the PLATO system (see Tatsuoka, 1983, 1985; Tatsuoka & Tatsuoka, 1997). Although I had experience in doing PLATO programming, I would not have been able to develop the tonal memory CAT without the help of Kumi, Maurice, and PLATO programmers such as Robert Baillie, Tom Cortese, and Kurt Huber.

The final CAT program was designed to be flexible in that the test user could specify which starting items and test termination rules to use. Ability estimates were derived using maximum likelihood procedures, and items were selected based on maximum information.[2] When taking the actual CAT, examinees would see a title page, test directions, practice items, actual items, and a results screen (see Vispoel, 1987a, pp. 142–154 for further details about this program). To play the test items, a special synthesizer box had to be attached to the PLATO terminal.

Despite the great time and effort that were devoted to building the PLATO version of the CAT, it enjoyed very limited use. After defending my dissertation, I immediately started a job as Director of Testing and Research at a high school district in the Northwest suburbs of Chicago, where I had no access to the PLATO system. Before leaving the University of Illinois in 1986, I had completed only one validation study for the CAT in a live testing setting (see Vispoel, 1992). In that study, 30 college student volunteers completed the tonal memory CAT, the Seashore Tonal Memory test (Seashore et al., 1960), the Drake Musical Memory test (Drake, 1957), and questionnaires assessing music experience and self-perceptions of music ability. Music experience indices, ability ratings, and Drake Musical Memory test scores served as criterion measures in a concurrent validity analysis. The results indicated that the CAT required an average of 72% fewer items to match the reliability of the Seashore Tonal Memory test and to exceed its concurrent validity.

I resumed my research into music CATs a few years later after I was hired as a faculty member at the University of Iowa. My efforts were hampered because the PLATO system was unavailable on campus and commercial packages for producing CATs such as MicroCAT™ (Assessment Systems Corporation,

---

[2]Maximum likelihood ability estimation procedures, as the label suggests, provide the ability estimate "most likely" to account for responses to the administered items. Maximum information item selection involves scanning unadministered items in the CAT bank for the remaining item that provides the most statistical information about the examinee's current ability estimate. See Wainer and Mislevy (1990) and Thissen and Wainer (1990) for more in-depth discussions of these ability estimation and item selection procedures.

1987) had limited capabilities for administering listening-type items. My first attempt at implementing the CAT on a microcomputer evolved out of a test development project for our dental school. Lynnea Johnson and James Fuller were using MicroCAT to develop mastery tests for dental pathology classes (see Fuller, Johnson, & Vispoel, 1992). The tests involved examinations of pictures of dental pathology that were stored on video disks. David Vale, the programmer for MicroCAT at that time, had developed customized subroutines to produce video images from video disk players, and he allowed us to field-test his new subroutines. Although the dental school tests did not involve sound production, audio tracks could be recorded on the video disks and reproduced using the new MicroCAT subroutines. I recorded my CAT item bank on a video disk at a studio on campus and succeeded in implementing a rough version of the CAT on MicroCAT. I was dissatisfied with the results because there were differential delays in the playing of test items, depending on how closely a given track was located to the previously played track on the video disk. Also I was limited to using only one computer at a time because a separate video disk and video disk player would be required at each computer work station.

After these experiences, I concluded that the best way to continue my research into music CATs was to develop my own software. I decided to develop software for IBM-compatible microcomputers because our computer research lab at that time had 10 of those computers. I had the good fortune of working with Roberto de la Torre, a graduate student in our measurement program, who was interested in doing a dissertation project related to CATs. For his dissertation, Roberto developed and evaluated the Computerized Adaptive Testing System (CATSYS)—a computer package for simulating and creating computerized tests (see, de la Torre, 1991; de la Torre & Vispoel, 1991). My colleagues and I have used this computer package extensively in our research involving CATs both within and outside of the music listening domain (see, e.g., Vispoel, 1993a, 1993b, 1998; Vispoel & Coffman, 1992, 1994; Vispoel, Rocklin, & Wang, 1994; Vispoel, Rocklin, Wang, & Bleiler, in press; Vispoel, Wang, & Bleiler, 1997; Wang & Vispoel, 1998).

The simulation part of CATSYS is largely menu driven, but creation of operational CATs requires some programming skill in Turbo PASCAL. In creating an operational CAT, separate files must be created for item parameters, test directions, practice items, actual test items, and reporting of results. Internal subroutines must be adjusted so that desired starting rules, ability estimation procedures, item selection rules, test termination rules, and other test options are implemented properly (permitting vs. not permitting answer feedback, permitting vs. not permitting answer review and change, etc.). In creating the music CAT, special subroutines were needed to play the items and display the text for the items. Music was played through the internal sound production capabilities of the IBM microcomputers. This was accomplished by using sound production commands accessed through Turbo PASCAL and attaching a special sound box with earphone jacks and a volume control to each computer. The sound production commands functioned in essentially the same way as had the music production commands used within the PLATO system.

Some of the advantages of the IBM-based CAT program were its flexibility in being able to alter CATs to address research questions of interest, its ability to produce sound with the use of limited special equipment, its ability to handle large item banks, and its ability to simulate tests prior to live testing. Before implementing the final IBM version of the CAT, I was able to recalibrate items from the CAT item bank using a sample of 731 high school and college students, 14% of whom were college music majors. All of these individuals volunteered to participate in the item calibrations, and many of them received course credit for doing so. Model fit analyses for these data showed that a modified 3-parameter item response model represented the data somewhat better than did the 2-parameter model used with the PLATO version of the CAT.[3] The new CAT had a pool of 278 items selected to provide good measurement precision over a wide range of ability levels.

My colleagues and I evaluated the administrative efficiency, reliability, and concurrent validity of the IBM-based CAT and several fixed-item tonal memory tests using both computer simulation and live testing data (see Vispoel et al., 1997). In the computer simulation study, 2,200 simulees completed the CAT and three fixed-item tests (the tonal memory subtests from the Seashore and Wing batteries and a computerized fixed-item test constructed from items in the CAT pool). The results showed that the CAT matched the measurement precision of the fixed-item tests using from 57% to 87% fewer items, and the CAT exceeded the precision of each fixed-item test when test length was held constant.

In the first of two live testing studies reported in Vispoel et al. (1997), 202 college student volunteers completed the CAT, the tonal memory subtests from the Seashore and Wing batteries, the Drake Musical Memory test (Drake, 1957), the *Advanced Measures of Music Audiation* (AMMA; Gordon, 1989), and a questionnaire assessing music experience (e.g., number of years one has played a musical instrument, number of college music courses one has taken, whether one currently plays a musical instrument or sings for enjoyment). Drake Musical Memory and AMMA test scores along with music experience indexes served as criterion measures in the concurrent validity analysis. Results showed that the CAT needed 76% to 93% fewer items to match or surpass the reliability and concurrent validity of the Seashore test and 73% to 87% fewer items to match or surpass the reliability and concurrent validity of the Wing test.

---

[3]The modified 3-parameter model involved estimating difficulty and discrimination parameters but fixing pseudo-guessing values for each item at the reciprocal of the number of response choices minus .05. An unmodified 3-parameter model would involve estimation of all three parameters for each item (difficulty, discrimination, and pseudo-guessing).

In the second live testing study reported in Vispoel et al. (1997), randomly equivalent groups of college student volunteers took either the tonal memory CAT ($n = 86$) or a computerized fixed-item tonal memory test constructed from items in the CAT pool ($n = 86$). Examinees in both groups also completed the tonal memory subtests from the Seashore and Wing batteries, the Drake Musical Memory test (Drake, 1957), the AMMA (Gordon, 1989), and the questionnaire assessing music experience used in the previous live testing study. Seashore, Wing, Drake, and AMMA test scores along with music experience indices served as criterion measures in the concurrent validity analysis. Results showed that the CAT needed 57% fewer items to match the computerized fixed-item test's reliability and 50% to 87% fewer items to match its concurrent validity. The CAT also provided higher reliability and concurrent validity than the computerized fixed-item test when test length was held constant.

The most recent version of the tonal memory CAT was developed by Timothy Bleiler and me for PowerMacintosh™ microcomputers using HyperCARD™. Compiled applications of the CAT program also can be implemented on other versions of Macintosh microcomputers (Powerbooks, CIs, CXs, FXs, SIs, SEs, etc.). We developed this version of the program in part because the IBM microcomputers in our lab were being replaced with Macintosh microcomputers, but also because we wanted to take advantage of the superior audio production, video production, and graphical display capabilities of the Macintosh computers when producing future tests. Our present HyperCARD testing programs allow us to implement a wide variety of computerized tests, but skill in HyperCARD programming is required to set up each operational test.[4]

In setting up the current HyperCARD version of the tonal memory CAT for administration, the test user would specify desired starting rules, item selection rules, test termination rules, and score reports to be produced. The program currently uses expected a posterior (EAP) Bayesian ability estimation and measurement error indices (see Bock & Mislevy, 1982) and maximum information-based item selection algorithms, but alternative procedures also are available.[5] A typical compiled version of the tonal memory CAT involves a stack of 283 cards, with one card for a title page, one card for directions, two

---

[4]Timothy Bleiler and I are also in the process of creating adaptive testing programs for Macintosh computers using SuperCAT™.

[5]Bayesian-based approaches to ability estimation incorporate assumptions about the nature of the population ability distribution into the ability estimate. Conceptually, these procedures yield ability estimates that combine information about the likelihood of getting items correct and incorrect with assumptions about the form, mean, and variance of the target population's ability distribution. Initially, it is typically assumed that the population ability distribution is normally distributed with a mean of 0 and variance of 1. This initial assumed ability distribution is called the prior distribution. After the examinee answers the first item, the likelihood associated with the response is combined with the information about the prior ability distribution to create an adjusted ability distribution called the posterior distribution. This posterior distribution then becomes the

You will be listening to examples of melodies that contain from 4 to 9 notes. A computer display containing a string of 4 to 9 numbers will be presented before a given example is played. This display will tell you the number of notes within the melody. For example, if the melody contains 6 notes, you will see the following display:

$$1 \quad 2 \quad 3 \quad 4 \quad 5 \quad 6$$

0 = No Change

Each melody will be played twice. Just listen to the melody the first time. As you listen, use the numbers on the computer display to help keep track of the number of each note. The melody will be replayed a second time but one note may be altered. As you listen to the melody the second time, follow along on the computer display again. Then, click on the number of the note that has been altered or click on "0 = No Change" to indicate that the melodies are the same.

We will now listen to a practice item. Click on the arrow below when you are ready to start.

➡

FIG 8.3.   Sample directions for the tonal memory CAT.

cards for practice items, 278 cards for the items in the test bank, and one card for test results. During the actual test, the examinee would see the title page, directions, practice items, actual items, and test results. The mechanisms for administering, selecting, and scoring the test items are linked to the cards through external command routines (i.e., small programs compiled to machine code that were originally written in programming languages such as PASCAL, C, or BASIC). The music items are played using the HyperCARD PLAY command, which functions in essentially the same way as did the music production commands used in the PLATO and IBM versions of the tonal memory CAT.

Figure 8.3 shows the initial directions that an examinee might see when taking the CAT. Figure 8.4 shows examples of test screens for a practice item and an actual CAT item. The screen for the practice item was printed after the

---

prior distribution to be combined with the likelihood associated with the examinee's responses to the second item. This process continues in a sequential fashion item by item with the posterior distribution from the previous step used as the prior distribution to be combined with the likelihood of the examinee's responses to the item taken at each subsequent step in the estimation process. The variance and standard deviation of the posterior distribution provide indices of the measurement error associated with the ability estimate. See Wang and Vispoel (1998) and Wainer and Mislevy (1990) for further discussion of the use of Bayesian procedures in CAT settings.

Practice Item

1   **2**   3   4   5   6

0=No Change

That is the correct answer.

Click on Begin Test to begin the actual test

Begin Test

Item Number 1.

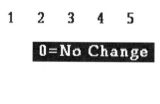

1   2   3   4   5

0=No Change

Click on Next Item to continue

Next Item

FIG. 8.4.   Screens for practice and actual tonal memory CAT items.

examinee had registered a response of 2 to the item and was told that the response was correct. During the actual test, no feedback about the correctness of answers would be given, although the test could be set up to provide such feedback if desired. The screen for the actual test item shown in Fig 8.4 was printed after the examinee had registered "0 = No change" as a response. Figure 8.5 shows an example of output derived for a CAT that was terminated after 15 items. In this example, both item-by-item and summary results are shown. The item-by-item output includes item sequence numbers, item pool

Test Results

Item by Item Data

Item Number	Pool Number	A Par.	B Par.	C Par.	Cor. Ans.	Exam. Ans.	Item Score	Ability estimate	Posterior Variance	Time in 1/100 sec.
1	6	2.00	-0.16	0.12	1	1	1	0.5091	0.6677	846
2	95	2.00	0.56	0.05	3	3	1	1.0148	0.4329	1153
3	25	2.00	1.88	0.05	9	8	0	0.6478	0.2621	1472
4	102	2.00	0.60	0.08	4	4	1	0.8715	0.1776	1313
5	138	2.00	0.63	0.09	1	1	1	1.0006	0.1435	917
6	14	1.75	0.98	0.06	4	0	0	0.8322	0.1059	1181
7	148	2.00	0.63	0.12	2	2	1	0.9177	0.0900	785
8	124	2.00	0.63	0.12	3	3	1	0.9822	0.0808	687
9	4	1.55	0.90	0.06	8	8	1	1.0578	0.0771	950
10	16	2.00	1.32	0.12	1	0	0	0.9851	0.0621	774
11	8	2.00	0.52	0.08	3	3	1	1.0183	0.0578	665
12	108	1.52	0.90	0.09	3	0	0	0.9407	0.0578	675
13	91	1.79	0.54	0.09	6	6	1	0.9715	0.0479	2175
14	53	1.49	0.87	0.09	4	1	0	0.9083	0.0431	1131
15	81	1.57	0.57	0.05	4	4	1	0.9387	0.0411	1132

Final Test Results after 15 items

Ability Estimate: 0.9387
Posterior Variance: 0.0411
Testing Time (sec):   158.56

Click on the arrow below when you want to exit the test.

➡

FIG. 8.5.   Sample score report for the tonal memory CAT.

numbers, item parameters, correct answers, examinee answers, item scores (1 = correct, 0 = incorrect), ability estimates, measurement error estimates (i.e., posterior variance), and item administration times. Note that the measurement error associated with the ability estimate gradually decreases as test length increases and that the differences in the ability estimates tend to get smaller and smaller as the test progresses. This illustrates the effectiveness of the CAT in efficiently "zeroing in" on the examinee's ability level. The summary test results for the examinee include: (a) the final ability estimate (0.9387), which is expressed on the norming sample's standard score scale ($M = 0, SD = 1$), (b) the posterior variance or measurement error associated with the ability estimate (0.0411, which is equivalent to a standard error of 0.203), and (c) the cumulative testing time excluding test directions (158.56 sec or 2 min and 38.56 sec).

If results were reported directly to an examinee at the end of a CAT, they typically would not be as extensive as those shown in Fig. 8.5. A typical score report given to an examinee might include percentile-rank scores and confidence intervals based on particular norm groups of interest (e.g., the total norm sample, high school students, college students, college music majors and college non-music majors). When given such scores, the examinees also would be reminded about the limitations of the norming samples.

FUTURE DIRECTIONS

My research into music CATs has been both rewarding and frustrating. The research suggests that CATs might be particularly effective in solving problems that have long hindered accurate measurement of music aptitude, but the data are limited to only one listening skill and to a modestly validated test that has not enjoyed widespread use. Nevertheless, the results have been consistently impressive despite having used limited size item calibration samples and having moved the CAT to three different computer platforms.

Although the potential for improved measurement is there, many obstacles to creating music CATs remain. First, music test developers seldom receive training in item response theory and related methods typically needed to implement CATs. Second, it is difficult to get large representative samples of examinees to take a large number of computerized test items for purposes of item calibration. Third, it is difficult and time consuming to create the large item pools typically needed for CATs. Fourth, it is difficult to obtain funding to promote music test development. Finally, there are still no commercially available CAT software programs that are set up to produce music listening items directly.

Despite these obstacles, the creation and implementation of music CATs is much simpler now than it was when I first started my research in this area. Many microcomputers today have built-in synthesizers, compact disk players, and earphone jacks that are ideally suited for the production and administration of music listening tests. The routines that my colleagues and I used to create the Macintosh tonal memory CAT can be incorporated into new HyperCARD-based adaptive tests as long as calibrated item banks are available. Given the technology currently available, it certainly would be possible to create the adaptive music test battery that I once envisioned to assess tonal memory, temporal tracking, rhythmic ability, and auditory cognition of relationships. It also would be possible to create adaptive versions of subtests from other music aptitude and achievement test batteries to improve their measurement precision and efficiency. Adaptive tests of such skills might be used for a variety of purposes including predicting future accomplishment in music-related activities, rank ordering examinees according to proficiency, diagnosing learning difficulties in music, targeting instruction to student skill levels, making mastery/nonmastery or other classification decisions, and assessing growth in music skills over time (see, e.g., Bowers, 1992; Bunderson,

Inouye, & Olsen, 1989; Tatsuoka, 1983; Vispoel, 1986; Weiss & Kingsbury 1984). In addition, the domains of possible music skill to assess can be expanded beyond listening through the use of Musical Instrument Digital Interface (MIDI) devices. Such devices are capable not only of producing sophisticated sound but also of recording input (dynamics, timing, pitches, etc.) from actual musical instruments. This opens up the possibility of adaptive assessment of music performance skills.

In the introduction to a special issue of the *Journal of Computer-Based Instruction*, Kate Covington (1989) noted that computers had made a major impact on music composition, performance, analysis, research, and teaching (p. 49). The potential is certainly there for computers to have a similar impact on the assessment and evaluation of music proficiency before the next millennium.

REFERENCES

Allvin, R. L. (1967). *The development of a computer-assisted music instruction system to teach sight-singing and ear-training*. Unpublished doctoral dissertation, Stanford University, Palo Alto, CA.

American College Testing. (1995). *COMPASS user's guide*. Iowa City, IA: Author.

Assessment Systems Corporation. (1989). *User's manual for MicroCAT™ Testing System* (2nd ed.). St. Paul, MN: Author.

Bahgi, H., Gabrys, R., & Ferrara, S. (1991, April). *Applications of computer-adaptive testing in Maryland*. Paper presented at the annual meeting of the American Educational Research Association, Chicago, IL.

Bentley, A. (1966). *Measures of musical abilities*. London: Harrap.

Bock, R. D., & Mislevy, R. J. (1982). Adaptive EAP estimation of ability in a microcomputer environment. *Applied Psychological Measurement, 37*, 431–444.

Boody, C. G. (1975). *Non-compositional applications of the computer to music: An evaluative study of materials published in America through June, 1972*. Unpublished doctoral dissertation, University of Minnesota, Minneapolis.

Bowers, D. R. (1992) Computer-based adaptive testing in music research and instruction. *Psychomusicology, 10*, 49–63.

Bunderson, C. V., Inouye, D. K., & Olsen, J. B. (1989). The four generations of computerized educational measurement. In R. L. Linn (Ed.), *Educational measurement* (3rd. ed., pp. 367–407). New York: Macmillan.

Buros, O. K. (Ed.). (1966). *The fifth mental measurements yearbook*. Highland Park, NJ: Gryphon Press.

Cattell, R. B. (1971). *Abilities: Their structure, growth, and action*. Boston: Houghton Mifflin.

Covington, K. (1989). Introduction to the special music issue. *Journal of Computer-Based Instruction, 16*, 49.

Davies, J. B. (1970). New tests of musical aptitude. *British Journal of Psychology, 62*, 557–565.

de la Torre, R. (1991). *The development and evaluation of a system for computerized adaptive testing.* Unpublished doctoral dissertation, University of Iowa.

de la Torre, R., & Vispoel, W. P. (1991, April). *The development and evaluation of a computerized adaptive testing system.* Paper presented at the annual meeting of the American Educational Research Association, Chicago, IL. (ERIC Document Reproduction Service No. ED 338 711)

Deihl, N. C., & Radocy, R. E. (1969). Computer-assisted instruction: Potential for instrumental music education. *Bulletin of the Council for Research in Music Education, 15* (Winter), 1–7.

Doucette, D. (Ed.). (1988). *Computerized adaptive testing: The state of the art in assessment at three community colleges.* Laguna Hills, CA: League for Innovation in the Community College.

Drake, R. M. (1957). *Drake musical aptitude tests.* Sarasota, FL: Raleigh M. Drake.

Fuller, J. L., Johnson, L. A., & Vispoel, W. P. (1992, March). *Dental anatomy testing using interactive videodisk.* Paper presented at the annual meeting of the American Association of Dental Science (AADS), Boston, MA.

Gershon, R. C. (1994). *CAT Software System* [computer program]. Chicago, IL: Computer Adaptive Technologies, Inc.

Gordon, E. E. (1965). *Musical aptitude profile.* Boston: Houghton Mifflin.

Gordon, E. E. (1979). *Primary measures of music audiation.* Chicago, IL: G. I. A. Publications.

Gordon, E. E. (1982). *Intermediate measures of music audiation.* Chicago, IL: G. I. A. Publications.

Gordon, E. E. (1989). *Advanced measures of music audiation.* Chicago, IL: G. I. A. Publications.

Haken, L., & Schmid, V. (1984). *The interactive music systems user's manual.* Urbana, IL: Computer-Based Educational Research Laboratory.

Hambleton, R. K. (1989). Principles and selected applications of item response theory. In R. L. (Ed.), *Educational measurement* (3rd. ed., pp. 147–200). New York: Macmillan.

Hambleton, R. K., Swaminathan, H., & Rogers, H. J. (1991). *Fundamentals of item response theory.* Newbury Park, CA: Sage.

Higgins, W. (1992). Technology. In R. Colwell (Ed.), *Handbook of research on music teaching and learning* (pp. 480–497). New York: Macmillan.

Horn, J. L. (1976). Human abilities: A review of research and theory in the early 1970s. *Annual Review of Psychology, 27,* 437–485.

Karma, K. (1985). Components of auditive structuring—Towards a theory of music aptitude. *Bulletin of the Council for Research in Music Education, 82,* 1–13.

Kingsbury, G. G. (1990). Adapting adaptive testing: Using the MicroCAT testing in a local school district. *Educational Measurement: Issues and Practice, 9*(2), 3–6.

Kostka, S. M. (Ed.) (1974). *A bibliography of computer applications in music.* Hackensack, NJ: Joseph Boonin.

Kuhn, W. E., & Allvin, R. L. (1967). Computer-assisted teaching: A new approach to research in music. *Journal of Research in Music Education, 15,* 305–315.

Kwalwasser, J., & Dykema, P. (1939). *Kwalwasser–Dykema music tests.* New York: Carl Fisher.

Legg, S. M., & Burr, D. (1987, November). *Final report: Feasibility study of a computerized test administration of the CLAST* (Contract: 5401473-12). Institute for student assessment and evaluation. University of Florida, Gainesville.

Long, N. H. (1965). *Indiana–Oregon music discrimination test*. Bloomington: Midwest Music Tests.

Lunz, M. E., Bergstrom, B. A., & Wright, B. D. (1992). The effect of review on student ability and test efficiency for computerized adaptive tests. *Applied Psychological Measurement, 16*, 33–40.

McBride, J. R., Corpe, V. & Wing, H. (1995, April). *Equating the computerized adaptive edition of the Differential Aptitude Tests*. Paper presented at the annual meeting of the National Council on Measurement in Education, San Francisco, CA.

Murphy, B. (Ed.). (1997). *Technology directory 1997–98*. Knoxville, TN: Association for Technology in Music Instruction.

Reese, C. (1992, April). *Development of a computer-based test for the GRE general test*. Paper presented at the annual meeting of the National Council on Measurement in Education, San Francisco, CA.

Seashore, C. E. (1917). Auditory memory. *Music Supervisors Journal, 4*, 6–11.

Seashore, C. E. (1919). *Manual of instructions and interpretations of measures of musical talent*. Chicago, IL: C. F. Stoelting.

Seashore, C. E., Lewis, D., & Saetveit, J. C. (1960). *Manual of instructions and interpretations of measures of musical talents* (2nd ed.). New York: Psychological Corp.

Segall, D. O. (1995, April). *Equating the CAT–ASVAB: Experiences and lessons learned*. Paper presented at the annual meeting of the National Council on Measurement in Education, San Francisco, CA.

Segall, D. O., & Carter, G. (1995, April). *Equating the CAT–GATB: Issues and approach*. Paper presented at the annual meeting of the National Council on Measurement in Education, San Francisco, CA.

Shuter-Dyson, R., & Gabriel, C. (1981). *The psychology of musical ability* (2nd ed.). London: Methuen.

Stankov, L., & Horn, J. L. (1980). Human abilities revealed through auditory tests. *Journal of Educational Psychology, 72*, 21–44.

Stankov, L., & Spilsbury, G. (1978). The measurement of auditory abilities of blind, partially sighted and sighted children. *Applied Psychological Measurement, 2*, 491–503.

Tatsuoka, K. K. (1983). Rule space: An approach for dealing with misconceptions based on item response theory. *Journal of Educational Measurement, 20*, 345–354.

Tatsuoka, K. K. (1985). A probabilistic model for diagnosing misconceptions in the pattern classification approach. *Journal of Educational Statistics, 10*, 55–73.

Tatsuoka, K. K., & Tatsuoka, M. M. (1997). Diagnostic adaptive testing: Effect of remedial instruction as empirical validation. *Journal of Educational Measurement, 34*, 3–20.

Thissen, D., & Wainer, H. (1990). Testing algorithms. In H. Wainer (Ed.), *Computerized adaptive testing: A primer* (pp. 161–186). Hillsdale, NJ: Lawrence Erlbaum Associates.

Thurstone, L. L. (1947). *Multiple factor analysis*. Chicago, IL: University of Chicago Press.

Urry, V. W. (1977). Tailored testing: A successful application of latent trait theory. *Journal of Educational Measurement, 14*, 181–196.

Vispoel, W. (1986). An application of rule space methodology to the assessment of tonal memory. In G. Hayes (Ed.), *Proceedings of the 28th International ADCIS Conference* (pp. 343–346). Bellingham, WA: ADCIS.

Vispoel, W. P. (1987a). An adaptive test of musical memory: An application of item response theory to the assessment of musical ability (Doctoral dissertation, The University of Illinois: Urbana-Champaign). *Dissertation Abstracts International, 49*, 79A.

Vispoel, W. P. (1987b). Improving the measurement of musical ability through adaptive testing. In G. Hayes (Ed.), *Proceedings of the 29th International ADCIS Conference* (pp. 221–228). Bellingham, WA: ADCIS.

Vispoel, W. P. (1990, March). *Computerized adaptive music tests: A new solution to three old problems*. Paper presented at the biannual meeting of the Music Educators National Conference, Washington, DC.

Vispoel, W. P. (1992). Improving the measurement of tonal memory with computerized adaptive tests. *Psychomusicology, 11*, 73–89.

Vispoel, W. P. (1993a). Computerized adaptive and fixed-item versions of the ITED Vocabulary subtest. *Educational and Psychological Measurement, 53*, 779–788.

Vispoel, W. P. (1993b). The development and evaluation of a computerized adaptive test of tonal memory. *Journal of Research in Music Education, 41*, 111–136.

Vispoel, W. P. (1997, October). *Improving the quality of music aptitude tests through adaptive administration of items*. Invited paper presented at Multidisciplinary Perspectives on Musicality: The Seashore Symposium, University of Iowa, Iowa City, IA.

Vispoel, W. P. (1998). Psychometric characteristics of computer-adaptive and self-adaptive vocabulary tests: The role of answer feedback and test anxiety. *Journal of Educational Measurement, 35*, 155–167.

Vispoel, W. P., & Coffman, D. D. (1992). Computerized adaptive testing of music-related skills. *Bulletin of the Council for Research in Music Education, 112*, 29–49.

Vispoel, W. P., & Coffman, D. D. (1994). Computerized adaptive and self-adapted tests of music listening skills: Psychometric features and motivational benefits. *Applied Measurement in Education, 7*, 25–51.

Vispoel, W. P., Rocklin, T. R., & Wang, T. (1994). Individual differences and test administration procedures: A comparison of fixed-item, adaptive, and self-adapted testing. *Applied Measurement in Education, 7*, 53–79.

Vispoel, W. P., Rocklin, T. R., Wang, T., & Bleiler, T. (in press). Can examinees use a review option to obtain positively biased ability estimates on a computerized adaptive test? *Journal of Educational Measurement*.

Vispoel, W. P., & Twing, J. S. (1990). Creating adaptive tests of musical ability with limited-size item pools. In David Dalton (Ed.), *ADCIS 32nd International Conference Proceedings* (pp. 105–112). Columbus, OH: Association for the Development of Computer-based Instructional Systems.

Vispoel, W. P., Wang, T., & Bleiler, T. (1997). Computerized adaptive and fixed-item testing of music listening skills: A comparison of efficiency, reliability, and concurrent validity. *Journal of Educational Measurement, 34*, 41–61.

Wainer, H. (1990). Introduction and history. In H. Wainer (Ed.), *Computerized adaptive testing: A primer* (pp. 1–21). Hillsdale, NJ: Lawrence Erlbaum Associates.

Wainer, H., & Mislevy, R. J. (1990). Item response theory, item calibration and proficiency estimation. In H. Wainer (Ed.), *Computerized adaptive testing: A primer* (pp. 65–102). Hillsdale, NJ: Lawrence Erlbaum Associates.

Wang, T., & Vispoel, W. P. (1998). Properties of ability estimation methods in computerized adaptive testing. *Journal of Educational Measurement, 35*, 109–135.

Ward, W. C. (1984). Using microcomputers to administer tests. *Educational Measurement: Issues and Practices, 3*, 16–20.

Webster, P. (1992). Research on creative thinking in music: The assessment literature. In R. Colwell (Ed.), *Handbook of research on music teaching and learning* (pp. 266–280). New York: Macmillan.

Weiss, D. J. (1982). Improving measurement quality and efficiency with adaptive testing. *Applied Psychological Measurement, 6*, 473–492.

Weiss, D. J., & Kingsbury, G. G. (1984). Application of computerized adaptive testing to educational problems. *Journal of Educational Measurement, 21*, 361–375.

Whellams, F. S. (1971). *The aural musical abilities of junior school children: A factorial investigation.* Unpublished doctoral dissertation, University of London.

Wing, H. D. (1948). Tests of musical ability and appreciation. *British Journal of Psychology: Monograph Supplements, 27.*

Wing, H. D. (1961). *Wing Standardised Tests of Musical Intelligence.* Windsor, England: NFER Publishing.

Wing, H. D. (1970). Tests of musical ability and appreciation (2nd ed.). *British Journal of Psychology: Monograph Supplements, 28.*

Wingersky, M.S., Barton, M. A., & Lord, F. M. (1982). *LOGIST user's guide.* Princeton, NJ: Educational Testing Service.

9

Development of an Interactive Video Assessment: Trials and Tribulations

Fritz Drasgow
University of Illinois, Urbana-Champaign

Julie B. Olson-Buchanan
California State University, Fresno

Philip J. Moberg
Wayne State University

Interactive video (IAV) computerized assessment uses full-motion video displayed on a computer monitor and sound provided via speakers or headphones. Assessees watch video clips that can be comparable in quality to color television and, at critical junctures, are asked multiple-choice questions. For some questions, the response option that is selected determines the next video clip to be viewed by the assessee.

Although the bells and whistles of multimedia technology are impressive, IAV assessment poses a number of challenges for test development and analysis. The production of an IAV assessment requires a development team with expertise in psychometrics, the substantive area of the assessment, video production, and multimedia software authoring. Indeed, coordinating such a diverse team and addressing various technical issues can be a daunting task (Dyer, Desmarais, Midkiff, Colihan, & Olson, 1992).

This chapter discusses several difficult issues encountered in developing, scoring, and validating video assessments. A number of alternative approaches for dealing with these critical issues are described. An example of an IAV assessment, the Conflict Resolution Skills Assessment (Olson-Buchanan et al., 1998), is presented to illustrate one approach to the development of IAV assessments.

MEASUREMENT OF SKILLS
USING IAV ASSESSMENT

Skills That Have Been Measured

Because the technology required for IAV assessment has been available for only a few years, relatively little research has been conducted in this area. Moreover, from our literature review, it appears that the bulk of this research is considered to be proprietary by its organizational sponsors. Thus, the research has been presented at conferences but relatively few published accounts are available.

One of the most carefully developed video assessments is the Workplace Situations test developed at IBM to assess situational judgment skills (Desmarais et al., 1992; Desmarais, Masi, Olson, Barbera, & Dyer, 1994; Dyer et al., 1992; Midkiff, Dyer, Desmarais, Rogg, & McCusker, 1992). This assessment presents a series of 30 short (typically less than 1 minute) scenes in a fictional organization named Quintronics. The scenes depict interpersonal issues arising in the manufacture of hypothetical electronics products called quintelles and alpha pinhole boards. The vignettes deal with such issues as poor training, demanding workloads, interpersonal conflict, sloppy work habits, and flawed work. After a video scene is presented, the computer presents five response options; each describes a way of responding to the workplace problem. Information about the psychometric characteristics of the Workplace Situations test is not available.

Another interesting and carefully developed video assessment is the Allstate Multimedia In-Basket (Ashworth & Joyce, 1994; Ashworth & McHenry, 1992). The hypothetical setting is an airline customer service organization; assessees must arrange and revise travel plans by calling customers, consulting flight schedules, and applying flight policy and regulations. A complex scoring procedure, derived from judgments of subject matter experts, has been developed to score assessees' responses. However, no information about the assessment's psychometric characteristics is available.

A video assessment, administered by VHS videotape rather than computer (and hence noninteractive), is the Teamwork assessment, which was developed as part of the American College Testing Program's (1995) Work Keys project. It was designed to measure an individual's skills in supporting team relationships while simultaneously accomplishing work objectives. The assessment contains 12 scenarios that depict teamwork situations varying in complexity. It is divided into two sections, each of which has 18 multiple-choice questions and takes about 40 minutes to complete. A Guttman scaling procedure is used for scoring four levels of competence; to attain a score level, an examinee must correctly answer seven of nine questions within that level and at least seven of nine questions in all lower levels. A minimum coefficient of reproducibility of .90 was used for the development of the Teamwork assessment.

Skills That Could Be Measured

Some insight into the range of traits sensibly assessed by IAV might be obtained by hypothesizing that an assessment's validity may be maximized by matching its administration medium to the skill that is measured (see also Drasgow, Olson, Keenan, Moberg, & Mead, 1993, and McHenry & Schmitt, 1994). For example, paper-and-pencil tests seem well suited for the assessment of intellective skills that are learned through the written word. On the other hand, validity may be attenuated when there is a mismatch between the skill assessed and the test's administration medium. Social skills, for example, are largely developed by interactions with other people and so it seems appropriate to measure skills in this domain via live or simulated interactions with others. Because assessments involving live interactions can be quite expensive (they ordinarily require one or more actors and one or more evaluators to observe and score each individual's responses), IAV appears to provide a reasonable methodology for assessing social skills.

An assessment of a social or interpersonal skill might be conceptualized as focusing on a set of specific job skills such as those required by a police officer interacting with suspects, a bank teller serving customers, or a nurse comforting hospital patients. Alternatively, an assessment could be viewed as measuring a latent trait such as the Conflict Resolution Skills assessment described here. Empowerment skills of a school principal or teamwork skills of workgroup members provide other examples of traits that could be measured by IAV. This job skill/latent trait distinction parallels the work-oriented/worker-oriented job analysis classification used in industrial–organizational psychology (e.g., Gatewood & Feild, 1994, p. 325).

The Conflict Resolution Skills Assessment

To illustrate the many issues and decisions that must be resolved during the creation of an IAV assessment, the development of the Conflict Resolution Skills Assessment (Olson-Buchanan et al., 1998) is described here. Conflict resolution is a construct that seems rather difficult to measure via a paper-and-pencil format. When we originally reviewed available tests and measures, the closest we could come to an assessment of conflict resolution skill was Putnam and Wilson's (1987) *Organizational Communication and Conflict Instrument* (OCCI), which assesses one's *preference* for how conflict is resolved (e.g., nonconfrontation, solution-oriented, control), not one's *skill* in conflict resolution. This distinction between preference and skill seems important; Moberg (1995) found no relation between OCCI scores and ratings by supervisors and coworkers of performance in on-the-job conflict resolution situations.

IAV technology seems well suited for the measurement of an interpersonal ability such as conflict resolution skill. Provided that the video is plausible, the assessee can become highly involved in the situations depicted. When asked what he or she would do in a conflict situation, some of the visceral processes that underlie behavior in real world settings may influence the assessee's response. Thus, the generalizability from the assessment setting to the setting of everyday life may be rather substantial. Note, however, that implausible situations or amateurish video clips are likely to reduce the validity of the IAV assessment.

A typical item on the Conflict Resolution Skills Assessment begins by presenting a conflict scene (1–3 minutes in duration) to an individual. At a critical point the scene is stopped and four options for addressing the conflict are provided; the assessee is asked to choose the option that best describes what he or she would do in this situation. Depending on the option chosen, the computer branches to an extension of the first scene depicting how events might unfold. Again, the conflict escalates, the scene is frozen, four options for addressing the conflict are presented, and the assessee decides which option would best resolve the conflict. The computer then branches to an entirely new conflict scene.

STIMULUS DEVELOPMENT
FOR IAV ASSESSMENTS

Alternatives

The dynamic nature of IAV assessment creates an additional set of challenges for the development of stimulus materials. Like conventionally administered tests, IAV assessments can contain some stimuli to which all test-takers will be exposed. However, IAV test developers can also create video clips that are administered conditionally, depending on the assessee's *interactions* with a previous video clip. Consequently, like computer adaptive tests (CATs), the test developer must create and develop more stimuli than a given assessee will experience. This task becomes more cumbersome as the number of response options increases and as the depth of the branching structure grows.

There are several different methods or approaches that could be used to develop the video for IAV assessment. One method involves converting materials from a preexisting assessment. For example, sometimes role-playing assessments are used to measure such constructs as communication skills, ability to handle discipline, and interpersonal conflict skills. To that end, actors often are trained to play a role as a disruptive student or an irate employee. Usually, scripts for these assessments include contingency dialogues—or a description of how the actor should respond depending on how the assessee attempts to handle the issue.

If such an assessment already exists, the test developer could convert the stimulus materials (the scripts or training manuals) to an IAV assessment. Indeed, this approach would cut development time and costs. Unfortunately, due to the relative scarcity of these types of preexisting assessments, this method is not feasible for many skills that could be measured via an IAV assessment. Moreover, the effectiveness of converting an existing paper-and-pencil assessment will depend on the extent to which the preexisting materials are well documented and the quality of the methods used in their development.

A second and perhaps more viable approach for stimulus development is the subject matter expert method used by Motowidlo, Dunnette, and Carter (1990) for their low-fidelity simulation. Their first step was to collect narrative reports of critical events pertaining to the skill to be assessed from job incumbents and their supervisors; they then used these reports to write situation descriptions. In the second step, the researchers asked another set of job incumbents to explain how they would respond to the situation descriptions created in Step 1; the researchers then grouped the responses into a smaller group of "general strategies" for each description. Finally, in Step 3, the researchers asked a group of subject matter experts to rate the effectiveness of the strategies identified in Step 2. These ratings were then used to develop the scoring key. Motowidlo et al.'s (1990) low-fidelity simulation (i.e., a paper-and-pencil test) successfully predicted supervisory ratings of performance.

Other researchers have adapted this subject matter expert method to develop *linear* video-based assessments (e.g., Desmarais et al., 1994). This method can be expanded to develop *interactive* video assessments by adding steps to develop branching items based on the situation descriptions (and options) of the strategies identified in the second step.

Motowidlo et al.'s (1990) three-step approach has several positive qualities. It should result in highly realistic, compelling stimuli because test material is developed from descriptions of real-life experiences of job incumbents. It also produces a scoring procedure for the assessment. However, a possible disadvantage is that the stimuli (and scoring procedure) may have limited generalizability to other organizations, particularly those with different cultures. In addition, this approach would not allow the developer to give specific feedback to assessees about *why* one response option is more or less correct than another. Although this may not be a concern when IAV assessments are used for the sole purpose of measurement, it would be paramount if the IAV were to be used for teaching, training, or development.

A third alternative is to use a preexisting theory or model of the construct to develop the test specifications and stimulus materials for an IAV assessment. To that end, the test developer would write materials that provide instantiations of the various components of the theory. Additional steps, such as asking experts to rate the extent to which the materials represent the theory, would be needed to refine the stimuli. This approach is advantageous in that it is based on previous theoretical and empirical work and would be particularly useful for providing feedback for training and development purposes. In addition, its base in theory may serve to increase its construct validity. However, an assessment developed through this method may not be particularly compelling or realistic because it may be based principally on the imagination of the test developer rather than the life experiences of students or job incumbents. Also, many skills that could be assessed by IAV do not have appropriate theoretical models, and the utility of this method would vary with the quality of the theoretical model.

Approach Used for the Conflict Resolution Skills Assessment

To develop this test, a combination of the subject matter expert judgment and theory-based methods was used. We began with a careful review of the mediation and conflict resolution literature, and used empirical findings from this domain to develop the Keenan–Olson (KO) model of conflict management (Keenan & Olson, 1991). The model classifies conflict in terms of three components: *short-term* issues such as the extent to which the conflict is disruptive immediately, *long-term* policy implications or long-term costs of the dispute, and *interpersonal* aspects of the conflict such as the level of emotional intensity of the disputants. The model then prescribes the type of actions a manager should take to resolve conflicts effectively and efficiently within an organization, while providing for participant satisfaction and perceptions of fairness (Lissak & Sheppard, 1983). Additional details about the conceptual model are provided in Olson-Buchanan et al. (1998). Following is a description of how we combined these two methods and a discussion of the problems we encountered in doing so.

Phase 1: Creating Items. The first two steps used to develop the Conflict Resolution Skills Assessment were similar to Motowidlo et al.'s (1990) procedure for creating a low-fidelity simulation. First, structured interviews with managers from several different organizations were conducted to solicit detailed examples of interpersonal, job-related conflict. After summarizing the interviews, and stripping them of any industry-specific information, similar conflict situations were combined and situations that could not be portrayed in a short video scene were eliminated. Next, a second sample ($N = 110$) of managers read the conflict summaries and described how they would handle each conflict. A group of nine researchers examined the managers' responses, sorted them into groups, and then wrote "options" that represented the content of the response groups.

Phase 2: Social Desirability Checks.   An important concern for IAV assessment is social desirability: Some options may seem obviously incorrect to examinees because they are less socially desirable than the correct option. That is, it is possible that an option is written in such a way that it can be rejected simply because it suggests an action that is less acceptable to society than other options. In an attempt to control the effects of social desirability, two additional studies were conducted. Survey A reduced the number of options to exactly four for each conflict situation by eliminating distractor options that were the least socially desirable. Entry-level managers read the candidate options and selected the one that best described what they would do in a given situation. The managers also were asked to indicate the option they thought others would be most likely to select. Options infrequently selected by the managers were eliminated. This revised set of options was used in Survey B, where a second group of entry-level managers read the descriptions and selected the option that best described what they would do in each situation and indicated the option they thought most other managers would select. Some conflict situations were eliminated from the assessment development process at this point due to very low variance of options selected in Survey B.

Phase 3: Linking to the Conceptual Model, Developing Branch Scenes, and Writing Scripts.   The next phase focused on linking the content of the assessment obtained from the interviews and surveys to the KO conceptual model. Each conflict situation was examined and classified according to the three components of the model (i.e., short term, long term, and interpersonal). Some of the conflict summaries were modified slightly to provide better coverage of the model.

Next, scripts for the main scenes were written from the conflict summaries. To enhance the interactive flavor of the assessment, "branch" scenes were written for each of the four multiple-choice options for the main scenes. Here, a likely consequence of each action contained in a multiple-choice option unfolds. Thus, after selecting a way of responding to the main scene, an assessee views a branch scene portraying a likely outcome. In addition, four multiple-choice options were written for each of the branch scenes.

The scripts for the main scenes were then systematically compared to the original conflict summaries and options to determine if the content of the original summaries (in terms of the model components) was accurately conveyed. Next, to verify the classification of the scripts, senior-level psychology students were trained on the KO model and asked to classify the scripts in terms of the model's components.

Problems Encountered and Recommendations

Conceptual Model.   Some of the problems we encountered with this approach were due to the conceptual model. The KO model was in its infancy when it was used to develop the assessment in 1990. Since that time, we have identified areas of the model that we would like to improve or change. However, we had to continue with the early version of the model because the developmental process used to create the assessment had proceeded to a point where we could not easily change course. Certainly, the next version of the Conflict Resolution Skills Assessment can and will accommodate these revisions. One possible solution to this type of problem is to rely on models that are already supported with a substantial amount of research. However, such well-established models are not available for many critical skills areas.

Script Development.   Some problems with the conflict descriptions elicited in the first step of development were encountered. When asked to describe conflicts they had to handle recently, the managers in our sample tended to provide examples of conflicts that were emotionally intense and costly to the organization in the short term and long term. This presented a problem because we were interested in designing an assessment that provided content coverage of the entire KO model, which includes conflicts that are not particularly emotional or necessarily costly in the short term and long term. Certainly, the test specifications could have been revised, but the ability to recognize and respond appropriately to lower levels of conflict also appears to be important. One possible solution involves changing the structured interview format used in the first stage so that interviewers specifically ask respondents to recall or describe conflicts with different levels of seriousness.

Labor Intensity.   The amount of time and effort that was required to develop stimulus materials for an IAV assessment was substantial. For example, the scripts must contain natural dialogue, maintain the integrity of the content with respect to the experts' input, and conform to the content specifications derived from the theoretical model. Juggling these diverse and often conflicting desiderata was a very difficult task that required numerous iterations and a great deal of input from a number of individuals, and took nearly 2 years. Test developers should plan for these labor requirements by setting a generous time schedule and spreading the work load as much as possible to prevent burnout.

As an alternative to the test developer writing scripts, it is possible to contract this work to professional writers. Scripts written by such professionals will sound more natural, but may be more likely to depart from the content specified by the subject matter experts and the theoretical model.

VIDEO PRODUCTION

Alternatives

There are basically two alternatives for creating a video from the stimulus materials. The test developer can (a) hire a professional production company, or (b) rent a studio and personally produce the videotape. Several production companies are experienced in developing video for multimedia technology, and some are solely dedicated to that purpose. Production companies can complete a range of tasks including developing or refining scripts, recruiting and auditioning actors and actresses, directing the video production, performing post-production editing, and preparing the videotape for laser disc or CD-ROM.

A professional production company offers several advantages. First, the final product is likely to be professional and should reflect the quality of video to which most assessees are accustomed to viewing (such as television). Second, a production company is likely to be well connected with talent sources (actors and actresses) that meet the test developer's specifications. Finally, a production company should be more efficient and possibly better able to meet a tight timeline.

However, hiring a professional production company to develop the videotape has its drawbacks. One disadvantage is cost. A professional videotape is expensive to produce, and may be beyond the reach of many researchers' budgets. Perhaps the most serious problem involves maintaining the integrity of the original material. Content requirements and psychometric considerations may be foreign to the artistic talent involved in video production, and the production company's final product can depart markedly from the test specifications. Thus, the test developer may need to be present at the auditions, videotaping, and even the post-production editing of the videotape.

The second alternative, "produce it yourself," may be more viable for academic researchers. With this method, the test developer would be responsible for recruiting and selecting actors, directing and videotaping, post-production editing, and preparing the videotape for laser disc or CD-ROM. Of course, the test developer could hire a video director to assist in the production.

Advantages and disadvantages of creating one's own video vary with the quality or level of talent available to the test developer. Smaller, semiprofessional production companies, such as what one might find in a university setting, can produce nearly professional video. The overall cost is likely to be much lower than the price of a professional production company. In addition, the test developer may have a greater degree of control over the stimulus material as it is prepared for video. However, the time requirements and frustration of this approach are likely to be higher. Also, there is a greater risk of producing a video that appears amateurish or less compelling to the assessees.

Approach Used for Conflict Resolution
Skills Assessment

We decided to rent a studio and create the video ourselves. One member of the research team had a theater background; she served as the director for the video production. Actors were recruited from the community and university. Consequently, the overall production cost was relatively low, and the production time from auditions to pressing laser discs was approximately 6 months.

Problems and Recommendations

Assessment Integrity.   In producing the videotape, we attempted to create the best artistic product possible within our budget. However, maintaining the integrity of the original script was of paramount and universal importance. If the videotape did not accurately convey the sense of the script as originally intended, it could limit or possibly eliminate the validity of the assessment. For example, sometimes a line was hard to deliver, did not make sense, or was not believable in the scene. In such cases, the actors often made suggestions for how a line could be rephrased or the dialogue could be delivered differently. However, the integrity requirement dramatically restricted the flexibility of the production. If deviations from the original script changed the scene, seemingly better alternatives from an artistic point of view were rejected.

One possible solution to this problem would be to have rehearsals spread out over a longer of period of time, or have a longer time period between the rehearsals and videotaping. Such a schedule would allow the test developer to experiment with script changes, and assess their impact on the integrity of the assessment by using rigorous methods before videotaping (e.g., how does such a script change affect the social desirability of response options?). If a professional production company is used, the staff may be able to critique the dialogue before rehearsals begin. This would allow the test developer an opportunity to evaluate the impact of dialogue modification before taping begins.

Directing Issues. IAV offers the advantage of realistic simulations of interpersonal interactions. One of the main reasons for IAV's realism is that the assessee is able to see body gestures and facial expressions as well as hear the intonation of voices. As the developers of the assessment, we envisioned how the lines would be delivered, how the actors' faces would appear on the screen, and so forth. However, actually creating this image on videotape was a different matter. Actors, as creative artists, are not programmable. Some actors performed well in rehearsal, only to freeze or change their lines under the pressure of taping. As studio time charges and payroll costs added up, and the production schedule became tighter, we reached a point where we had to settle for less than our planned vision. These problems are endemic in video production.

HARDWARE IMPLEMENTATION ISSUES

Learning about the computer technologies required for IAV was one of the major challenges of this work and therefore this section briefly summarizes some of the main hardware considerations. The continuing development of computer hardware has caused an evolution of problems faced by measurement specialists using multimedia methods. Fortunately, hardware manufacturers have attempted to reduce the problems encountered in presenting video via computer.

Alternatives

As a simple alternative, a video assessment can be delivered on an ordinary television with a videocassette recorder (VCR). Here the test administrator plays a videoclip. Questions are asked about the clip either via videotape or by a printed test form; examinees respond by paper-and-pencil. After making sure that all examinees have finished responding to a video clip, the test administrator plays the next clip. Dynamic branching is not possible and test scoring proceeds as with conventional paper-and-pencil tests.

Two technologies allow full-screen (640 x 480 pixels), full-motion (30 frames per second) video on a personal computer (PC). In the older approach, analog images were stored on a laser disc. A laser disc player, which is about the size of a VCR, was attached by cable to a full-motion video board (such as IBM's M-Motion Video Adaptor card) installed in a 16 bit slot of the PC. Software instructs the PC to play a series of frames, which results in full-motion video on the PC's monitor. A one-sided laser disc can store 54,000 frames, thus allowing 30 minutes of full-motion video (30 frames per second x 60 seconds per minute x 30 minutes = 54,000 frames).

The newer approach is digital. Video images are digitized and stored, typically on a CD or a digital video disk (DVD). The central problem in this approach is the size of the files containing the digitized video. For example, if video were digitized for a screen containing 640 x 480 pixels, and 8 bit color was used (i.e., each pixel would be displayed as one of 256 colors), a single screen would require 307,200 bytes, one second of video would require 9,216,000 bytes, and a minute of video would need 552,960,000 bytes. A CD, which holds about 680 megabytes (MB), would be limited to just over 1 minute of video!

Due to the enormous size of video files, attention has been focused on compression algorithms. *Intraframe compression* exploits consistencies within a given frame (e.g., a part of the frame that is a solid color) to reduce storage requirements. *Interframe compression*, on the other hand, capitalizes on the fact that frequently only a few pixels change from one frame to the next. Taken together, these two forms of compression can achieve compression ratios on the order of 50:1 to 100:1.

Several compression algorithms have achieved some prominence, including DVI (digital video interactive), AVI (audio video interactive), and MPEG (Motion Picture Expert's Group). A problem for each of these algorithms occurs during playback: Decompression of the compressed file requires extensive calculations. To solve this problem, MPEG decompression boards, such as Sigma Designs's RealMagic™ board, were developed. These boards intercept the compressed video file, decompress it in real time, and pass the full-motion video to the PC's video adaptor board via a feature connector. Alternatively, Intel introduced the MMX instruction set for its Pentium microprocessors; these instructions are designed to facilitate full-motion video. Thus, a hardware decompression board is not needed with a Pentium microprocessor with MMX.

The DVD format allows roughly 5 gigabytes (GB) to be stored on a high density CD. This format was designed to be able to play a full-length movie with broadcast quality resolution using MPEG-2 compression. DVD drives incorporate an MPEG-2 decoder, so no additional hardware is needed to play video clips.

Approach Used for the Conflict Resolution
Skills Assessment

When we began this research in 1990, the only viable technology for IAV was laser disc. Therefore, we attached laser disc players to PCs using IBM's M-Motion Video Adaptor card. When CDs became common and the MPEG format was introduced, we upgraded to this approach.

Problems Encountered and Recommendations

There are a variety of problems with the laser disc approach to IAV. Laser discs are awkward and require a laser disc player that is almost as large as a PC. The laser disc player is difficult to connect to a PC (IBM's M-Motion Video Adaptor card can only be connected to a nonstandard data bus). Compatibility problems were a problem with different types of laser disc players (software that ran flawlessly with a Sony player would not run with a Pioneer player). In addition, the costs were prohibitive; the laser disc player and associated video card cost about $3,000.

The CD-ROM approach to IAV is superior on several fronts. Pentium computers with MMX, a CD drive, a sound card, and speakers are readily available. An internal CD drive does not consume any additional desktop space as does a laserdisc player. Compatibility issues for CD drives have been largely resolved due to their wide use.

SOFTWARE ISSUES

Alternatives

There are two approaches to software development. Test developers can use either a programming language such as Visual Basic or Pascal, or they can use specialized multimedia authoring software (e.g., Macromedia's Authorware™). A programming language provides great flexibility, but it is difficult to find information about accessing hardware such as a laser disc player. Multimedia authoring software, on the other hand, is designed to allow simple and speedy development of IAV applications. Sophisticated tools, such as fades and dissolves, are provided in most authoring packages, which cost from about $1,000 to $5,000.

Approach Used for the Conflict Resolution Skills Assessment

When presenting Conflict Resolution Skills Assessment via laser disc, we wrote software using Pascal. This approach worked well for us because we wanted to simply play a video clip and then present multiple-choice options on screen. When we converted to the CD format, we rewrote our software using Asymmetrix's Multimedia Toolbook™, CBT Edition. This authoring software allows sophisticated video presentations to be developed relatively quickly and efficiently.

PSYCHOMETRIC ISSUES

Alternatives

Scoring an assessment of a social skill seems to be more difficult than scoring items on an intellective skill. Item writers for, say, tests of science knowledge are often required to provide a citation to a specific page in a textbook showing that a particular option is the correct answer. On the other hand, textbooks describing findings based on rigorous research that are widely accepted by a community of scholars generally do not exist for interpersonal skills.

A variety of approaches can be taken in domains where answer keys are open to question. Three methods are common. A scoring key can be based on judgments of subject matter experts, derived from a conceptual model, or computed from data. Hybrid approaches that combine methods are also possible.

Approach Used for the Conflict Resolution Skills Assessment

Keying and Validity.   Other multimedia assessments have found key development to be a significant challenge (Ashworth & Joyce, 1994; Desmarais et al., 1994) and we had a similar experience. We began with a key based on the KO model of conflict resolution (Keenan & Olson, 1991). This model uses a contingency framework; for example, to address a conflict with little short-term pressure, but with important long-term implications, the KO model suggests that a problem-solving approach should be used to develop policy (see Olson-Buchanan et al., 1998, for further details). Response options consistent with the KO model's prescriptions were scored as $+1$, options that contradicted the model were scored as -1, and options describing actions irrelevant to the model were scored as 0.

The KO model key was evaluated in a sample of 347 examinees from six organizations. The criterion variable was a composite of 10 items asking about the examinee's on-the-job performance in handling conflict. The examinee's supervisor made confidential ratings of the examinee on these items; these ratings were used for our research only and never disclosed to the examinee or any other person in the organization. The internal consistency reliability of the criterion measure was .85. A statistically significant but rather modest validity coefficient of .14 was obtained for the KO model key.

An empirical approach was then used to determine whether a more effective keying could be found. In the empirical keying, we created a dummy (0/1) variable for each option of each item; the dummy variable was coded as 1 if an examinee selected that option, as 0 if the examinee selected another option for that scene, and as missing if the scene was not presented due to the branching nature of the IAV assessment. Each of the dummy variables was correlated with the criterion variable. The option was keyed $+1$ if its dummy variable had a correlation of .05 or larger with the criterion, -1 if the dummy variable had a correlation of -.05 or smaller, and 0 otherwise, provided an adequate number of responses were available when computing the correlation (some branch scenes were viewed very rarely). This empirical key produced a correlation of .37 with the criterion measure.

It is difficult to interpret a validity coefficient obtained in this manner: Evaluating validity in the same sample used to key a test results in capitalization on chance. Therefore, we used an iterative analysis similar in spirit to jackknifing to obtain an "honest" estimate of validity (Breiman, Friedman, Olshen, & Stone, 1984). Here, we removed the first examinee from the sample, and keyed the assessment using the other 346 respondents. Then, we used this keying to compute a test score for the first examinee. Note that there was no capitalization on chance because the first examinee was, in essence, a holdout sample of size $N = 1$. Then, the first examinee was returned to the sample, the second examinee was removed, and the assessment was rekeyed. The second keying was applied to the second examinee to obtain a test score that did not capitalize on chance. This process was continued, until 347 separate keyings were obtained; each respondent thus served as a holdout sample of $N = 1$.

We then correlated the holdout score for each of the 347 examinees with their on-the-job performance rating. The iterative rekeying analysis yielded a cross-validated correlation of .26.

The empirical key just described begins with each option scored as zero; if the option was found to have a positive (negative) correlation with the criterion, its keying was revised to $+1$ (-1). In our *hybrid* keying, we began the keying process with the KO model key; if the option was found to have a positive (negative) correlation, we added $+1$ (-1) to the KO key; however, the sum was capped at $+1$ (-1) so that no scoring weight was larger in absolute value than 1. This hybrid scoring method also produced a cross-validated validity of .26.

As reported by Olson-Buchanan et al. (1998), the Conflict Resolution Skills Assessment was unrelated to two measures of cognitive ability (i.e., tests of quantitative and verbal abilities) for the sample of 347 assessees. Thus, this assessment would be expected to add to the validity of a battery of cognitive tests by an amount equal to its simple correlation with the criterion. Olson-Buchanan et al. found no evidence of adverse impact on females or African Americans. In fact, African Americans obtained significantly higher scores than Whites on the Conflict Resolution Skills Assessment for the empirical and hybrid keyings.

Reliability.   Determining the internal consistency reliability of a branching test is difficult because there is a great deal of "missing data." For example, our assessees answered questions based on the main scene and one of four branch scenes; thus, three of every set of five questions were not answered (i.e., the questions from three branch scenes that were *not* presented).

To estimate reliability, we computed coefficient α for the nine main scenes and then applied the Spearman–Brown prophesy formula for a test of double length. The resulting reliability coefficient, approximately .30, was disappointing.

We therefore attempted to find a means of scoring the assessment that would improve homogeneity; a sample of 306 examinees from five organizations was used for these analyses. We started with the Olson-Buchanan et al. (1998) model-based key and again created a dummy variable for each option of every item. A total score for the assessment was computed using the KO key, and option-total correlations were computed for the dummy variables. For a given item, the option with the largest option-total correlation was taken as the keyed response provided that it had been selected by enough respondents for meaningful analysis. A new total test score was formed based on this keying, option-total correlations were recomputed, and the key was revised. This process was repeated for three cycles.

Table 9.1 contains the number of individuals who attempted each item, the percent correct, and item-total point–biserial correlations (where the total score has been corrected to eliminate any part–whole confound) for the answer key obtained by the process just described. To protect the security of the assessment, scorable items were recoded so that option A was the correct response (see Table 9.1).

Table 9.1 shows that all 306 assessees responded to Item 1, which was the first main scene. 261 individuals selected the keyed response (which was recoded to be option A of Item 1), and then viewed the corresponding branch scene, which is denoted Item 2; 31 individuals selected response option B and then viewed branch scene 2 (Item 3); 13 individuals selected response option C and then viewed branch scene 3 (Item 4); finally, only one person selected option D and was routed to branch scene 4 (Item 5). All 306 assessees then viewed the second main scene (Item 6) and again a branch scene was selected depending on the assessee's response option.

Table 9.1 shows rather low item-total correlations. Item-total point–biserial correlations for tests of academic skills are frequently between .30 and .50; the point biserials for the Conflict Resolution Skills Assessment are well below this range. Thus, it appears to be impossible to develop a scoring key that yields high internal consistency for this assessment.

Table 9.1 clearly illustrates an additional problem for IAV assessment: Even though the overall sample size was moderate, the sample sizes for many of the branch scenes were inadequate for statistical analysis. Thus, 15 of the 45 items were not analyzed due to sample size considerations.

TABLE 9.1
Item Statistics for Conflict Resolution Skills Assessment

Item	N	% Correct	r_{pb}	Item	N	% Correct	r_{pb}
1	306	.85	.13	26	306	.50	.13
2	261	.58	.11	27	154	.33	.21
3	31	a	a	28	33	a	a
4	13	a	a	29	77	.35	.17
5	1	a	a	30	42	a	a
6	306	.38	.07	31	306	.47	.16
7	117	.64	.12	32	77	b	b
8	131	.56	.26	33	144	b	b
9	7	a	a	34	69	.51	.23
10	51	.33	.30	35	16	a	a
11	306	.45	-.01	36	306	.13	.14
12	137	.23	.09	37	40	.48	.21
13	24	a	a	38	68	.68	.14
14	118	.70	.10	39	77	.12	.09
15	27	a	a	40	121	.25	.11
16	306	.60	.03	41	306	.51	.09
17	183	.27	.13	42	157	b	b
18	28	a	a	43	43	a	a
19	3	a	a	44	8	a	a
20	92	b	b	45	92	.70	.04
21	306	.40	.10				
22	123	.76	.12				
23	14	a	a				
24	112	.66	.12				
25	57	a	a				

DISCUSSION

This chapter provides a first look at the development of an IAV assessment. Because research describing other IAV tests has not been published, it is not possible to know whether our experiences are normal for this assessment medium. The finding that the Conflict Resolution Skills Assessment was uncorrelated with general cognitive ability is very interesting and suggests that social skills may be fundamentally distinct from intellectual ability. Moreover, the significant correlations with the criterion measure suggests that IAV may provide a means for predicting what Borman and Motowidlo (1993) call *contextual job performance*. Further research with IAV assessments is needed to determine whether these characteristics of the Conflict Resolution Skills Assessment are typical for this medium of measurement.

Our work to date seems to have generated as many questions as it has answered. One important issue lies in item construction. At the time we began development of the Conflict Resolution Skills Assessment, the best hardware technology for presenting full-motion video was laser disc. With this technology, creating a master disk was rather expensive ($2,000), which led us to consider our nine main scenes and 36 branch scenes as chiseled in stone (or, more precisely, stamped in plastic). With the introduction of full-motion video on CD-ROM and the Pentium microprocessor with MMX, the costs of computer presentation of full-motion video have dropped. Thus, it is more feasible to develop and pretest a larger number of scenes than desired for the final assessment, and then delete poorly functioning vignettes. Of course, the costs of developing additional scripts and producing the corresponding video can be a serious concern.

Another interesting question concerns the robustness of the conflict situations to minor nuances of the actors. To what extent will the psychometric properties of a vignette change if one actor is replaced by another? If rather substantial changes occur, it would be very difficult to develop alternative tests that are virtually parallel and then equate forms.

An important limitation on our conceptualization of conflict resolution skills lies in our use of a dimensional model (i.e., scores on the Conflict Resolution Skills Assessment vary along a continuum from low to high). For tests of academic skills, models that use a unidimensional latent trait representation (e.g., item response theory or IRT) have served many functions admirably. However, it is less clear that dimensional models are most appropriate for domains such as interpersonal behavior. A latent class model, or even a hierarchical tree analysis (Breiman, Friedman, Olshen, & Stone, 1984), might provide a better representation.

The results presented here provide a first look at the psychometric properties of IAV items. Because analyses of other IAV tests are not available, it is not possible to know whether these results are typical for this assessment medium.

It is clear, however, that these results seem more similar to item analyses obtained from biographical data ("biodata"; see Mumford & Stokes, 1992) than item analyses for academic skills tests. The Conflict Resolution Skills Assessment is similar to most biodata inventories in its lack of a strong first factor, low item-total correlations, and weak internal consistency. Biodata instruments highlight the distinction between internal consistency reliability and test–retest reliability in that they can have low coefficient αs but high test–retest reliability. Further research is needed to determine whether the Conflict Resolution Skills Assessment and other IAV assessments will be similar.

Finally, perhaps the most auspicious finding for the Conflict Resolution Skills Assessment was its cross-validated validity of .26. Moreover, because the assessment was uncorrelated with verbal and quantitative skills, it appears likely that substantial incremental validity will result when the Conflict Resolution Skills Assessment is used to supplement a battery of cognitive tests. Note, however, that such validity gains may be more likely when predicting criterion measures that fall into Borman and Motowidlo's (1993) contextual performance category than in their task performance category.

In sum, these results should encourage researchers to explore video assessment as a means of expanding the types of individual differences used to understand human behavior. The assessment described in this chapter was unrelated to cognitive ability but contributed incremental validity to the prediction of an important job performance dimension. Further research is clearly needed to explore individual differences in social skills and the relations of these differences to job behaviors and job performance.

REFERENCES

American College Testing Programs. (1995). *Work keys*. Iowa City IA: Author.

Ashworth, S. D., & Joyce, T. M. (1994, April). *Developing scoring protocols for a computerized multimedia in-basket exercise*. Paper presented at the Ninth Annual Conference of the Society for Industrial and Organizational Psychology, Nashville, TN.

Ashworth, S. D., & McHenry, J. J. (1993, April). *Developing a multimedia in-basket: Lessons learned*. Paper presented at the Eighth Annual Conference of the Society for Industrial and Organizational Psychology, San Francisco, CA.

Borman, W. C., & Motowidlo, S. J. (1993). Expanding the criterion domain to include elements of contextual performance. In N. Schmitt & W. C. Borman (Eds.), *Personnel selection in organizations* (pp. 71–98). San Francisco, CA: Jossey-Bass.

Breiman, L., Friedman, J. H., Olshen, R. A., & Stone, C. J. (1984). *Classification and regression trees*. Belmont, CA: Wadsworth.

Desmarais, L. B., Dyer, P. J., Midkiff, K. R., Barbera, K. M., Curtis, J. R., Esrig, F. H., & Masi, D. L. (1992, May). *Scientific uncertainties in the development of a multimedia test: Trade-offs and decisions*. Paper presented at the Seventh Annual Conference of the Society for Industrial and Organizational Psychology, Montreal, Quebec.

Desmarais, L. B., Masi, D. L., Olson, M. J., Barbera, K. M., & Dyer, P. J. (1994, April). *Scoring a multimedia situational judgment test: IBM's experience*. Paper presented at the Ninth Annual Conference of the Society for Industrial and Organizational Psychology, Nashville, TN.

Drasgow, F., Olson, J. B., Keenan, P. A., Moberg, P., & Mead, A. D. (1993). Computerized assessment. In G. R. Ferris & K. M. Rowland (Eds.), *Research in personnel and human resources management*, Vol. 11 (pp. 163–206). Greenwich, CT: JAI Press.

Dyer, P. J., Desmarais, L. B., Midkiff, K. R., Colihan, J. P., & Olson, J. B. (1992, May). *Designing a multimedia test: Understanding the organizational charge, building the team, and making the basic research commitments*. Paper presented at the Seventh Annual Conference of the Society for Industrial and Organizational Psychology, Montreal, Quebec.

Gatewood, R. D., & Feild, H. S. (1994). *Human resource selection* (3rd ed.). Chicago IL: Dryden.

Keenan, P. A., & Olson, J. B. (1991, April). *Multimedia-based measurement of conflict management*. Paper presented at the Sixth Annual Conference of the Society for Industrial and Organizational Psychology, St. Louis, MO.

Lissak, R. I., & Sheppard, B. H. (1983). Beyond fairness: The criterion problem in research in dispute intervention. *Journal of Applied Social Psychology, 13*, 45–65.

McHenry, J. J., & Schmitt, N. (1994). Multimedia testing. In M. G. Rumsey, C. D. Walker, & J. H. Harris (Eds.), *Selection and classification research: New directions* (pp. 193–232). Hillsdale, NJ: Lawrence Erlbaum Associates.

Midkiff, K. R., Dyer, P. J., Desmarais, L. B., Rogg, K., & McCusker, C. (1992, May). *The multimedia test: Friend or foe?* Paper presented at the Seventh Annual Conference of the Society for Industrial and Organizational Psychology, Montreal, Quebec.

Moberg, P. J. (1995). *Social skills, personality, and occupational interests: A multivariate structural analysis*. Doctoral dissertation, Department of Psychology, University of Illinois.

Motowidlo, S. J., Dunnette, M. D., & Carter, G. W. (1990). An alternative selection procedure: The low-fidelity simulation. *Journal of Applied Psychology, 75*, 640–647.

Mumford, M. D., & Stokes, G. S. (1992). Developmental determinants of individual action: Theory and practice in applying background measures. In M. D. Dunnette & L. M. Hough (Eds.), *Handbook of industrial and organizational psychology* (2nd ed., vol. 3, pp. 61–138). Palo Alto, CA: Consulting Psychologists Press.

Olson-Buchanan, J. B., Drasgow, F., Moberg, P. J., Mead, A. D., Keenan, P. A. & Donovan, M. A. (1998). Interactive video assessment of conflict resolution skills. *Personnel Psychology, 51*, 1–24.

Putnam, L. L., & Wilson, C. E. (1987). *Organizational Communication and Conflict Instrument—Form B2*. West Lafayette, IN: Authors.

10

Computerized Assessment of Skill for a Highly Technical Job

Mary Ann Hanson
Walter C. Borman
Personnel Decisions Research Institutes, Tampa, FL

Henry J. Mogilka
Carol Manning
Federal Aviation Administration, Oklahoma City, OK

Jerry W. Hedge
Personnel Decisions Research Institutes, Minneapolis, MN

Computerized testing is becoming increasingly popular in a variety of settings. Much of the available research has explored issues related to computerizing paper-and-pencil tests or developing computer adaptive tests (see Mead & Drasgow, 1993, for a review). Less attention has been given to capitalizing on the potential of computers for measuring skills and abilities that are difficult, extremely expensive, or even impossible to measure using traditional testing formats. Computer administration provides a great deal of flexibility both for presenting test stimuli and for collecting responses, and thus avoids many of the limitations inherent in paper-and-pencil administration. For example, computers can present visual stimuli that are moving and changing and can also present audio (e.g., verbal) stimuli. Responses can be made using a standard keyboard, a computer mouse, or specialized testing apparatus. Computers are also capable of collecting information concerning the time to respond and/or limiting the time allowed for responding to test items. The type of dynamic stimulus and response capabilities offered by computer administration makes the measurement of perceptual and psychomotor abilities much more practical (e.g., Peterson et al., 1990) and also allows for more efficient administration of work sample tests (e.g., Schmitt, Gilliland, Landis, & Devine, 1993).

This chapter describes the development of a work sample test that capitalizes on the capabilities of computers to present stimuli that are dynamic *and* includes audio in addition to visual stimuli. This test was developed for the air traffic control specialist (ATCS) job at the Federal Aviation Administration (FAA). Much of the research on computerized testing has focused on the prediction of job performance. The research described here focuses on *measuring* job performance. This test, the Computer Based Performance Measure (CBPM), was developed to serve as a criterion measure of job performance. It was developed as part of a large-scale project to develop and validate selection tests for controllers: the Air Traffic Selection and Training (AT-SAT) project (Ramos, 1999). Briefly, the CBPM is administered on a standard personal computer. Examinees watch an evolving air traffic control scenario and respond in a multiple choice format concerning what should be done to handle the problems presented.

The Air Traffic Selection and Training Project

The goal in the AT-SAT project was to develop and validate a comprehensive battery of computerized cognitive, perceptual/spatial and temperament/interpersonal instruments to identify individuals likely to be successful in the air traffic controller job. This battery included relatively pure measures of many abilities, such as memory and reasoning, and also some more complex tests designed to measure several different cognitive and perceptual abilities. An example of the latter type of test is the "letter factory" test, in which respondents monitor activities in a fictitious factory and use a mouse to perform multiple and often concurrent tasks. Information concerning the experimental selection battery is available in (Ramos, 1999).

To obtain an accurate picture of the experimental tests' validity for predicting controller performance, it was important to have reliable and valid measures of controller job performance. A concurrent validation approach was used to assess whether scores on these tests are, in fact, related to performance in the air traffic controller job. This involved correlating predictor scores for controllers in the validation sample with criterion performance scores. If these performance scores are not accurate, inferences about predictor test validities are likely to be incorrect. Thus, criterion performance measurement was an extremely important element of the AT-SAT predictor development and validation project.

The Air Traffic Control Specialist Job

The job of air traffic controller is complex and potentially difficult to capture in a criterion development effort. Air traffic controllers in the FAA are assigned to one of three general areas of specialty: en route, terminal, or Flight Service Station (FSS). En route controllers ensure the separation of aircraft traveling between airports, and terminal controllers ensure the separation of aircraft approaching or departing from airports. These controllers provide aircraft with instructions regarding appropriate altitudes and directions of flight (i.e., issue clearances) for safe and efficient air traffic movement. FSS specialists provide services to pilots such as giving weather briefings, filing flight plans, and helping to locate lost aircraft. The research described in this chapter focuses on en route controllers only. However, en route and terminal controllers perform similar job functions, so it is likely that a test battery developed for selecting en route controllers will be useful for selecting terminal controllers as well.

En route airspace is divided into sectors and these sectors are grouped into areas of specialization (made up of between five and eight sectors). An en route controller is assigned a single area of specialization and is responsible for learning to control traffic in all sectors within that area. During times of slow traffic, a single controller works in a sector of airspace; at other times, a team of two or even three controllers work each sector. This controller or team of controllers performs a variety of duties including identifying potential problems, formulating clearances to ensure separation, issuing these clearances to pilots via radio, handing off responsibility for an aircraft to another controller, communicating information not directly related to aircraft separation to pilots and other controllers, entering data into the computer, ensuring that records of flight progress are available and up to date, and so forth.

In order to accomplish these tasks, controllers continually monitor radar displays. Aircraft on these displays are associated with data blocks, which provide information such as the aircraft call sign, altitude, etc. Additional information is available in a paper format, with one or more "flight strips" for each aircraft currently in the controller's sector or scheduled to enter that sector in the near future.

Extensive training is required to become a full performance level (FPL) air traffic controller. Controllers must learn a great deal of information concerning general air traffic control rules and procedures and the sectors of airspace in their areas. Once controllers demonstrate that they can control traffic in all sectors in their area of specialization they become FPL controllers. It takes an average of about 2.5 to 3 years to reach FPL status in the en route option.

Measurement of Air Traffic Controller Performance

As mentioned, the CBPM was developed to measure en route air traffic controller performance. Considerable research is available concerning performance measurement in the air traffic controller job, and this section provides a very brief review of this research. Several methodologies have been used to evaluate controller performance. Supervisory ratings of how well individual controllers work in their particular geographic sectors of airspace have been used for both research and operational purposes and have been described as the most frequently used measure of performance for this job (Greener, 1984). Ratings by peers (i.e., other controllers) have also been collected in both research (e.g., Cobb, Nelson, & Mathews, 1973) and operational settings (e.g., Manning, 1991).

Air traffic control simulators with various levels of realism have been used to assess controller performance in dealing with standardized samples of simulated air traffic. It is difficult to compare the performance of controllers from different areas of specialization or different facilities when they are controlling actual or "live" air traffic, because they are likely to control different numbers of aircraft in sectors of airspace that vary in complexity. Simulation allows for standardization of the stimuli presented. In addition, simulators have been developed that provide a high degree of realism both in the stimuli presented (i.e., air traffic scenarios) and in the responses made by examinees (Tucker, 1984).

Some simulation work has been aimed at assessing the performance of the larger air traffic control system and evaluating the effects of changes in procedures or workload on system performance (e.g., Boone, Van Buskirk, & Steen, 1980). Other research has focused more directly on assessing individual controller performance (e.g., Buckley, DeBaryshe, Hitchner, & Kohn, 1983; Buckley, O'Connor, Beebe, Adams, & MacDonald, 1969; Sollenberger, Stein, & Gromelski, 1997). Performance in these simulations has been assessed by collecting computerized information concerning the locations of the simulated aircraft (e.g., separation, the efficiency with which they move through the airspace) and control actions taken by the assessees (e.g., communications with pilots). Performance has also been assessed by trained raters watching "over the shoulder" of the controllers being assessed and providing ratings of their performance. Results indicate that trained observers' ratings of simulator performance are highly related to various aircraft safety and expeditiousness measures (i.e., separation and efficiency; e.g., Buckley et al., 1983).

Part-task simulations have also been used to assess individual controller performance. For example, Buckley and his colleagues developed a motion picture test in which assessees are asked to monitor an evolving air traffic situation on a radar screen and indicate when they first notice a potential confliction, that is, two or more aircraft that will pass dangerously close to each other unless control actions are initiated (Buckley & Beebe, 1972). Although only a few studies have examined correlations between scores on part-task simulations and other measures of performance, these correlations have usually been significant and often substantial (e.g., Buckley, O'Connor, & Beebe, 1969; Milne & Colmen, 1972). In general, these results suggest that a lower-fidelity simulation can capture important air traffic controller judgment and decision-making skills.

Job Simulations and Fidelity

Standardized work samples or job simulations have been used in many contexts as criterion measures of job performance, and some would even argue that a properly constructed work sample measure is the ultimate criterion against which all other criteria should be judged (Green & Wigdor, 1988). An important question regarding these work sample or simulation performance measures is the level of realism or fidelity required. More realistic simulations are likely to provide better measures of individual differences in job performance, but are often expensive and/or time consuming to develop and administer. This makes lower-fidelity simulations an attractive alternative. Motowidlo, Hanson, and Crafts (1997) described the levels of fidelity that can be incorporated in a simulation, ranging from actual job performance to verbal descriptions of job situations with verbal descriptions of responses from the examinees. In general, the fidelity can be viewed as made up of two components: the realism of the situation presented and the fidelity of the examinee responses collected. For example, the work sample interview approach, developed by Hedge and Teachout (1992), involves presenting highly realistic work samples and then simply asking examinees to verbally describe how they would perform the work tasks. This approach provides a high degree of realism in the situation and a lower degree of realism in the responses.

The Situational Judgment Approach

Situational judgment tests present respondents with realistic, job-related situations, usually described in writing. Respondents are asked what should be done to handle each situation effectively. These tests are typically multiple choice. That is, examinees are asked to choose among several possible responses or courses of action for each situation. Thus, this type of situational judgment test approach can be viewed as providing an even lower level of fidelity, and these test are sometimes referred to as low-fidelity simulations (Motowidlo et al., 1997). However, a few situational judgment tests have employed a video format (e.g., Dalessio, 1994). In these tests, respondents are asked to watch a videotaped scenario of actors portraying an evolving situation.

The screen freezes at the point in the situation where the respondent must make a decision. Then, the respondent is asked to choose from a series of either written or videotaped responses. Although research is not available comparing video and written formats for situational judgment tests, the ability of the video format to portray the often subtle and complex nature of interpersonal situations at work offers exciting possibilities. In the Motowidlo et al. framework, the fidelity of the stimulus is enhanced.

Scoring situational judgment tests is not as straightforward as scoring more traditional multiple choice tests. Real life situations are complex, and often there is not one answer that is clearly "correct" while the rest are clearly "wrong." Rather, the possible actions in response to the sort of difficult, job-related situations included in most situational judgment tests vary along a continuum of effectiveness, ranging from very effective to very ineffective. Judgments obtained from job experts concerning the effectiveness of each possible action or response option can be used to assign item-level scores; that is, examinees are assigned the average effectiveness rating of the response they choose as their item-level score. This gives examinees more credit for choosing "wrong" answers that are relatively effective than for choosing wrong answers that are very ineffective. These item-level scores can then be averaged to generate an overall test score. Research has shown that this type of effectiveness weighting can result in more reliable situational judgment test scores than simple number correct scoring (Hanson, 1994), and thus scores with more potential for usefulness.

Situational judgment tests have been found useful primarily for jobs that have large interpersonal components, especially managerial jobs. The type of judgment-based key used to score these tests can be viewed as more accurately reflecting the complexities of responding in difficult interpersonal or managerial situations. Situations typically encountered in the air traffic controller job are quite different from the types of interpersonal situations typically included in situational judgment tests. However, air traffic situations are certainly difficult and complex. In addition, these situations do not typically involve responses that are simply correct or incorrect, but rather responses or courses of action that vary along a continuum of effectiveness. Thus, it seems reasonable to expect that a situational judgment approach would be appropriate for a comparatively low-fidelity simulation of air traffic controller performance.

Role of the CBPM in the AT-SAT Project

Task-based job analysis information (Nickels, Bobko, Blair, Sands, & Tartak, 1995) and a critical incidents study (Hedge, Borman, Hanson, Carter, & Nelson, 1993) were available to guide criterion development efforts in the AT-SAT project. Initial job analysis work suggested a model of air traffic controller performance that included both maximum and typical performance (Bobko, Nickels, Blair, & Tartak, 1994; Nickels et al., 1995). More so than with many jobs, maximum "can-do" performance is very important in controlling air traffic. There are times on this job when the most important consideration is maximum performance—does the controller have the technical skill to keep aircraft separated under very difficult conditions? Nonetheless, typical performance over time is also important for this job. Basically, the plan for AT-SAT criterion development was to develop multiple measures of controller performance.

To tap typical performance over time, a set of rating scales was developed and used to collect performance ratings from peers (i.e., other controllers) and supervisors. The intention here was to develop behavior-based rating scales that would encourage raters to make evaluations as objectively as possible. An approach to accomplish this is to prepare scales with behavioral statements anchoring different effectiveness levels on each dimension so that the rating task is to compare observed ratee behavior with behavior on the scale (Borman, 1979). This matching process should be more objective than, for example, using a 1 = very ineffective to 7 = very effective scale. Ten rating scales were developed, and will be referred to as the Behavior Summary Scales. A second part of this approach was to orient and train raters to use the behavioral statements in the manner intended, and a rater training program was developed to accomplish this. Discussions with controllers in the rating scale development workshops suggested that both supervisors and peers (i.e., fellow controllers) would be appropriate rating sources. Because gathering ratings from relatively large numbers of raters per ratee is advantageous to increase levels of interrater reliability, we requested that two supervisor and two peer raters be asked to contribute ratings for each controller ratee in the study. Administration procedures included training designed to help raters avoid typical rating errors (Pulakos, 1984). Details concerning the development of these rating scales and administration procedures are available in Borman et al. (1998).

Technical skill, especially the ability to keep planes separated even under difficult conditions, is a critical part of the ATCS job, and thus important to include when assessing controller performance. One approach to measuring technical skill is hands-on (i.e., work sample) performance measurement. As discussed previously, standardized hands-on performance measurement in the controller job requires simulation, because the nature of the aircraft controlled and the airspace features cannot be standardized across controllers using a live traffic approach.

The high-fidelity simulation approach to air traffic controller performance measurement is extremely expensive and time consuming. Controllers work with complex equipment and communicate verbally with pilots and other controllers. In addition, there is a great deal of air traffic control job knowledge that is unique to controlling traffic in a specific sector of airspace (e.g., the map, local obstructions). In order to obtain a standardized measure of performance that can be used to compare the technical skills of controllers who normally work in different sectors of airspace, it is necessary to use simulated air traffic problems staged in a single "generic" airspace. This means that sophisticated simulators and multiple test administrators are needed for perform ance measurement, and also for familiarization sessions before performance measurement to allow controllers to learn the generic airspace.

It was not practical to administer such a high-fidelity simulation to the entire concurrent validation sample in the AT-SAT project. Even so, a high-fidelity air traffic control simulation was developed and administered to a relatively small subset of the controllers in this sample in order to evaluate the construct validity of the other criterion measures. The fact that only a subset of the validation sample had scores on this test limited its usefulness for validating the predictors. This test, the High Fidelity Performance Measure or HFPM, required examinees to travel to the location of the simulators (the FAA Academy in Oklahoma City) and participate in 1½ days of training and 1 full day of testing. Details concerning the HFPM can be found in Borman et al. (1998).

The goal in the development of the lower-fidelity CBPM was to measure as many of the most critical tasks performed by controllers as possible, without the expense and administrative difficulties involved in full-scale simulation of the job. In other words, the CBPM was designed to be a practical, economical measure of technical proficiency that could be administered to the entire concurrent validation sample.

DEVELOPMENT OF THE CBPM

Overview of the Approach

Again, the intention in the present effort was to develop a computerized performance test that as closely as possible assessed the very important technical proficiency part of the controller job that involves separating aircraft. Thus, the target performance constructs included judgment and decision making in handling air traffic scenarios, procedural knowledge about how to perform technical tasks, and "confliction prediction" (i.e., the ability to know when a confliction is likely to occur sometime in the near future if nothing is done to address the traffic situation).

The CBPM was basically patterned after the situational judgment test method. However, providing examinees with a verbal description of the situation seemed particularly deficient for the controller job. The evolving air traffic situations controllers face on their jobs would be difficult or impossible to describe verbally (e.g., the positions of aircraft, call signs, the timing of voice communications from pilots). Thus, the plan was to use personal computers (PCs) to administer the test and to incorporate as much realism as possible into the test stimuli. The idea was to have an air traffic scenario appear on the computer screen, allow a little time for the problem to evolve, and then freeze the screen and ask the examinee a multiple-choice question about what he or she would do in response to the problem. A standard PC with a large monitor can be used to provide a very realistic depiction of the radar screens controllers monitor in their daily jobs. A PC can also be used to present audio stimuli (e.g., voice communications from pilots and other controllers, etc.) and to collect examinee responses.

As mentioned previously, there is a great deal of technical knowledge involved in controlling air traffic. Thus, test development required extensive input from air traffic control subject matter experts (SMEs). Three experienced controllers worked closely with the researchers throughout the development and pilot test of the CBPM. Test development involved several phases. First, the content of the evolving scenarios and the test items was developed and refined in a paper-and-pencil format. Second, a preliminary version of the test was computerized. Third, this initial computerized version of the test was reviewed by two groups of SMEs and further refined. Fourth, another group of controller SMEs independently rated the effectiveness of each response option for each test item. Finally, a pilot test was conducted at two Air Route Traffic Control Centers. A final set of revisions was made based on the results of the effectiveness rating workshops and the pilot test before the final CBPM was used as a criterion measure of performance in the AT-SAT concurrent validation study. The following sections provide details concerning each of these five developmental steps.

Developing the CBPM Item Content

Development of the CBPM item content involved the three air traffic control SMEs working closely with psychologists to build difficult situations and test items, along with possible responses that varied in effectiveness. The first issue in developing this test was the airspace in which the test would be staged. There is a great deal of air traffic controller job knowledge that is unique to controlling traffic in a specific airspace (e.g., the map, local obstructions, etc.). As discussed previously, each air traffic controller is trained and certified on the sectors of airspace in which he or she works. Our goal in designing the CBPM airspace was to include a set of airspace features (e.g., flight paths, airports, special use airspaces, etc.) sufficiently complicated to allow for development of difficult, realistic situations or problems, but to also keep the airspace relatively simple, because it is important that controllers who take the CBPM learn these features very quickly. Figure 10.1 shows the map of the CBPM airspace and Fig. 10.2 is a summary of important features of this airspace that do not appear on the map.

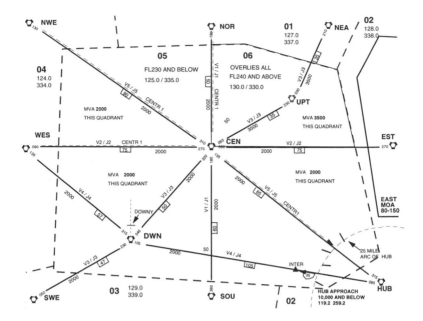

FIG. 10.1. Map of the CBPM Airspace.

1. True north and magnetic north are the same.

2. There is an airport co-located with each displayed Navaid _except_ CEN. There are three primary airports:

Uptown: UPT	Downtown: DWN	Hubsville: HUB
FSS only.	VFR tower.	Hubsville approach owns 10,000 and below.
IFR approach is VOR for RWY 27.	IFR approach is ILS to RWY 18. IAF is DOWNY.	STAR: north, northwest, & west. Jet arrivals via CENTR1cross at 11,000 @ 250 knots, propellors cross at 10,000; HUB's control on contact. Departures via V4/J4 climb to 10,000; your control on contact.
Missed approach altitude is 3500.	Missed approach altitiude is 2000.	

3. "DPT" indicates a departure from outside depicted airspace; "DESTN" indicates an arrival at an airport outside depicted airspace.

4. Tick marks on CENTR1 arrival are 10 miles apart, and airways start 5 miles from the Navaids.

5. Each full data block has a one minute velocity vector and three histories.

FIG. 10.2. Summary of important features of CBPM Airspace.

206

After the airspace was designed, the three air traffic SMEs were provided with detailed instructions concerning the types of scenarios and questions appropriate for this type of test. These SMEs then developed several air traffic scenarios on paper and multiple-choice items for each scenario. The plan was to generate many more items than would be needed on the final test, and then select a subset of the best items later in the test development process. Also, based on the job analysis (Nickels et al., 1995), a list of the 40 most critical en route air traffic controller tasks was available, and one primary goal in item development was to measure performance in as many of these tasks as possible, especially those that were rated most critical.

At this stage, each scenario included a map depicting the position of each aircraft at the beginning of the scenario, flight strips providing detailed information about each aircraft (e.g., the intended route of flight), a status information area (describing weather and other pertinent background information), and a script describing how the scenario would unfold. This script included the timing and content of voice communications from pilots and/or controllers, radar screen updates (which occur every 10 seconds in the en route environment), other events (e.g., hand-offs, the appearance of unidentified radar targets, emergencies, etc.), and the exact timing and wording of each multiple-choice question (along with possible responses). For example, a scenario could begin with 10 aircraft (i.e., radar targets) displayed. After a few moments, a pilot's voice could be heard making initial contact. The first question then might ask the controller what should be said in response to this pilot communication. A second question could ask what altitude this aircraft should be assigned. After the situation has evolved a little further, the controller might be asked how he or she would sequence arrivals into one of the displayed airports.

After the controllers had independently generated a large number of scenarios and items, we conducted discussion sessions in which each SME presented his scenarios and items, and then the SMEs and researchers discussed and evaluated these items. Discussion included topics such as whether all necessary information was included, whether the distractors were plausible, whether or not there were "correct" or at least better responses, whether the item was too tricky (i.e., choosing the most effective response did not reflect an important skill), or too easy (i.e., the correct response was obvious), and whether the item was fair for all facilities (e.g., might the item be answered differently at different facilities because of different policies or procedures?). As mentioned previously, the CBPM was patterned after the situational judgment test approach. Unlike other multiple choice tests, there was not necessarily only one correct answer, with all the others being wrong. Some items had, for example, one best answer, and one or two others that represented fairly effective responses. These test development sessions resulted in a total of 30 scenarios and 99 items, with between 2 and 6 items per scenario.

Computerizing the Scenarios

A "radar engine" was available that had been previously developed for the FAA for training purposes. This software tool allows programmers to develop fictitious sectors of airspace and display the resulting radar screens on a standard PC. The radar engine also depicts the movement of aircraft (i.e., radar targets with data blocks) on these radar screens with a fairly high degree of realism. The CBPM scenarios were initially programmed using this radar engine. Once the scenarios had been programmed into the radar engine, the SMEs watched the scenarios evolve on the PC and made modifications as necessary to meet the measurement goals.

After realistic positioning and movement of the aircraft had been achieved, the test itself was programmed using Authorware (Macromedia, 1995). Authorware was chosen for several reasons. It is one of the leading authoring environments for computer-based training. Authorware is also a program that the FAA uses for training program development. Finally, it allows for straightforward integration of graphics, audio, and user interaction into a single program. In order to maximize the fidelity of the final test and achieve accurate positioning and movement of the aircraft, screens were output from the radar engine into Authorware. Graphics were then created in Authorware with the radar engine screens as a background. The Authorware program was then used to present the radar screens, voice communications, and multiple choice questions, and also to collect the multiple choice responses. The audio portions of the program were recorded directly into the computer, using a professional microphone. An audio editing package was used to add background noise where appropriate (e.g., to the pilot communications).

The test was programmed to run on a standard PC with Pentium processor, a 17" high-resolution monitor, and a standard keyboard. This platform was chosen for two reasons. First, this is the platform that was used for the predictor measures in the AT-SAT validation study, so it was a practical choice. Second, the large monitor was needed to realistically depict the display as it would appear on an en route radar screen. Finally, the completed program was written to a CD-ROM, so a CD drive is also needed for administration.

However, not all of the information concerning these scenarios was presented via computer. Flight strips are normally available in a paper format on the controller job, so it seemed most appropriate that flight strips be provided in a paper format for our test as well. Similarly, the map of the airspace is displayed above the radar display on the actual job, so it seemed most appropriate to include this map in a paper format as well. Thus, the flight strips and status information areas were compiled into a booklet, with one page per scenario. Typing stands were used to display these "bays" of flight strips and the sector map near the computer during test administration. Although the format and positioning of these items was not identical to that found on the job, an effort was made to keep them functionally equivalent (i.e., the controller could easily glance over at the map or down at the flight strips while monitoring the radar display). Controllers were provided with scratch paper for taking notes, and asked not to make markings on the booklet of flight strips (so they could be reused).

During test administration, controllers are given up to 60 seconds to review each scenario before it begins. During this time, the frozen radar display appears on the computer screen, and examinees are allowed to review the flight strips and any other information they believe is relevant to that particular scenario (e.g., the map or airspace summary). The scenarios themselves are generally short in duration, lasting at most a couple of minutes. Once the test items have been presented, respondents are given 25 seconds to answer each question. This is analogous to the controller job, where controllers are expected to "get the picture" concerning what is going on in their sector of airspace, and then sometimes required to react quickly to evolving air traffic control situations. The controllers who developed the CBPM items discussed and agreed on 25 seconds as a reasonable amount of time to make the sort of decisions required in the CBPM. The CBPM radar screen remains displayed while controllers are choosing their response to each question, again to be as consistent as possible with the actual job requirements. Examinees are asked to press the letter corresponding to their response on the keyboard and then either confirm that response by pressing *enter* or choose a different response if they wish. Once they have chosen a response (or time has expired), examinees are not allowed to return to previous items or scenarios to review information or change their answers.

A training module was included at the beginning of the test to familiarize test takers with the airspace and to provide detailed instructions concerning how to take the test. As mentioned previously, an effort was made to keep the airspace features simple. We did not want performance on the test to be unduly affected by memorization ability. The orientation to the airspace provided in the training module is very thorough and includes all important information about the airspace (e.g., arrival routes, letters of agreement with adjacent facilities, etc.). In addition, we provided all of this important information concerning the airspace on the sector map (described previously) or in the airspace summary, which is also displayed near the computer during test administration. One practice scenario was also included at the beginning of the test, to ensure that examinees become familiar with test taking procedures.

Another potential confound was reading ability. The scenarios themselves are presented using a radar display and spoken verbal communications, but the items and response options are in a written format. In order to minimize the effect of reading ability on test scores, each item and the associated response options are read aloud. The response options appear as they are read aloud, and examinees are not allowed to choose an answer until all responses have appeared. We were initially concerned that examinees would want to read ahead and might find the voice annoying or confusing. However, the feedback from controllers was generally positive. This could have been at least partly due to the fact that we used a professional "voice" that was very pleasant sounding.

Refining the CBPM Items

After preparing these materials, we gathered a panel of four experienced controllers who were teaching at the FAA Academy and another panel of five experienced controllers from several different field facilities to review the scenarios and items. Specifically, each of these groups was briefed regarding the project, trained on the airspace, and then shown each of the scenarios and items. Their task was to rate the effectiveness of each response option for each item. Ratings were made independently on a scale from 1 to 7. The first two columns in Table 10.1 summarize the intraclass correlation interrater agreement across items for the two groups.

TABLE 10.1
CBPM Scaling Workshops: Interrater Reliability Results

	Number of Items			
Level of Reliability[a]	Initial Scaling Group 1 (N = 4)	Initial Scaling Group 2 (N = 5)	Final Scaling Participants (N = 12)	Scoring Key for 84 Item CBPM (N = 12)
Reliability < 10	9	7		
Between .10 and .19	1	4		
Between .20 and .29	3	1		
Between .30 and .39	4	2		
Between .40 and .49	4	8	5	1
Between .50 and .59	1	3	1	
Between .60 and .69	8	7	1	
Between .70 and .79	10	12	7	1
Between .80 and .89	18	26	22	13
Reliability > .90	41	29	58	46
Total Number of Items	99	99	94	61[b]

[a]Reliabilities are k-rater intraclass correlation coefficients; these coefficients reflect the reliability of the mean ratings. [b]61 of the 84 CBPM items are scored based on panel effectiveness ratings; the 23 remaining items were either knowledge, "confliction prediction," or memory items and effectiveness weights were not used in scoring.

After this initial rating session with each of the groups, the panel members compared their independent ratings and discussed discrepancies. In general, two different outcomes occurred as a result of these discussions. In some cases one or two panel members failed to notice or misinterpreted part of the item (e.g., did not examine a very important flight strip). For these cases, generally no changes were made to the item. In other cases, there was a legitimate disagreement about the effectiveness of one or more response options. Here, we typically discussed revisions to the item or the scenario itself that would lead to agreement between panel members (without making the item overly transparent). In addition, discussions with the first group indicated that several items were too easy (i.e., the answer was obvious). These items were revised to be less obvious. Five items were dropped because they could not be satisfactorily revised. These ratings and the subsequent discussions resulted in substantial revisions to the CBPM. These revisions were accomplished in preparation for a final review of the CBPM by one additional panel of SMEs.

Developing a Scoring Key

For this final review session, 12 controllers from several different field facilities were identified who had extensive experience as air traffic controllers, and had spent time as either trainers or supervisors. The final panel was also briefed on the project and the CBPM and then reviewed each item. Recall that during the previous workshops there was some disagreement in the ratings because one or two panel members had failed to notice or misinterpreted part of an item. In order to ensure that this type of misunderstanding did not influence the final scoring key, short briefings were prepared for each item highlighting the most important pieces of information. These briefings were designed to highlight key information that impacted the effectiveness of the various responses. It is possible that including the item briefings biased this final panel of judges or somewhat inflated the interrater reliability, but it seemed more important to ensure that the scoring key was based on an accurate and complete understanding of each situation. Each member of the panel independently rated the effectiveness level of each response option. This group did not review each other's ratings or discuss the items.

Interrater agreement data for this final group appear in the third column of Table 10.1. These results are quite impressive. The agreement certainly improved for the revised CBPM. Five items were dropped because there was still a great deal of disagreement among raters. These final scaling data were used to score the CBPM. For each item, examinees are assigned the mean effectiveness of the response option they choose, with a few exceptions. First, 9 items actually tapped knowledge of air traffic control procedures, and for these knowledge items, there was actually one correct response. Similarly, for the 11 "confliction prediction" items, there was one correct response. In addition, it is arguably more effective to predict a confliction when there is not one (i.e., be conservative) than to fail to predict a confliction when there is one. Thus, a higher score was assigned for an incorrect conservative response than an incorrect response that predicted no confliction when one would have occurred. Finally, there were 3 items that tapped memory of events occurring earlier in the scenario. The controller SMEs generated rational keys for these 23 knowledge, confliction prediction, and memory items. The last column of Table 10.1 shows the reliability results for just those effectiveness ratings that were used in the CBPM scoring key. These latter items can be viewed as measuring judgment concerning how to respond effectively in difficult air traffic control situations. Finally, if examinees do not respond to an item (i.e., the time expires and a response has not been made), they are assigned the lowest possible score for that item (i.e., the score assigned to the least effective response option).

Conducting a Pilot Test

The CBPM and the performance rating program were pilot tested at two FAA Air Route Traffic Control Centers: Seattle and Salt Lake City. Administration materials were prepared and two criterion research teams traveled to the pilot test sites. Data were gathered on a total of 77 controllers at the two locations. Test administrators asked pilot test participants for their reactions to the CBPM, and many of them reported that the situations were realistic and like those that occurred on their jobs. In general, procedures for administering these two assessment measures proved to be effective.

Results for the CBPM are presented in Table 10.2. The distribution of total scores was promising in the sense that there was variability in the scores. The internal consistency (coefficient α) was moderate, as we might expect from a

TABLE 10.2
CBPM Pilot Test Results

Percentage of Maximum Score	Number of Controllers
69% or lower	1
70%–74%	1
75%–79%	9
80%–84%	36
85%–89%	28
90% or higher	2

Note. $N = 77$; mean score (i.e., percentage) = 84.4; standard deviation = 4.0; coefficient α reliability = .53.

test that is likely multidimensional. Based on the pilot test results, one additional CBPM item was dropped because it had a negative item-total score correlation. That is, controllers who answered this item correctly tended to have low total CBPM scores. In addition, for some CBPM items, a fair number of controllers in the pilot test sample "timed out" without providing a response. Lengthening the time allowed to respond to each item was considered but rejected, because we wanted to measure the ability to react quickly to evolving air traffic control situations. In order to ensure that controllers did not accidentally time out because they were not watching the time, we added an audio chime to warn examinees when they have only 5 seconds remaining to respond. We also lengthened the time allowed to review the scenario/flight strips for the example item, to make sure examinees had plenty of time to become familiar with the test-taking process.

DESCRIPTION OF THE CBPM TEST

The final CBPM is basically a situational judgment-type test. Figure 10.3 shows an example of a CBPM item. This test presents difficult, realistic air

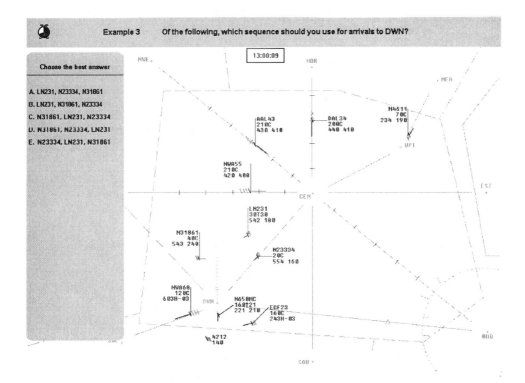

FIG. 10.3.   Example of CBPM item.

traffic control situations on a simulated radar screen, and asks controllers to answer several multiple choice questions concerning each situation. Each situation shows an evolving air traffic scenario. Some situations include voice communications from pilots and other controllers and some provide multiple updates of the radar screen (i.e., the aircraft move). Each situation has a series of flight strips that show the positions of the radar targets and their intended flight paths and a status information area that provides weather and other relevant information. An airspace map and a summary of important airspace features are displayed near the computer during administration. The final CBPM is made up of 29 scenarios and 84 test items. One of the original 30 scenarios and the 4 items associated with it were used as an example (and not scored in the final test).

The CBPM runs off a CD-ROM on a standard personal computer with a 17" monitor. Responses are collected in a multiple choice format. Thus, the CBPM is essentially self-administering. In fact, at one point the program asks the examinee to confirm that the supporting materials (i.e., flight strips, map, airspace summary, etc.) are available near the computer. Examinees are allowed to take as many breaks as needed, but required to take breaks only at specified points in the program (i.e., between scenarios). The CD administration allowed for test security, because the CD can be removed and kept in a secure location.

CONSTRUCT VALIDITY OF THE CBPM

The CBPM was administered to a total of 1,046 controllers in the AT-SAT concurrent validation sample. Time to complete the test ranged from less than 1 hour to almost 2 hours, with an average time of about 1.5 hours. Performance ratings for a total of 1,227 controllers, including 1,043 of the controllers who completed the CBPM, were provided by 535 supervisor and 1,420 peer raters. Table 10.3 shows the number of supervisors and peers rating each controller. For a sample of 107 of the controllers in the validation sample, scores were also available on the high-fidelity simulation of controller performance (the HFPM). Briefly, these controllers spent 1½ days becoming familiar with a simulated generic airspace, and 1 day having their ability to control traffic in this environment tested. Scores for the HFPM consisted primarily of "over the shoulder" ratings of performance made by trained observers. More detail concerning the concurrent validation results for the Behavior Summary Statement ratings and the HFPM is available in Borman et al. (1999).

Table 10.4 shows the distribution of CBPM scores for the concurrent validation sample. As with the pilot sample, there is a reasonable amount of variability. Also, item-total score correlations ranged from .01 to .27 (mean = .11). The coefficient α was .63 for this 84 item test. The relatively low item-total correlations and the modest coefficient α suggest that the CBPM is measuring more than a single construct.

TABLE 10.3

Number of Behavior Summary Statement Ratings Obtained
for Participants in AT-SAT Concurrent Validation

Number of Supervisor Raters/Ratee	N	Number of Peer Raters/Ratee	N	Total Number of Raters/Ratee	N
0	33	0	74	1	40
1	92	1	87	2	79
2	1,064	2	1,044	3	93
3	34	3	21	4	974
4	4	4	1	5	39
				6	2

Note. Mean number of supervisor raters per ratee = 1.90. Mean number of peer raters per ratee = 1.82. Mean total number of raters per ratee = 3.73.

TABLE 10.4

CBPM: Distribution of Scores
in AT-SAT Concurrent Validation Sample

Percentage of Maximum Score	Number of Controllers
69% or lower	5
70%–74%	35
75%–79%	214
80%–84%	490
85%–89%	280
90% or higher	22

Note. $N = 1,046$; mean score (i.e., percentage) = 82.68; standard deviation = 4.17; coefficient α reliability = .63.

Table 10.5 depicts the relationships between scores on the 84-item CBPM, the supervisor/peer Behavior Summary Statement ratings, and a "Core Technical Proficiency" score from the HFPM. This latter score is the average HFPM rating across several different over-the-shoulder rating scales across several different scenarios. Factor analysis indicated that the Behavior Summary Statement performance rating data could be summarized by forming

TABLE 10.5

Intercorrelations Between AT-SAT Criterion Scores

| | Performance Ratings (Behavior Summary Statements) | | | CBPM | HFPM |
	Technical Performance	Technical Effort	Teamwork	Total Score (84 items)	Core Technical Proficiency
Performance Ratings					
Technical Performance	(.94)				
Technical Effort	.78**	(.88)			
Teamwork	.60**	.63**	—		
CBPM					
Total Score (84 items)	.19**	.24**	.13**	(.62)	
HFPM					
Core Technical Proficiency	.47**	.28**	.10	.50**	(.89)

Note. Sample sizes for correlations involving the HFPM range from 106 to 107; sample sizes for remaining correlations range from 1,043 to 1,227. Internal consistency reliabilities appear on the diagonal.

*p < .05, one tailed. **p < .01, one tailed.

three composites. The first composite was labeled Technical Performance, and is made up of ratings on rating scales labeled Maintaining Safe and Efficient Air Traffic Flow, Prioritizing, Managing Multiple Tasks, Reacting to Stress, and Adaptability and Flexibility. The second composite, labeled Technical Effort, is made up of ratings on Maintaining Attention and Vigilance, Communicating and Informing, Coordinating, and Technical Knowledge. The final composite is made up of a single rating scale: Teamwork. Controller scores on these composites were averaged over raters, across peers and supervisors, and across the rating scales included. The interrater reliabilities of three composites are .72, .69, and .63, respectively.

Regarding Table 10.5, first, the correlation between the CBPM total score and the HFPM Core Technical Proficiency score, arguably our purest measure of technical proficiency, is .50. This provides strong evidence for the construct validity of the CBPM. Apparently, this lower-fidelity measure of technical proficiency taps much the same technical skills as the HFPM, which had controllers working in an environment highly similar to their actual job setting.

Correlations between the Behavior Summary Statement ratings and the CBPM are as expected. Ratings on the technical proficiency categories relate moderately with the CBPM, with the correlation between Teamwork and the CBPM total score being lower. Overall, there is impressive evidence that the CBPM and the ratings measure the criterion domains they were targeted to measure.

In order to assess the extent to which the CBPM taps the intended content domain, a panel of 10 controller SMEs was asked to perform a judgment task with the 84 CBPM items. These controllers were divided into three groups, and each group was responsible for approximately one third of the 40 critical tasks that were targeted by the CBPM. They reviewed each CBPM scenario and the items, and indicated which of these important tasks from the job analysis were involved in each item. These ratings were then discussed by the entire group until a consensus was reached. Results of this judgment task show that the CBPM taps 39 of the 40 most critical tasks, with the one task not measured ranking 19th in criticality.

At this point, and as planned, we examined individual CBPM items and their relations to the other criteria, with the intention of dropping items that were not contributing to the desired relationships. For this step, we reviewed the item-total score correlations, and CBPM item correlations with the HFPM score and the rating categories. Items with very low or negative correlations with total CBPM scores, the HFPM score, and the first two rating category composites were considered for exclusion from the final CBPM scoring system. Also considered were the links to important tasks. Items representing one or more highly important tasks were given additional consideration for inclusion in the final composite. These criteria were applied concurrently and in a compensatory manner. Thus, for example, a quite low item-total score correlation might be offset by a high correlation with HFPM scores.

This item review process resulted in 38 items being retained for the final CBPM scoring system. The resulting CBPM composite has a coefficient α of .61 and correlates .60 with the HFPM Core Technical Proficiency score, and .21, .26, and .14 with the three rating categories. Thus, the final composite is related more strongly to HFPM performance and correlates a bit more highly with the two technical rating categories. We believe this final CBPM composite has even better construct validity in relation to the other criterion measures than did the total test, and this 38-item composite was used in validation analyses for the AT-SAT experimental selection battery (Ramos, 1999).

CONCLUSIONS

The CBPM demonstrates the ability of personal computers to simulate important decision-making processes in a highly technical job, by presenting a realistic set of stimulus materials. The multiple-choice response format lacks fidelity, but the use of a situational judgment test approach allows this test to capture the important judgment and decision-making aspects of the air traffic controller job at a relatively low cost.

The 38-item CBPM composite provides a very good measure of the technical skills necessary to separate aircraft effectively and efficiently on the "real job." Its .60 correlation with the highly realistic HFPM is especially supportive of its construct validity for measuring performance in the very important technical proficiency-related part of the job. Additional ties to the actual controller job are provided by the links of CBPM items to the most important controller tasks identified in the job analysis.

The CBPM was designed to serve as a criterion measure of job performance in a concurrent validation study for an experimental selection battery. Thus, the goal was to develop a practical, economical measure of technical proficiency that measures as many of the most critical tasks performed by controllers as possible. Clearly, this goal was achieved. Practical measurement of technical proficiency has many other potential uses as well, including certification of competence, promotion decisions, and identification of training needs.

ACKNOWLEDGMENTS

The authors thank Nick Atiyeh and Skip Miller from Performance Technologies International, who programmed the CBPM test. We also thank Paul DeBenneditis and Marc McKinney for their tireless efforts as air traffic control subject matter experts in developing the CBPM. We also acknowledge several researchers from Personnel Decisions Research Institutes (PDRI) who contributed to this effort: Ken T. Bruskiewicz, who helped develop the High Fidelity Performance Measure used in this research; and Laura B. Bunch and Kristen

E. Horgen, who conducted the analyses. Finally, we are grateful to Phil Bobko and Ed Buckley, who provided crucial guidance and insight at many stages in this research.

REFERENCES

Bobko, P., Nickels, B. J., Blair, M. D., & Tartak, E. L. (1994). *Preliminary internal report on the current status of the SACHA model and task interconnections: Volume I.* Bethesda, MD: University Research Corporation.

Boone, J., Van Buskirk, L., & Steen, J. (1980). *The Federal Aviation Administration's radar training facility and employee selection and training* (FAA-AM-80-15). Washington, DC: U. S. Department of Transportation, Federal Aviation Administration, Office of Aviation Medicine.

Borman, W. C. (1979). Format and training effects on rating accuracy and rater errors. *Journal of Applied Psychology, 64,* 410–421.

Borman, W. C., Hedge, J. W., Hanson, M. A., Bruskiewicz, K. T., Mogilka, H. J., Manning, C., Bunch, L. B., & Horgen, K. E. (1999). Development of criterion measures of Air Traffic Controller performance. In B. Ramos (Ed.), *Air Traffic Selection and Training (AT-SAT) final report.* Federal Aviation Administration. Manuscript in preparation.

Buckley, E. P., & Beebe, T. (1972). *The development of a motion picture measurement instrument for aptitude for air traffic control* (FAA-RD-71-106). Washington, DC: U.S. Department of Transportation, Federal Aviation Administration, Systems Research and Development Service.

Buckley, E. P., DeBaryshe, B. D., Hitchner, N., & Kohn, P. (1983). *Methods and measurements in real-time air traffic control system simulation* (DOT/FAA/CT-83/26). Atlantic City, NJ: DOT/FAA Technical Center.

Buckley, E. P., O'Connor, W. F., & Beebe, T. (1969). *A comparative analysis of individual and system performance indices for the air traffic control system (Final report)* (NA-69-40; RD-69-50; Government accession #710795). Atlantic City, NJ: Department of Transportation, Federal Aviation Administration, National Aviation Facilities Experimental Center, Systems Research and Development Service.

Buckley, E. P., O'Connor, W. F., Beebe, T., Adams, W., & MacDonald, G. (1969). *A comparative analysis of individual and system performance indices for the air traffic control system* (NA-69-40). Atlantic City, NJ: DOT/FAA Technical Center.

Cobb, B. B., Nelson, P. L., & Mathews, J. J. (1973). *The relationship of age and ATC experience to job performance ratings of terminal area traffic controllers* (FAA-AM-73-7). Washington, DC: U. S. Department of Transportation, Federal Aviation Administration, Office of Aviation Medicine.

Dalessio A. T. (1994). Predicting insurance agent turnover using a video-based situational judgment test. *Journal of Business and Psychology, 9,* 23–32.

Green, B. F., & Wigdor, A. K. (Eds.). (1988). *Measuring job competency: Report of the Committee on the Performance of Military Personnel National Research Council.* Washington, DC: National Academy Press.

Greener, J. M. (1984). Post-training criterion measures in validation of controller selection procedures. In S. B. Sells, J. T. Dailey, & E. W. Pickrel (Eds.), *Selection of air traffic controllers* (FAA-AM-84-2; pp. 241–262). Washington, DC: U.S. Department of Transportation, Federal Aviation Administration, Office of Aviation Medicine.

Hanson, M. A. (1994). *Development and construct validation of a Situational Judgment Test of Supervisory Effectiveness for first-line supervisors in the U. S. Army*. Unpublished doctoral dissertation, University of Minnesota, Minneapolis.

Hedge, J. W., Borman, W. C., Hanson, M. A., Carter, G. W., & Nelson, L. C. (1993). *Progress toward development of ATCS performance criterion measures* (Institute Report #235). Minneapolis, MN: Personnel Decisions Research Institutes.

Hedge, J. W., & Teachout, M. S. (1992). An interview approach to work sample criterion measurement. *Journal of Applied Psychology, 77*, 453–461.

Macromedia. (1997). *Macromedia Authorware 4.0*. San Francisco, CA: Author.

Manning, C. A. (1991). *Relationships between performance in air traffic control specialist technical training and supervisory selection programs*. Paper presented at the 6th Annual Meeting of the Society for Industrial and Organizational Psychology, St. Louis, MO.

Mead, A. D., & Drasgow, F. (1993). Equivalence of computerized and paper-and-pencil cognitive ability tests: A meta-analysis. *Psychological Bulletin, 114*, 449–458.

Milne, A. M., & Colmen, J. (1972). *Selection of air traffic controllers for FAA*. Washington, DC: EPA (Education and Public Affairs, Inc.) (Contract #DOT=FA7OWA-2371).

Motowidlo, S. J., Hanson, M. A., & Crafts, J. L. (1997). Low-fidelity simulations. In D. L. Whetzel & G. R Wheaton (Eds.), *Applied measurement methods in industrial psychology*. Palo Alto, CA: Consulting Psychologists Press.

Nickels, B. J., Bobko, P., Blair, M. D., Sands, W. A., & Tartak, E. L. (1995). *Separation and Control Hiring Assessment (SACHA), final job analysis report*. Bethesda, MD: University Research Corporation.

Peterson, N. G., Hough, L. M., Dunnette, M. D., Rosse, R. L., Houston, J. S., Toquam, J. L., & Wing, H. (1990). Project A: Specification of the predictor domain and development of new selection/classification tests. *Personnel Psychology, 43*, 247–276.

Pulakos, E. D. (1984). A comparison of rater training programs: Error training and accuracy training. *Journal of Applied Psychology, 69*, 581–588.

Ramos, B. (Ed.) (1999). *Air Traffic Selection and Training (AT-SAT) final report*. Federal Aviation Administration. Manuscript in preparation.

Schmitt, N., Gilliland, S. W., Landis, R. S., & Devine, D. (1993). Computer-based testing applied to selection of secretarial applicants. *Personnel Psychology, 46*, 149–165.

Sollenberger, R. L., Stein, E. S., & Gromelski, S. (1997). *The development and evaluation of a behaviorally based rating form for assessing air traffic controller performance* (DOT/FAA/CT-TN96-16). Atlantic City, NJ: DOT/FAA Technical Center.

Tucker, J. A. (1984). Development of dynamic paper-and-pencil simulations for measurement of air traffic controller proficiency. In S. B. Sells, J. T. Dailey, & E. W. Pickrel (Eds.), *Selection of air traffic controllers* (FAA-AM-84-2; pp. 215–241). Washington, DC: DOT/FAA/OAM.

11

Easing the Implementation of Behavioral Testing Through Computerization

Wayne A. Burroughs
Janet Murray
S. Scott Wesley
Debra R. Medina
Stacy L. Penn
Steven R. Gordon
Michael Catello
Wilson Learning Corporation, Orlando, FL

The growth objectives of corporations today are astounding. After more than a decade of downsizing to improve productivity and efficiency, companies are determined to seize opportunities for substantial growth and to stake out an increased share of the markets of the future. The trend toward growth is liberating after the reductionist mid-1980s and 1990s, but the pace, complexity, unpredictability, and sheer aggression of the competitive environment are unprecedented (D'Aveni, 1994). The ability of corporations to grow in this turbulent and uncertain environment rests squarely on the ability of their human assets to carry out shifting and increasingly sophisticated organizational strategies. The balance of strategic leverage in organizations today has migrated from planning to *execution*. What corporations need are engaged, accountable, and skilled employees who understand the big picture strategy and are willing to

221

invest the discretionary effort and energy to personalize it and make it happen. Yet, downsizing has taken an enormous toll on the intellectual and emotional energy that employees are willing to commit to their work. What employees hear is that they are the company's most valuable resource; what they have learned is that they are the most expendable.

What does any of this have to do with innovations in computerized assessment? First, it defines the context in which employee assessment is now conducted. Second, it is a driving force for continued innovation in assessment methodologies. As companies move from strategy planning to strategy execution, it is imperative that they select, develop, and promote employees well. Individuals who provide and conduct assessments must step up to the challenge of selecting the best people, developing those who have the most promise, promoting those who are most capable, and doing all of this faster and with fewer resources. In the lean organizations of the 1990s and beyond, mistakes in employee assessment cannot be easily overcome. Put simply, there is no one on the bench to come in for a poorly performing starter. Thus, there is now, more than ever, a compelling business reason for reliable, valid, and cost-effective assessments. The opportunity for innovation is beating at the practitioner's door.

The lean organization has also expanded the roles that employees must play. Employees must be more than technical specialists. They must exhibit a considerable behavioral range as well. Knowledge workers need to be skilled in communication, collaboration, leadership, decision making, adaptability, and planning.

If these are important skills for employment, then the assessment question is how they should be measured. The easy answer is that these behavioral skills should be measured *behaviorally*. Organizational researchers have found that assessment centers effectively meet this need. An assessment center typically consists of a set of exercises designed to assess a variety of skills related to job performance. It usually contains simulation exercises, in which some important aspect of the job is portrayed in a situation to the participant. Simulation exercises often involve role plays, in which the participant interacts with one or more individuals. Another common assessment center exercise is the in-basket, in which the participant analyzes various documents such as letters, memos, facsimiles, e-mail, reports, and charts and takes action on the issues embedded therein. If the definition of behavioral skills is broadened to include behavioral intentions, then behavioral judgment assessments (e.g., situational judgment tests, audio- and video-based tests) are also appropriate tools for assessing behavioral skills.

As practitioners know, behavioral testing can be both costly and highly labor intensive. For example, the traditional approach to conducting assessment centers often requires assessors to work 12 to 14 hours each day of an assessment center administration cycle (usually 2 to 3 days in succession). Moreover, the training period for new assessors typically involves 4 to 5 days of similarly intense work. Behavioral judgment tests, although they afford some economy in operation, can be just as labor intensive and costly to develop.

The traditional assessment center approach includes other challenges, which are directly and indirectly associated with this labor intensity. First, and perhaps most important to the assessee, is the lag time between assessment and feedback. With a traditional approach, feedback may be provided a week or even a month after the assessment. The developmental value of the assessment deteriorates as the lag time increases (Bernardin & Beatty, 1983; Mosel, 1961). In addition to time, quality is an important consideration for feedback. It can be very difficult to ensure a high level of quality and consistency in written feedback reports. The feedback must be tied both to the actual performance during the assessment center and to specific developmental activities that the individual can engage in afterward.

To accomplish this in a consistent fashion for multiple assessees, both within and across assessment center administrations, the observers must adhere to strict guidelines for writing the reports, and extensive quality control measures must be applied. This check-and-balance process adds significantly to the cost, labor, and time involved in the center. Finally, there is the issue of data integration and subsequent interpretation. When multiple exercises or varied formats are used in an assessment center, the observers must integrate the data for each assessee. To ensure that process is fair, the integration must be done consistently for each candidate. The integrated data must then be consistently interpreted and linked to appropriate feedback. This is made even more complicated when multiple assessors are involved in the integration and interpretation.

These issues became apparent to professionals in the assessment center business over 10 years ago. At Wilson Learning Corporation, we decided then that what organizations and assessment center practitioners needed was a way to streamline the entire process without sacrificing the quality of the experience or the validity of the technique. At that time, computerization seemed like the ultimate panacea. It was, and it was not. Over the years, Wilson Learning has also developed other technology-aided judgment assessments (e.g., video and audio tests, computerized simulations). In this chapter, we describe what we have discovered in developing computer-based and technology-aided behavioral assessment systems. We also describe how our clients have benefited from these computer-aided assessment systems, and some future directions that take the current business climate into consideration.

DEVELOPMENT OF COMPUTERIZED
BEHAVIORAL TESTING SYSTEMS

We started developing computer-based behavioral testing because our clients wanted to have the capability to understand and predict criterion (job) behavior in more economical ways. Time and money were extremely important. In conceptualizing this process of streamlining behavioral testing, we considered three basic questions:

1. How will the stimulus material be presented?
2. How will the behavioral response be captured?
3. How will the behavioral response be scored?

In attempting to answer these questions, we uncovered three more fundamental underlying issues:

1. What do people do best?
2. What do machines do best?
3. What is practical or what makes sense for this application?

The practicality issue cannot be ignored. Consider, for example, a bank that hires 3,000 tellers annually. Here, the use of a traditional assessment center or even a live simulation may not be practical. To hire 3,000 tellers, the bank might need to evaluate 8,000 candidates. The overriding issue becomes how to quickly measure this number at a reasonable price. In such a case, the stimulus would probably best be presented by means of a paper-and-pencil or video-based test. To capture their behavior, candidates would likely be asked to select from alternative answers to multiple choice questions. Their responses would be processed, scored, and reported by computer. The practicality requirements of the situation dictate these approaches. There is room for creativity in the process, but certain options are eliminated by the constraints of the business problem.

Consider the conceptual process for computerizing a traditional assessment center. In contrast to the bank teller example, suppose an organization has been assessing approximately 200 supervisors and managers each year for purposes of development. The process is labor intensive but the organization sees great value in the live, real-time simulation mode of stimulus presentation (high-stimulus fidelity). This organization also wants to capture candidates' actual behavior in writing reports, interacting with others, and making oral presentations (high-response fidelity). For both financial and developmental reasons, the organization is using higher level employees as assessors. To increase efficiency in this scenario, we must decide what people (assessors) do best and what computers do best in this process.

Deciding What People Do Best

Assuming that we have developed the assessment center exercises from a thorough job analysis and have accurately clustered the job tasks into competencies, that we have developed detailed lists of behaviors or standards of performance to aid in the evaluation process, and that we have trained assessors and they are prepared to assess candidates, then we can turn our attention to the operation of the assessment center. The following list represents the chronological flow of activities in a traditional assessment center:

- Assessors observe candidates during simulation exercises and take notes to document behavior.
- Assessors use their notes to complete exercise reports. (Usually the report is a detailed list of behaviors exhibited during the exercise or a narrative report summarizing the behaviors).
- Assessors rate the candidates' performance in each competency measured in the exercise to complete the exercise reports.
- The assessor team, typically three people, meets to review the candidates' performance and to reach consensus on assigned ratings. This process usually takes 45 to 90 minutes for each candidate and includes:
  - Reading each exercise report aloud.
  - Listening for evidence to support assigned ratings.
  - Considering all the exercises to determine an overall rating for each competency (typically done first independently and then as a team).
- Assessors individually prepare for face-to-face feedback sessions with their assigned candidates. This preparation usually takes 30 minutes per candidate.
- Assessors conduct individual feedback sessions for candidates, which typically require 1 hour each.
- Assessors summarize each candidate's performance in a written final report that requires an additional 2 to 3 hours.

Which of these activities do *people* do best? The strength of the assessment center process lies in how well assessors observe and document candidate behavior in several simulation exercises designed to provide ample opportunity for candidates to demonstrate job-related behaviors. We have found that people are best at:

- Observing behavior.
- Taking extensive notes on what they observe.
- Completing exercise reports using their notes.
- Rating exercise performance according to predetermined criteria and using their trained best judgment.
- Providing face-to-face feedback to candidates regarding their performance.

We believe these functions are best performed by people for several reasons. First, without using accurate, documented observations to produce thorough exercise reports that support accurate ratings, assessment center results would have little value. Computers are not yet capable of observing, categorizing, and evaluating human performance. Second, in the case of feedback, we have found that candidates generally prefer to receive sensitive information from a well-trained assessor (Ilgen, Fisher, & Taylor, 1979). Candidates most often tell us that the detailed, personalized feedback they receive on their performance is the most valuable piece of the assessment experience. In fact, many candidates state that the feedback is the richest developmental information they have ever received. Obviously, these important functions require the skills and abilities of people, and cannot (yet) be performed by computer. But the assessment center process involves many other functions as well.

Deciding What Computers Do Best

After analyzing the steps involved in the operation of an assessment center and being very careful *not to use computers unless they truly add value or efficiency* to the process, we believe that computers can do the same or a better job of performing the following activities traditionally performed by assessors:

• Providing "expert ratings" of candidate performance in each exercise for purposes of comparison to assessor ratings. The computer ratings are generated from assessor rating judgements, which are entered as +'s and −'s (i.e., effective and ineffective behaviors) for each competency in each exercise. The computer employs rules (i.e., an equation) to calculate "expert" numerical ratings. The computer applies these rules consistently, thus eliminating the occurrence of human error from inconsistent application of the rules. The "expert" ratings are shown on-screen *after* the assessor enters the candidate's rating for each competency. The assessor compares his or her rating with the "expert" rating. Although the assessor has the right to overrule the computer, this helps enormously to minimize inaccurate ratings and to maximize consistency across assessors.
• Combining exercise ratings to yield overall competency ratings. The computer can perform this function, which traditionally involves lengthy team meetings during which assessors read aloud the content of each exercise report. The computerized mechanical combining of data is more consistent than the team meeting because the same rules are applied each time. Also, several empirical investigations have strongly supported the use of mechanical versus clinical (i.e., more subjective) processes for combining the data (Borman, 1982; Feltham, 1988; Gilbert, 1982; McEvoy, Beatty, & Bernardin, 1987; Pynes, Bernardin, Benton, & McEvoy, 1988; Sackett & Wilson, 1982; Schmitt,

1977; Tziner & Dolan, 1982; Wingrove, Jones, & Herriot, 1985). In fact, the *Guidelines and Ethical Considerations for Assessment Center Operations* (Task Force, 1989) were changed to permit the mechanical (i.e., statistical) integration of exercise data to yield overall competency ratings based on this empirical evidence.

•   Synthesizing and generating feedback support information. Because the computer can compile all of the report form information, each assessor can designate the information to be covered in the feedback session, and the computer can list and print this information by competency for each exercise. Thus, any information that might have been generated by discussion in the team meeting will not be lost during the mechanical combining of the data.

•   Generating the final summary report. Traditionally, this report has been written after the assessment center cycle has been completed. Typically, a trained assessor spends from 2 to 3 hours completing the final report. Because this report represents the integration of data from the separate exercise reports, the computer can compile, integrate, and cross-reference these data with greater speed, accuracy, and consistency regarding length and style than can people. Computerizing this activity represents huge savings in time.

Conceptualizing the Computerization of Behavioral Judgment Tests

As is the case in computerizing a traditional assessment center process, computerizing behavioral judgment tests emphasizes the *scoring* of the responses and the *reporting* of information. However, once the decision is made to depart from real-time simulation exercises where, for example, one candidate interacts with one role-player, a number of additional potential efficiencies emerge. For example, if we present the stimulus via video, large numbers of candidates can view it at the same time or at multiple times and at different locations. Similarly, if we structure the candidates' response options or limit them in some way (e.g., multiple choice questions or extended response lists of alternative actions), panels of Subject Matter Experts (SMEs) can evaluate the appropriateness of the responses before the test. These experts can establish the value of various responses, and then the computer can be used to consistently apply these prescribed values to candidate answers. The computer can then generate reports that summarize component or subtest scores in any format desired. In determining how stimulus material should be presented, there are a variety of options that differ in fidelity but share the fact that administration to large numbers of candidates becomes possible. The most frequently used options for presenting a stimulus are paper-and-pencil, video, and audio.

If we must administer the test to large numbers of candidates at the same time, then we must structure the responses in some way to allow for computer or mechanical scoring. To score the responses, the computer or machine uses the values established in advance by *people*. This approach permits testing of very large numbers of candidates and reduces the costs by as much as 90%, depending on the particulars of the situation. For example, a typical 1-day assessment center with three simulations might cost $1,000 per candidate (at a minimum). Even a video-based test might cost less than $100 per candidate, assuming the candidate volume is sufficient to defray the high cost of development.

In considering the validity of tests that present highly structured response alternatives, the validity of traditional assessment centers might be used as a reference point. Although they are relatively expensive to administer (e.g., $1,000 to $3,000 per candidate), traditional assessment centers typically produce criterion-related validity in the range of $r = .40-.43$ (Gaugler, Rosenthal, Thornton, & Bentson, 1987; Hunter & Hunter, 1984; Schmitt, Gooding, & Noe, 1984). Validity coefficients of a wide variety of situational judgment tests, including video formats and paper-and-pencil tests, typically fall in the range of $r = .25-.40$ (Motowidlo, Dunnette, & Carter, 1990; Weekley & Jones, 1997). Thus, it seems that little validity is sacrificed to obtain very great savings in time and money.

ESTABLISHING DESIGN PARAMETERS

General Considerations

Assuming that a behavioral test that can be computer scored (or computer assisted in some way) is being designed, there are three parameters to which attention should be paid: stimulus presentation; response format; and response capture, storage, integration, analysis, and reporting.

As mentioned earlier, the method used to present the stimulus or test situation has extremely important implications for the practical use of the measure. In the traditional process of assessment center technology, it is very important to create the highest possible degree of realism and fidelity in the stimulus material; if the candidate is presented with realistic situations to which he or she must respond, it is more likely that behavioral samples similar to ones that will later occur in the target job will be observed. This logic is well supported in the literature, but the most important question might be "How much fidelity is needed to predict behavior?" If we can reduce costs by lowering stimulus fidelity with minimal declines in validity, then it seems prudent to consider alternatives to the traditional assessment center (Motowidlo, Dunnette, & Carter, 1990). However, the exercise designer must pay close attention to the job analysis data, the job context, and particular situations in which critical job skills are necessary in order for performance to be effective. For example, presentation of stimulus material via audio recording would not be realistic for many jobs. However, in police or fire service work, in which much communication occurs via radio, audio material might be very realistic and cost-effective. Of course, what makes sense and has high fidelity in one predictive situation may be inappropriate in another.

At one end of the continuum for response options are the totally open-ended, behavioral responses that occur in assessment centers. The scoring of these responses can be aided by the creation of detailed lists of behaviors, which can be presented to assessors on the computer screen to reduce the amount of categorizing and summarizing of responses that must be done.

Another response option includes multiple choice questions that occur at critical times in the development of a scenario presented via video, audio, or paper. For example, to assess customer service skills, we might present a video clip of a disgruntled customer speaking to a customer service representative about an unsatisfactory purchase. At a critical juncture in the conversation, the video action would pause and the candidate would be asked to answer to a multiple-choice question about how best to respond to the customer.

Still another, albeit underutilized, option includes the development of an extended list of possible actions that can be taken in a particular set of job situations. For example, Wilson Learning has developed simulation exercises that use a master list of 60 to 90 actions that can be taken in police or fire tactical situations. Although this is a lot of actions to develop, this master list can be used across situations and as a result, ease the scoring process.

Data analysis and reporting requirements present still another challenge. In the most complex assessment center, data capturing comes from human input that must be stored according to very specific rules. The computer follows these rules to establish data files that can later be used to produce ratings of performance, lists for feedback purposes, or final summary reports. In less complex situations, the computer assigns values to choices that the candidate has made to arrive at an overall numerical score, which is then used to select qualified candidates or provide feedback for purposes of development. Another tremendous advantage of computerization involves the combining of data from different sources in consistent ways. Humans often combine information in different ways depending on a number of factors.

Designing Applications With Differing Levels of Complexity

Wilson Learning's experience has shown that the simplest assessment system to design and develop is one where the stimulus is provided through a means other than the computer (i.e., paper, audio, video, or live action). The adminis-

tration component of this system provides a form for entering registration information. The data collection component provides a data entry format for
entering a single response to each item. The processing component assigns a
value to each response option, links each response option to a single competency being measured, and averages the values for each competency to calculate the competency ratings. Finally, the reporting component prints a report
summarizing the competency ratings.

This simplistic design requires development of very few on-line screens
while still utilizing the computer for what it traditionally does best—tracking,
processing, and reporting data. This type of application is very adaptable, and a
significant portion of the original programming can be reused, even when the
assessment stimulus and response alternative changes. The assessment content is designed completely independent of the software, thus allowing the
two elements to be developed simultaneously and then integrated for pilot
testing of the system.

We have also developed a more complex, fully computerized system that
involves combining results from two different assessment methodologies.
One measure is a timed in-basket simulation, and the other is a structured
interview. The stimulus component for the in-basket simulation displays
multiple documents and provides the capability for the participant to move
from one to another and back again at will. The data collection component
for the in-basket simulation displays the response options on the screen
while allowing the participant to review the various documents, as needed.
The stimulus component for the structured interview presents the interview questions and guidelines for scoring candidates' responses. For the
purposes of data collection, a single screen is provided, on which the inter-
viewer enters rating judgments. The processing component for the system
combines the values associated with the responses from both assessments
to calculate competency and behavioral level scores as well as an overall rating. The reporting component produces an administrative report, displays
ranking the participants by their overall ratings, and creates a feedback report for each participant that includes overall, competency, and behavioral
level results across both assessments.

This complex application benefited from piloting the in-basket stimulus
content and response options on paper before inserting them into the system.
We gave careful consideration to the type of monitors participants would use.
In addition, we used recommendations from SMEs and end-users to establish
the design parameters for font size, colors, and document length. The need to
utilize an unbiased testing medium that does not provide an advantage for one
participant over another adds to the complexity of designing this type of application. The interface was designed so that a computer novice and a computer
expert would have equal opportunity to succeed. It was also structured to em-

ulate the work environment in that maneuvering through the computer screens is actually a significant part of the target job.

Our fully computerized assessment center system took considerably longer to develop. Initial development, implementation, and testing occurred concurrently in three phases over a period of 18 months. A phased development process was planned to achieve incremental benefits as each phase was completed. The phased approach facilitated the use of concurrent manual and automated assessment systems to ensure that the computerized application produced accurate results when compared to the traditional approach. For example, to test the processing component, the assessors first determined competency scores in the traditional manner. These scores were then compared to the computer-generated scores. To test the reporting component, the assessors used the traditional method to write a final report, which was compared to a system-generated final report.

Testing of this nature continued through the entire development process. New functions and changes to the user interface were continually demonstrated to the design team for their feedback. Input gathered from assessors and administrators before and after the system was released into production led to the design and delivery of system enhancements, including simplification of the administrator's data entry function, cultural adaptation of screens and reports, additional report formats, and data export capabilities.

DETERMINING SCORING METHODS AND RULES

Once the logic has been established that permits the computer to capture, store, and process information obtained in the test situation, the bulk of the work involved in the design process is complete. What about this "logic," and where does it come from?

In 1963, Gerald Whitlock published a creative empirical article in which he reported consistently supportive data for Stevens' psychophysical law that "equal ratios in stimulus produce equal ratios in response." Translated to performance appraisal situations, this means that a rater's observations get combined in very predictable ways to yield performance evaluations. Wilson Learning considers the assessment center process similar to a performance evaluation, but it has a shorter format and controlled environment that involves simulation exercises. If this is accurate, then Whitlock's research model using observation of performance "specimens" as the core of information could be useful. The equation that describes the relationship between an overall judgment and the observations that preceded it is:

$$y = kx^n,$$

where y is the overall judgment, k is a constant depending on the type of rating scale used, x is the ratio of effective to ineffective (E/I) performance observations, and n is the fractional power to which x is raised (Whitlock, 1963). The object is to use the right side of the equation as a mathematical model to predict the left side of the equation. In an assessment center situation, a detailed list of behaviors can be used as the criteria for evaluating observations in the form of E/I.

To see whether this model applied to assessment center situations, we set out to investigate the extent to which assessors' ratings of exercise performance on each competency could be predicted by Whitlock and Stevens' psychophysical equation. We used data from four different assessment centers, each of which measured nine competencies of performance. A total of 75 exercise reports was used. Twenty-four professionally trained assessors who worked on one or more of the projects served as raters for the project and most of the assessors worked on two of the four projects. The centers were conducted in a traditional way where assessors documented their observations and then assigned ratings. During the rating process, assessors were required to identify behaviors that were effective or ineffective in helping the organization meet its goals. It was, therefore, necessary to analyze reports to calculate the numbers of effective and ineffective observations for each competency. This was accomplished by two professionally trained assessors who had not participated in any of the centers in question. A 7-point scale was used in these centers, where 7 represented extremely effective performance and 1 represented extremely ineffective performance. The equation that best predicted competency ratings in each exercise by the assessors was:

$$y = 4.04 \ (E/I)^{.23}$$

The y values (ratings) generated by this equation led to correlations with the competency ratings assigned by assessors in each exercise ranging from $r = .80$–$.85$. This indicates that the professional raters were using the ratio of effective to ineffective observations in quite similar ways.

This also means that an algorithm based on data (i.e., observations by professional raters) can be developed, which can then be applied by the computer in exactly the same way for all candidates. In other words, the human assessor observes and the computer uses the observations in perfectly consistent ways. Since this research was completed, Wilson Learning has worked on a number of other algorithms in an attempt to simplify programming requirements and still maintain very high levels of consistency.

Scoring methods and rules for other applications such as multiple choice or extended list formats are much more straightforward in their design. In these cases, total scores or component scores are usually obtained by counting the number of "effective" answers or assigning point values to chosen alternatives.

In the latter case, each of these responses is assigned a value ranging from +2 to -2 for each of three tactical scenarios. The scenarios might be expressed in text, photographs, audio, video, or a combination of these media. The test requires the candidate to choose the 10 most important actions to take in a situation. As each alternative has already been assigned a point value for each scenario by the SME panel, the candidate's score is the total points assigned to his or her choices. This type of exercise requires the same rigorous development as an assessment center exercise, but scoring is extremely efficient. The specific weighting of the response options can be determined by SMEs of the target position or by the customers of the target position (Weekley & Jones, 1997). Complexity can increase if detailed scores for each competency of performance are required. Yet, even this problem is basically a counting and sorting function that can be addressed by the software.

DEVELOPING SOFTWARE APPLICATIONS FOR BEHAVIORAL ASSESSMENT

The benefits of successful automation of a manual assessment process are many. Wilson Learning has recognized significant benefits from automating the calculation of assessment scores, combining results across multiple simulations and multiple assessments, and producing detailed reports. The benefits include rapid production of final results, simplified data retrieval, reduced redundancy, increased accuracy of results, and greater consistency throughout the process.

Wilson Learning has identified factors that should be considered to ensure the successful design of a computerized assessment application. The application should provide a simple, easy-to-follow user interface in which actions are clear, commands are consistent, and keystrokes are minimized. By identifying and modeling the effective components of the manual process, efficiency can be maximized and the users' learning curve minimized. Redesign should provide options for easy customization to accommodate the varying system and data requirements that occur in different assessments. For example, it is critical to have the flexibility to evaluate a differing number of dimensions, simulations, and participants without major software changes.

Before the system is developed, it is important to determine what information must be input to the system, what processes the system must perform, and what outputs must be produced. Example of these are:

Inputs: Participant name, participant ID number, demographic information, date of assessment, name of assessment, participant's responses to questions, and assessors' evaluations.

Processes: Sort and select data by participant information, calculate a score from the participant's responses or the assessor's evaluations, and convert numerical score to a scaled score.

Outputs: Print raw data, print/display reports for a single participant or for groups of participants, and print behavioral examples of performance.

After identifying the needs of the application, the next step would be to determine the organization and flow of the system's functions. Designing the user interface (screens and menus) and the database (storage and access to information) follows the identification of the source, sequence, and relationships among the data. Design of the processing rules (e.g., transformation of data, assignment of values to responses, and calculation of scores) can proceed after the input and outcome specifications are defined.

As the design progresses, it is useful to think of the application as several interdependent components that link together to achieve a desired result. An example of system components might be:

1.   The *administration component* is where participant registration and demographic information is recorded and data from assessment sessions are stored. The information stored in the administration component is available to the other components of the application and can be used to build tables for sorting results and provides selection options to generate reports and score matrices.

2.   The *stimulus component* enables a participant to view the test stimulus on the computer screen. As described earlier, the stimulus may be provided via paper, audio, video, or live interaction or through the application software. Applications with a stimulus component are more complex to program and, therefore, more costly to develop. However, having the stimulus self-contained in the application simplifies the administration of the test.

3.   The *data collection component* enables a participant or evaluator to enter the responses to the assessment items into the system for processing. The participant will enter responses where the application contains the stimulus component. The assessor or evaluator will enter behavioral observations and ratings when the stimulus is presented live rather than electronically. Even though a participant or an evaluator may be expected to record their responses directly into the system, there should be a method for someone else to enter responses from a paper record (data entry) in the event that the system is not available to the participant or evaluator. To minimize error and to optimize efficiency, the format of the data entry screen matches the format of the paper record from which the responses are read. Alternate data entry methods such as loading information from scanned documents and from electronic mail files can also be designed as options.

4. The *processing component* applies the scoring rules to the participants' responses or assessors' behavioral ratings to calculate the results or scores of the assessment. Processing takes place automatically, either when a participant's data are saved or when a report is requested. When an application requires the participants' unprocessed responses (the raw data) to be loaded from an external source (e.g., from a scanned document or from the Internet), the application usually allows selection of an individual participant or a group of participants for processing.

5. The *reporting component* displays the results on the screen and generates print commands to print reports of individual and summary performance. Text paragraphs, bar charts, and graphs can be generated by selecting response options. Statistical analyses can be performed and reported as desired. The reporting and printing capability can be entirely contained in the assessment application, or it may call on a word processing or spreadsheet application to generate the reports.

Consistency of the user interface across all of the components is critical to the application's ease of use. Conforming to currently accepted interface guidelines is also crucial to the acceptance and usability of the application, that is, placement of icons and use of commands, labels, prompts, and messages differs depending on whether the application is being written for a Windows, Apple, or Internet interface.

TESTING APPLICATIONS

A draft version of the screens and menus for the administration and data collection components is often programmed in advance of, or concurrent with, the processing and reporting components. This allows testing and revision of screen flow and general usability before linkages are made among all of the components.

Extensive testing of the processing and reporting components is critical to ensuring the integrity of the data saved, generated, and retrieved. This requires creation of test data and manual calculation of the expected results for comparison with the computer-generated results.

When all components are linked together, every action a user is expected to perform (and those they are not expected to perform) should be tested to ensure the correct results before the application is actually put to use. When the system tests are consistently successful and user documentation is developed, the system is then introduced to a sample user population for further testing (beta sites). This allows a controlled move from the development environment to a production environment while testing continues. Quirks or bugs in the system, as well as suggestions from those who will be using the application, are identified, and the data that are collected are used to build normative data-bases for use in the production release.

Expectations for the testing by beta-site participants, and a means for them to provide specific feedback to the developers, are clearly communicated. After a period of testing, revisions are made to the system and the documentation, and the beta-testing process may be repeated. This loop of testing and revision continues until the system delivers the desired results with a high level of confidence. The system is now ready for production release.

This description of application testing is a perfect-world scenario. Often constraints of speed and cost must be factored into the development cycle and, generally, the first component of software development to suffer is the testing and quality assurance process. The risks associated with this can be minimized by using high-quality developers who understand the business process as well as the development of software products. The more a developer is able to understand the customer's situation and how the product will be ultimately used, the better the chances are that the software will perform properly when it is finally installed. Another way to minimize impact of shortened testing cycles is to fully disclose the risks to the customer. If, in exchange for lower cost and shorter development time, the customer agrees to a procedure for the fixing of any bugs or issues that may appear after the software has been installed, then shortening the testing cycle may be acceptable. Regardless of the level of testing done, some understanding of the after-installation "bug fix" procedure should be discussed with the customer. In that way, when, not if, a bug arises, it will be addressed in a timely and acceptable fashion.

EASING THE PAINS OF SOFTWARE DEVELOPMENT

Wilson Learning's experience in designing and developing computerized applications for assessment systems has led to the following learning points:

• Consideration of the hardware, software, and operating systems available to the user population today must be balanced with a view to what will be state-of-the-art tomorrow in order to maximize the longevity of the application. When designing a new software application, the decision to support older hardware and operating systems should be made with great care. Given the speed with which technology is advancing, beginning your product in an older paradigm will immediately outdate it when it is released. Instead, we recommend developing a leading-edge product that gives the user base a reason to update their computers.

• The type and volume of data to be collected and the information that needs to be readily accessible versus accessible through archives may affect the type of database used. More sophisticated database solutions generally require a lengthier installation process and often require experts for their ongoing maintenance. However, these solutions will enhance the ability to do queries and advanced analysis on large data sets. Simplified storage solutions, such as saving information in a data file designed specifically for the application, may give the application more portability (e.g., the ability to run from, and save information on, a single floppy diskette) but will lack in the ability to access large amounts of information. Combined solutions can be very effective where people gathering the information use portable computers and enter data that will be transferred to a main computer for storage in a large database for analysis and group reporting.

•   The amount of flexibility required in the system (e.g., rating scales, weighting schemes, competency labels and components, and report formats) must be factored into the design process. The balance here is between up-front development time versus time for ongoing maintenance and administration time of the software. For example, if ratings scales are hard-coded into the application, when a modification is required for a future situation, a software developer must make the necessary alterations to the software. This may be very time consuming and increases the risk of introducing new "bugs" into the system. For any component or feature of the system that is likely to change, it is strongly recommended that an administrator interface be developed to allow an advanced system user to make the required modifications. Over the lifecycle of the software, the administrator interface can be enhanced to allow more flexibility and to expose additional portions of the system for administrator modification.

•   New tools are available every day and should be explored. Many of the advancements being made in software development tools are designed to increase the productivity of the developer. Whenever possible, you should take advantage of these features to allow for the rapid development of contemporary-looking applications.

•   Data security requirements ensure that the assessment content and participant performance results will remain confidential. Security of the data can range from being maintained by process solutions to technology solutions. Process security can be established by determining who has access to the data and under what circumstances. Such systems require an established trust agreement on ethics among the administrators and users of the system. Software security may include advanced password protection schemes and the encryption of data. Process control is the least expensive method of security but requires a high level of integrity among the users of the system. In contrast, application security can be very costly as it may involve the development and maintenance of password access, encryption of data and logging of users activity in the software, and so forth. However, it can afford a much greater level of security for the sensitive information being collected.

• The makeup of the development team should include computer systems analyst(s), computer programmers, project coordinator(s), and documentation writer(s). Representatives from the user population and the content development team should be included as well. Each of these people brings a unique perspective and a different set of skills to the group when designing an application. Having a well-rounded and well-chosen team will help to ensure the success and acceptance of the software solution developed.

• The implementation team is a critical part of the project and should include system installation technical support, end-user support, and technical trainers. Even if the system developed is the best of its kind, a poor implementation can damage acceptance and overall effectiveness. A carefully designed and executed implementation plan can impact the overall success of the system as much as the design of the system itself.

The design and development techniques for computer applications continue to evolve daily and the capabilities of computer technology continue to expand geometrically. Keeping up with these changes is critical to maximizing the benefits realized through automation of assessment applications.

IMPACT OF COMPUTERIZATION
ON TEST DELIVERY

The previous sections of this chapter have presented some of the many variables organizations must consider when making decisions regarding the selection/assessment process they wish to use, and whether that process should be computerized. This section addresses logistical issues regarding computerized assessment measures that impact those decisions. The computerization of testing practices impacts all aspects of the test delivery process, including administration of the measures, training of raters (and in some cases, of the participants), and the potential for increased complexity of the logistics of delivering the test. These factors, as well as the intent of the test (i.e., selection decision vs. developmental feedback) and the need for high-stimulus and high-response fidelity should be taken into consideration when making decisions regarding the type of tests to implement and whether or not to computerize these measures.

Administration

Computerized test delivery and scoring requires proportionately the same involvement of the administrator as comparable noncomputerized tests. Consider the relative simplicity of administering a paper-and-pencil test or a situational judgment test delivered by means of an audio or video stimulus. One administrator can distribute materials, queue up the test, monitor the process, and then score responses as easily for 1 participant as for 50. In such a

case, the training and involvement of the administrator is relatively uncompli-
cated. The administration of a more complex test, such as an assessment center, requires much greater involvement on the part of the administrator and
therefore, additional training.

The comprehensiveness and detail of the results from various test formats
falls on a continuum that ranges from the numeric point value awarded to test
item responses to the behavioral narrative of an assessment center. The degree
of involvement and training requirements of the administrator of these measures varies in the same way. Once the score sheets are delivered and the test is
queued up, audio- or video-based situational judgment tests require very little
involvement on the part of the administrator. Tests where both the stimulus
and the response set are delivered via computer require some additional involvement from the administrator but still in a passive, monitoring role. These
tests do not require any involvement from human raters. On the other extreme, computerized assessment centers require much more intense involvement from both administrators and assessors.

Training

As when using traditional assessment center methodology, the administrator
prepares the site and the materials, distributes materials throughout the day,
and coordinates intricately timed schedules. Administrators for computerized
assessment centers require more extensive training than with most other test
formats. This is because of their added responsibilities, which include register-
ing participants and entering their demographics into the system, creating
scoring diskettes, processing those diskettes, printing a variety of reports, and
troubleshooting any software and hardware problems. Wilson Learning rec-
ommends that administrators attend the assessor training and then at least one
additional day of hands-on training and practice with the software and hardware used to implement computerized assessment centers.

The high-stimulus and high-response fidelity of an assessment center requires extensive training of the raters or assessors. The typical 5-day assessor
training Wilson Learning conducts for a traditional assessment center is condensed to 3 days when using a computerized scoring and reporting system. The
assessors are trained on the traditional activities of observing and documenting
behavior, rating the effectiveness of behaviors, and delivering feedback. A major portion of assessor training with the traditional method is geared toward
generating the behavioral simulation reports, and then interpreting and incor-
porating the reports of two other assessors to determine ratings, deliver feedback, and write a summary report. The computerized assessment center
program provides each assessor with an extensive list of expected behaviors to
ensure that he or she considers the same elements in evaluating each participant. The assessors no longer need extensive practice on categorizing behaviors

to the appropriate competency or reaching consistency in how each behavioral statement and the final report should be written. The assessors are trained to use the software and practice interacting with the computer-assisted scoring aspect of the program. With a computerized assessment process, the primary focus of training is attaining a higher level of interrater agreement by using the computer-assisted scoring software and participating in rating exercises and discussions. Assessor trainees also spend time reviewing computer-generated feedback preparation reports and practicing conducting feedback sessions rather than perfecting their writing skills.

When using most computerized testing methods, the orientation or training of participants becomes a critical part of the process to ensure consistency and fairness for all participants. At a minimum, when administering a video-based situational judgment test, participants should be given an opportunity to preview the format of the stimulus and response mechanisms. When the participant is required to interact with a computer, such as during computer-generated stimulus situations, a hands-on practice session should be provided to all participants. This is necessary to ensure that the testing process is fair for participants regardless of their computer experience. Such participant training should include viewing samples of the assessment material, practicing moving within the screen and from one screen to another, using the keyboard and mouse, and understanding time limits for completing various elements of the simulation. Each participant should complete a 10- to 15-minute practice session prior to beginning the actual assessment. Computerized assessment centers do not require special training for the participants, as the computerized aspect of the test does not involve the participants. Wilson Learning conducts a 30- to 45-minute orientation session for participants to familiarize them with the process and logistics of the assessment center, regardless of whether or not the system is computerized.

Test Security

With computerized testing, participants may remain anonymous to the assessors by assigning them a testing identification number, such as part of their social security number or some other code. Results may then be examined without compromising the identity of individual respondents. Results may also be reported by grouping the respondents on the basis of various demographic factors. Demographics typically identified are gender, race, ethnic origin, region, position title, training completed, or number of years in the organization. Data are collected in a database, and reports of results are easily compiled for specific demographic groups. Valuable conclusions can be drawn by reviewing and contrasting test results for selected clusters of candidates, for example, individuals having different lengths of tenure in a target position or groups that differ in the number of training courses they have completed.

Test security is optimized with computerized testing. Behavioral evaluations and specific test results may be removed from computers and archived electronically in a secure place to be easily retrieved when needed. When the stimulus and response are both computer generated, both the participants' specific responses and the ratings can be easily stored on diskette. Not only does this provide security of the results, but it eliminates the retention of participant testing material on paper, which can quickly accumulate to warehouse-size proportions.

Implementation

The logistics for location and materials needed should also be taken into consideration when deciding whether or not to use a computerized testing method. There is a broad range of equipment needs required for the various computerized testing methods. Minimal hardware is needed to administer audio- or video-based situational judgment tests. Large groups of participants can be tested using one audio or video cassette player and one or more video monitors. Computer-generated stimulus tests require one computer workstation per participant. The software is designed to be used on a wide range of low-end hardware so that state-of-the-art equipment is not a requirement or barrier. Participants must be spaced an appropriate distance from one another or partitions provided to allow for ample workspace and privacy. An additional computer and a high-speed printer are necessary for the administrator to register participants, process assessment responses, and print their reports. A workroom can be set up for assessors to use their laptops or PCs and for the administrator to use a computer and printer during the assessment process.

Computerizing assessment measures involves trade-offs in many areas. Although the involvement and training of the administrator may become more complex, the involvement and training of the assessors is condensed or in some cases, eliminated. The need for additional hardware may increase the initial investment necessary to implement computerized processes, but the immediate availability of reports and feedback, and the increased reliability of the test results provide a substantial return on that investment when a long-range perspective is taken. The next section addresses the options and value that computerization brings to the feedback portion of assessment.

IMPACT OF COMPUTERIZATION ON FEEDBACK

Although some performance improvements have been noted simply as a result of assessing one's skills, little positive change is likely to occur without feedback on test performance and developmental action. Multilevel feedback reports can be obtained from a wide variety of behavioral assessments (e.g., situational judgment tests, structured response tests, assessment centers). Feedback can be simple and consist of standardized high-level descriptions (i.e., labels such as exceeds expectations or meets standard requirements) of an individual's performance based on a numeric score for a given set of behaviors or items related to a competency. More specific feedback based on the behaviors elicited or responses selected for each assessment stimulus or test item can also be provided. The level of detail is primarily dependent on the purpose and planned use of the results. If an organization needs test results to make an overall selection decision but does not require an understanding of the candidate's specific skill profile (i.e., strengths and developmental opportunities), then a high-level description (verbal or numerical) of the candidate's performance will suffice. A one-page matrix of competency scores is typical for this level of reporting. However, if the organization seeks to understand both the candidate's general employability (i.e., whether the candidate has met minimal proficiency in the skill areas essential to the position) and specific behavioral strengths and developmental needs, a more detailed feedback report is needed.

Several different types of reports are available when using a computerized assessment center process. A matrix of the overall results or a highly specific, behavioral-level feedback report can be created with the ease of a keystroke. Wilson Learning typically provides behavior-specific feedback reports that present a formal summary of a participant's performance across all the simulation exercises and competencies assessed. Another readily available report is used by assessors and test administrators to conduct individual feedback sessions with participants. This feedback preparation report typically includes a summary of the participant's performance in each simulation exercise, a listing (by competency) of the participant's behaviors and scores (sorted high to low into performance categories for each exercise), specific participant behavioral examples and quotes, assessors' comments, numeric scores for each competency and a brief summary of the participant's patterns of performance expressed in terms relevant to development action.

Computer-assisted scoring and quick access to printed feedback reports facilitates finely tuned differentiation of performance levels among candidates. Through detailed documentation of performance patterns, an individual's skill level can be highlighted and more fully understood. For example, it may be useful to know that a candidate's decision-making score was high in a noninteractive in-basket exercise but rather low in a highly interactive group discussion exercise. This inconsistent pattern of performance might indicate that the assessment situation impacted the way in which the candidate made critical decisions and the quality of those decisions.

In addition to assessing meaningful differences in performance among participants, computerization also facilitates the integration of performance results from varied test formats. Through computerization, the results from different test formats can be easily and quickly integrated at the competency level to yield an overall skill profile for an individual. For example, the data collected from a structured interview, a computer-scored in-basket simulation and two role-play simulations can be combined into one report. Using the resulting overall skill profile and the details of the candidate's performance from the various tests, qualified selection decisions can be made and/or developmental prescriptions can be identified. The specific developmental information can recommend just-in-time training, meeting both the budget constraints of organizations today and the time constraints of employees.

A feedback report is one of the most valuable aspects of the behavioral assessment process but can be very time consuming to produce in noncomputerized assessments. The average time required to prepare the feedback report in a traditional assessment center is 2.5 hours. With a computerized process, the various reports can be printed in minutes. The primary benefit from computerizing the scoring and reporting functions is the immediate generation of reports, which minimizes lag time between testing and feedback.

Performance improvement is best fostered by specific verbal feedback provided as close in time to the exhibited behavior as possible (Bernardin & Beatty, 1983; Mosel, 1961). The shorter the delay in feedback, the sooner employees can take action—and the sooner organizations will benefit from performance improvements. Even a time difference of 1 or 2 weeks can have a substantial business impact when hundreds of people are going through the testing process. Immediate provision of results has benefits for the candidate as well. When given a choice, individuals will invariably select quick feedback over delayed feedback (Reid & Parsons, 1996). Intrinsically, people seem to understand that they will learn more and the test results will have more meaning for them if the feedback is not delayed.

In addition to reducing the time needed to generate the feedback report, the computerization of the reporting function also ensures the consistent and high quality of the documents produced. The computerized feedback report allows for standardized text to be complemented with dynamic text, based on an individual's assessment performance. It also permits access to varied report formats at the touch of a button. Finally, computerization provides an automatic means for electronic storage of the test responses and results for each individual, controls access to the test results, and enables results to be linked to other organization databases for personnel record storage.

TIME SAVINGS WITH COMPUTERIZATION

We have analyzed the overall impact of computerizing the assessment center with respect to the amount of assessor time that is spent on each candidate. The savings from computerization are dramatic. In fact, it reduces the time spent by almost 50%. Table 11.1 compares assessor time on several activities for the traditional and computerized approaches in a three-simulation assessment center.

TABLE 11.1

Assessor Activity Hours in Traditional Versus Computerized
Assessment Centers

Assessor Activity	Traditional	Computerized
Observing and documenting performance	3	3
Recording and evaluating performance	4.5	3
Conducting team meeting and preparing for feedback	4	1
Conducting feedback	1	1
Writing the final report	2.5	0
Total	15	8

Note. Hours are based on an assessment center containing three simulations.

Overall, computerization reduces the amount of time spent per candidate from 15 hours to 8. In a typical assessment center cycle of 12 candidates, computerization leads to a time savings of 84 hours (180 with traditional vs. 96 with computerization). The activities that yield savings are: recording and evaluating performance, conducting the team meeting and preparing for feedback, and writing the final report. These are all activities in which the computer can play a significant role to increase efficiency. In contrast, computerization does not reduce assessor time in the following activities: observing and documenting performance and conducting feedback. At present, these two activities are best performed by people.

CONCLUSIONS

This chapter describes some practical advice about the conceptualization, design, and development of computerized and technology-aided behavioral assessment systems. This advice is born of Wilson Learning's experiences with computerized assessment centers and audio- and video-based tests over the past 10 years. The lessons learned are summarized next.

First, the assessment system in question should be analyzed in terms of stimulus presentation, response capture, and response scoring. Questions about how these actions should be performed in a computerized system can be answered by looking at what people do best, what machines do best, and what is practical, given the business situation. Once these questions are answered, the design of the system can begin. In the design of the system, we have learned that three factors are key to a successful design: (a) a simple, easy-to-follow user interface, (b) an automated process that leverages the strengths of the manual process, and (c) options for easily customizing the system to handle varying system and data requirements. In developing the system, other practical issues become important. These include the hardware, software, and operating system that is available to those who must interact with the system, the type and storage requirements of the data to be collected, the data security measures, and the flexibility required of the system. Computerization also has implications for test delivery and implementation of the system. The keys to successful implementation are sufficient training of the administrator and assessors, including considerable hands-on practice, test security procedures to ensure the confidentiality of those being assessed, and logistical considerations such as equipment needs and physical facilities. And finally, feedback on performance in a computerized assessment should adhere to certain principles; for example, the level of specificity and the content should be guided by the purpose of the assessment and the intended audience of the feedback.

FUTURE DIRECTIONS

Having been in the business of computerized and technology-aided assessment for some time now, we should know better than to predict future directions of this rapidly changing area. Nevertheless, we believe that certain technologies have great potential in the future of behavioral assessment. First, and most promising, is the Internet. Already, video, audio, graphics, and text can be presented, and multiple types of responses can be collected. With transmission speed increasing, the Internet seems a logical delivery vehicle for behavioral judgment assessments. On a more local level, many companies are building their own intranets, which can provide the same functionality as the Internet but with greater limitations on access. This seems like a particularly useful mechanism for using assessment as a tool for employee development.

Another technology that Wilson Learning believes has some application in behavioral assessment includes PDAs (personal digital assistants) and touch-screen computers. These devices could be used by assessors to facilitate behavioral observation. Assessors could type or write their behavioral notes or even highlight certain prespecified behaviors that appeared in a checklist. The data could then be downloaded to a central computer for storage and reporting.

And finally, Wilson Learning believes that CD-ROM has some potential in this arena. The technology has become widely available at a time when employees are taking increasing responsibility for their own development and training. The CD-ROM technology can present very sophisticated training with embedded behavioral assessment that individuals can access at their convenience.

One note of caution to practitioners: Do not become blinded by or enamored with the technology. Using technology to perform a task simply because it can be done that way is not sufficient justification. The purpose, not the tool, of the assessment must guide the design, development, and implementation of the assessment system. At present, many tasks involved in conducting behavioral assessment are still best performed by humans, imperfect as we are.

REFERENCES

Bernardin, H. J., & Beatty, R. W. (1983). *Performance appraisal: Assessing human behavior at work.* Boston: Kent Publishing.

Borman, W. C. (1982). Validity of behavioral assessment for predicting military recruiter performance. *Journal of Applied Psychology, 67,* 3–9.

D'Aveni, R. A. (1994). *Hypercompetition: Managing the dynamics of strategic maneuvering.* New York: The Free Press.

Feltham, R. (1988). Assessment centre decision making: judgemental vs. mechanical. *Journal of Occupational Psychology, 61,* 237–241.

Gaugler, B., Rosenthal, D., Thornton, G., & Bentson, C. (1987). Meta-analysis of assessment center validity. *Journal of Applied Psychology, 72,* 493–511.

Gilbert, P. J. (1982). *A comparison of clinical and mechanical combination of assessment center data.* Unpublished master's thesis, University of Central Florida, Orlando, FL.

Hunter, J. E., & Hunter, R. F. (1984). Validity and utility of alternative predictors of job performance. *Psychological Bulletin, 96,* 72–98.

Ilgen, D. R., Fisher, C. D., & Taylor, M. S. (1979). Consequences of individual feedback on behavior in organizations. *Journal of Applied Psychology, 64,* 349–371.

McEvoy, G. M., Beatty, R. W., & Bernardin, H. J. (1987). Unanswered questions in assessment center research. *Journal of Business and Psychology, 2,* 97–111.

Mosel, J. N. (1961). How to feed back performance results to trainees. In E. A. Fleishman (Ed.), *Studies in personnel and industrial psychology* (pp. 173–181). Homewood, IL: The Dorsey Press.

Motowidlo, S. J., Dunnette, M. D., & Carter, G. W. (1990). An alternative selection procedure: The low-fidelity simulation. *Journal of Applied Psychology, 75,* 640–647.

Pynes, J., Bernardin, H. J., Benton, A. L., & McEvoy, G. M. (1988). Should assessment center competency ratings be mechanically derived? *Journal of Business and Psychology, 2,* 217–227.

Reid, D. H., & Parsons, M. B. (1996). A comparison of staff acceptability of immediate versus delayed verbal feedback in staff training. *Journal of Organizational Behavior Management, 16,* 35–47.

Sackett, P. R., & Wilson, M. A. (1982). Factors affecting the consensus judgment process in managerial assessment centers. *Journal of Applied Psychology, 67,* 10–17.

Schmitt, N. (1977). Interrater agreement in dimensionality and combination of assessment center judgments. *Journal of Applied Psychology, 62,* 171–176.

Schmitt, N., Gooding, R. Z., & Noe, R. A. (1984). Metaanalyses of validity studies published between 1964 and 1982 and the investigation of study characteristics. *Personnel Psychology, 37,* 407–422.

Task Force on Assessment Center Guidelines. (1989). *Public Personnel Management, 18,* 457–470.

Tziner, A., & Dolan, S. (1982). Validity of an assessment center for identifying future female officers in the military. *Journal of Applied Psychology, 67,* 728–736.

Weekley, J. A., & Jones, C. (1997). Video based situational testing. *Personnel Psychology, 50,* 25–49.

Whitlock, G. H. (1963). Application of psychophysical law to performance evaluation. *Journal of Applied Psychology, 47,* 15–23.

Wingrove, J., Jones A., & Herriot, P. (1985). The predictive validity of pre- and post-discussion assessment centre ratings. *Journal of Occupational Psychology, 58,* 189–192.

12

Blood, Sweat, and Tears: Some Final Comments on Computerized Assessment

Fritz Drasgow
University of Illinois, Urbana-Champaign

Julie B. Olson-Buchanan
California State University, Fresno

The contributing authors in this book are pioneers in the true sense of the word. Despite the prevalence of personal computers in educational and organizational settings, their use as tools for innovative assessment has been limited. Consequently, there is very little information available about how to address the psychometric, administrative, and technological issues raised by nontraditional computerized assessment. However, this book's chronicling of the authors' experiences in this unchartered territory can serve as a blueprint for others who may be interested in computerized assessment.

The chapters in this book described the long and exacting process of developing computerized tests. As the authors recounted their trials and tribulations, a number of common themes and surprises emerged. One theme running through all the chapters involves the amount of effort needed to develop a computerized assessment of high quality: *A great deal of work is required.* There are countless decisions to be made, each of which must be carefully considered.

In particular, several researchers devoted considerable time and effort to the psychometric issues raised by innovative assessments. For example, Segall and Moreno's chapter on the CAT–ASVAB (chapter 3, this volume) described a long series of empirical studies undertaken by military researchers to provide definitive answers to the dilemmas that were encountered as this test was developed. Mills (chapter 6, this volume) described a set of studies designed to answer important questions concerning the computerization of the GRE. Similarly, Zickar, Overton, Taylor, and Harms (chapter 2, this volume) explained how they designed and conducted several studies to ensure the psychometric integrity of the CAT version of their math reasoning ability test for computer programmers.

Other researchers considered the potential reactions to the computerized assessment. For example, Bergstrom and Lunz (chapter 4, this volume) discussed licensees' possible reactions to fixed- versus variable-length tests. Kingsbury and Houser (chapter 5, this volume) discussed a dilemma they encountered in developing CATs for school-age children: Would such tests would be more frustrating to students than conventional (i.e., nonadaptive) tests?

It is interesting to note the lack of emphasis on software development in the chapters of this book. Computer programming was obviously critical for all of the tests and certainly constituted a major element of the development process. Indeed, several chapters (e.g., chapters 8 & 9, this volume) noted how rapid improvements in computer technology made some early programming efforts obsolete for later versions of the assessments. However, in general, it seems that the test development teams were able to anticipate the effort level required for software development and planned accordingly.

On the other hand, some issues that need very little attention for paper-and-pencil tests loom large in the development of computerized tests. For example, an examinee who does not complete a traditional exam can be assigned a score that is based on the number of items he or she answered correctly (or perhaps the number correct minus some proportion of the number of incorrect answers given); this is the same scoring procedure used for examinees who complete the test. Computerized adaptive tests are ordinarily scored using an estimate of the item response theory ability parameter, θ. As described in chapters 3 and 6, an approach that simply uses the current ability estimate for examinees who do not complete the exam would allow sophisticated strategies for inflating one's score. Thus, the test developers had to carefully devise procedures for scoring incomplete exams that were fair, yet precluded strategic nonresponding.

Costs and Benefits of Computerized Assessment

After reading about the computerized tests described in the preceding chapters, it is useful to return to the basic question of whether the advantages of these assessments justify their costs. In addressing this question, it is useful to divide computerized tests into those that cost less than their alternatives and those that cost more.

Some of the computerized assessments and assessment procedures described in this book cost less, on a per-examinee basis, than traditional assessment. Burroughs et al. (chapter 11, this volume) presented a very careful analysis of how to use computers in a variety of ways to reduce the overall cost of assessment. Hanson et al. (chapter 10, this volume) gave an example where a hands-on assessment is simply too time-consuming and expensive to use routinely; their computerized assessment provides high-fidelity simulation of the hands-on measure and greatly reduces costs. The per-assessee cost of the interactive video assessment described by Drasgow, Olson-Buchanan, and Moberg (chapter 9, this volume) is also much lower than the cost incurred in an assessment center using a role-play exercise with actors and trained observers. In each of these cases, computerization reduces costs with little or no degradation (or, perhaps, even improvement!) in the quality of measurement. In these cases, it is obvious that computerized assessment is cost effective.

On the other hand, the initial investment required for computerized versions of many multiple-choice tests is much larger than the corresponding costs for paper-and-pencil forms. Clearly, a number two lead pencil costs less than a computer! In such cases, a cost-benefit analysis is needed to ascertain whether computer administration is economical. Such a cost-benefit analysis should comprehensively examine the expenses and the benefits of both assessment formats.

An extraordinarily detailed economic analysis was conducted by Wise, Curran, and McBride (1997) for the CAT–ASVAB; this study, described in chapter 3, revealed that the U.S. Department of Defense would save approximately five million dollars a year by computerizing their enlistment testing program. These savings accrued, in part, because CAT–ASVAB takes less time to administer than the paper-and-pencil ASVAB. In addition, the individualized administration of CAT–ASVAB allows walk-in testing (i.e., the test can be administered whenever an applicant arrives at the testing site); in contrast, the paper-and-pencil ASVAB is administered as a group test, and an applicant who arrives 10 minutes late must wait until the next administration begins. Note that applicants are often accompanied by recruiters, and so the time devoted to enlistment processing is directly related to cost.

Some benefits of computerized assessment are difficult to enter into a cost-benefit analysis. For example, test scores can be made available as soon as a computerized exam is completed; moreover, the scores can be automatically entered into a database and become accessible to personnel offices at geographically dispersed locations. Consequently, the time from the beginning of the job application process to hiring might be substantially reduced. Although this increased speed might be very important to unemployed job applicants, its influence on a cost–benefit analysis may be minimal.

As described by Kingsbury and Houser, educational institutions can receive similar benefits from the speed and flexibility of computerized assessments. For example, transfer students can be individually assessed via a CAT in a relatively short amount of time, with little administrative cost. These scores can then be used immediately for placement purposes. Thus, after the initial development of the CAT, educational institutions may enjoy financial savings from the reduced time and effort needed to evaluate continuing and new students.

It is interesting to note that all three of the chapters that describe innovative visual, audio, or audio–video assessments were based on projects conducted in academic settings. This is somewhat surprising, given the reputation of multimedia assessments as rather expensive. Perhaps the availability of relatively inexpensive graduate student labor makes such projects feasible on a shoestring budget. Accordingly, such projects are more likely to enjoy desirable cost–benefit ratios.

Many other benefits have been described in the chapters of this book. Rather than exhaustively listing them, we shall simply say that advantages of computerized testing are as diverse as the testing programs themselves. Analogous to the ways in which personal computers have come to serve a wide variety of functions in the corporate world and in private life, the flexibility of computerized testing allows it to be shaped to the particular needs of different testing programs. Thus, walk-in testing may be the critical advantage of computerized testing in one organization, immediate feedback to examinees may be the most highly valued feature in another, automatic updating of a wide-area database may be most important to a third organization, and so forth.

Future Directions

Computerized assessment seems limited only by the creativity, energy level, and financial limitations of test developers. It is well established now that test developers can create computerized versions of power tests that are essentially parallel forms of traditional paper-and-pencil tests. Mead and Drasgow (1993) performed a meta-analysis that substantiated this fact and CAT–ASVAB (Segall & Moreno in chapter 3, this volume) and the GRE-CAT (Mills in chapter 6) provide two prominent examples.

The possibilities for new assessments that are not parallel to any paper-and-pencil test form seem extraordinary. Vispoel's assessment of musical ability (chapter 8, this volume) provides an excellent example as does Ackerman, Evans, Park, Tamassia, and Turner's (chapter 7, this volume) test of diagnostic skills for dermatological skin disorders. These assessments use computers to provide high-fidelity information to the examinee in ways that are simultaneously individualized and standardized. Such assessment tools seem fundamentally superior to earlier tests using more restrictive formats.

It is easy to envision a wide range of measures that use multimedia computer technology to improve assessment. Consider, for example, vocational interest measurement. Measurement in this domain is typically via paper-and-pencil, and numerous assessment tools ask the respondents whether they are interested by the work in specific occupations (e.g., psychologists, accountants, etc.). Unfortunately, many young people know very little about the world of work and hence have little idea about what psychologists or accountants actually do in the workplace. A multimedia computerized assessment of vocational interest could show short video clips of a clinical psychologist with a client, an accountant with a spreadsheet, and so forth. Thus, a young person could respond to the questions on the vocational interest measure with a much clearer understanding of what the questions really ask.

As an example of another assessment tool, consider teamwork skills. Many work organizations have changed their structures to emphasize teams and teamwork. Assessment tools in this domain have lagged behind changes in the corporate world, and the assessment of teamwork skills has been little studied. A multimedia assessment tool for teamwork skills could be developed along the lines of the Conflict Resolution Skills Assessment (Olson-Buchanan et al., 1998) described in chapter 9. Here video clips showing scenes involving teams could be displayed and, at critical junctures, the assessee would be asked what he or she would do in that situation.

Educational measurement provides another context for improved assessment. Although there have been repeated calls for "authentic assessment," hands-on performance tests in some domains are expensive and sometimes dangerous. Video clips could be used to display, for example, chemistry experiments and again, at critical points, the student could be asked pertinent questions. The Department of Chemistry at the University of Illinois has used this approach to assessment with considerable success.

It is possible to continue to enumerate domains where computerized assessment might prove very successful. These examples, then, should suffice to make the point that measurement of workplace skills, vocational interest, and educational achievement might all be computerized in ways that improve the assessment process. Moreover, other domains, such as personality and psychopathology, might also consider replacing or at least augmenting self-report paper-and-pencil questionnaires with multimedia computerized assessment tools.

In conclusion, personal computers became viable for assessment just a few years ago and several programs of research and development subsequently took root. The chapters in this book recount the experiences of these pioneers and illustrate that, with both inspiration and perspiration, computerized assessments can be developed and implemented with great success. We hope that these chapters encourage others to consider computerized assessment for their measurement needs.

REFERENCES

Mead, A. D. & Drasgow, F. (1993). Equivalence of computerized and paper-and-pencil cognitive ability tests: A meta-analysis. *Psychological Bulletin, 114,* 449–458.

Olson-Buchanan, J. B., Drasgow, F., Moberg, P. J., Mead, A. D., Keenan, P. A., & Donovan, M. A. (1998). The Conflict Resolution Skills Assessment: Model-based, multimedia measurement. *Personnel Psychology, 51,* 1–24.

Wise, L. L, Curran, L. T., & McBride, J. R. (1997). CAT–ASVAB cost and benefit analyses. In W. A. Sands, B. K. Waters, & J. R. McBride (Eds.), *Computerized adaptive testing: From inquiry to operation* (pp. 227–236). Washington, DC: American Psychological Association.

Author Index

255

Subject Index